Tell Me Everything

Also by Erika Krouse

Contenders

Come Up and See Me Sometime

Tell Me Everything

The Story of a Private
Investigation

Erika Krouse

FLATIRON
BOOKS
NEW YORK

Designed by Donna Sinisgalli Noetzel

ISBN 9781250240309

For the women

Although this is a work of nonfiction, the author has changed dates, timelines, and the names of individuals portrayed in this work, except for the identities of certain public officials. To further protect privacy, she also changed characters' physical appearances and circumstances, or has created composite characters or events. The author has elected not to use the name of the university that functions as one of the main characters in this work. Dialogue has been reconstructed to the best of the author's recollection, or contains the gist of what she heard.

I wonder which is preferable—to walk around all your life swollen up with your own secrets until you burst from the pressure of them, or to have them sucked out of you, every paragraph, every sentence, every word of them, so at the end you're depleted of all that was once as precious to you as hoarded gold, as close to you as your skin—everything that was of the deepest importance to you, everything that made you cringe and wish to conceal, everything that belonged to you alone—and must spend the rest of your days like an empty sack flapping in the wind, an empty sack branded with a bright fluorescent label so that everyone will know what sort of secrets used to be inside you?

—Margaret Atwood, *The Blind Assassin*

Tell Me Everything

1

The Face

I became a private investigator because of my face. It's an ordinary-looking face, but if I ask "How are you?" sometimes people start crying. "I'm getting a divorce," they say. "He ended our marriage by text." Or "I was just diagnosed with late-stage Lyme disease." Or a man grips a packet of peas in the frozen food aisle and asks, "How do you cook these? My wife died last month."

Or an immaculately dressed woman suddenly tells me, "I hate my job so much I want to kill myself. I've been saving up Ambiens."

Then we sit on a concrete curb, or stand in line at a train station, or clutch clear plastic cups at a party as the near-stranger in front of me dabs away mascara with a cocktail napkin and dumps out her mind like it's her purse, like I'm the one who can sift through the dust and used tissues to find what she's looking for.

Demographics don't seem to matter. Young, old, women, men, nonbinary, gay, straight, rich, poor, East, West—everyone tells me things. A woman with twenty-six grandchildren and fifteen great-grandchildren whispered to me at her 101st birthday party that she wished she never had kids, that she had wasted her life on all these people. After I volunteered at an elementary school, a six-year-old followed me all the way to the bathroom to tell me in Spanish that her daddy's not going to come home anymore.

Even as a kid, I was a storage locker for people's secrets. Grown-ups confessed their affairs, lost fetuses, traumas. When I was seven, my maternal grandmother told me her husband chased her with a knife. One of my elementary school teachers told me he was leaving his wife because she hoarded pizza boxes and dead bugs. When I was fourteen, my mother's friend yanked me aside and said, "I just want to say your mother is a bitch. You *know* she's a bitch, right?" When I was seventeen, X, my abuser, blurted that he had denied a promotion to a friend at work because he was Black. This wasn't intimacy; we hated each other.

I thought that was just how other people were, confessing things all the time, that everyone experienced these constant revelations from both kin and strangers. Except people would always say, "I don't know why I'm telling you this," or "I've never told this to anyone before." Nobody told my older sister or younger brother these things, even though we looked similar. So it must be me, something I was doing, right or wrong or neither. Something in my face bore the shape of a key, or a steel table on which to lay something heavy.

"Where do I know you from?" strangers ask brightly. One surreal morning on a springtime park bench, three strangers in a row insisted they knew me as each sat down in turn. "Do you work at the library? Do you know Pat? Do you eat at Dot's?" I said no, I just have a familiar face, this happens to me all the time. One woman said, "With that face, you must have a tough time even going outside without people bugging you."

Does a familiar face imply a forgettable one? One ex-boyfriend forgot my name. "This is, um," he said, actually snapping his fingers, trying to introduce me to his new girlfriend. Another ex-boyfriend remembered my name, but forgot we had been together for a year. "What's it like to date you, I wonder," he flirted over the phone until I reminded him we did date not long ago, and he had sorta-kinda proposed to me amid a wash of emotion he felt after a screening of *Moulin Rouge*. But how could I get mad at him? Nobody remembers a mirror.

When I was thirteen, my family moved to Japan for four years.

The first year, nobody seemed to understand anything I said. "No, no," they said, waving their hands in front of their faces. "No speak English." "But I'm speaking in Japanese," I said in Japanese and they stared blankly at my casual body, my oddness.

At some point, without realizing it, my gestures morphed from American to Japanese ones. I covered my teeth when I smiled, nodded in short bows, kept my fingers pressed tightly together, pinned my elbows to my sides. My Japanese hadn't improved much, but people now called me fluent, *pera pera*. They would talk and talk and talk to me, way beyond my capacity to comprehend the language. They insisted I was half-Japanese, *"Hafu-desu!"* My mimicry was getting me adopted.

Keep your friends close, but keep your enemies closer, even if you have to become just like them. As a child, whenever I had to take car trips with X, it was safer to sit directly behind him because he couldn't hit me without having to pull over and haul me out. Sitting there, I felt like his lesser shadow. I couldn't read a book because it made me carsick, so I spent the time memorizing the back of the head I hated most. If the car came to a sudden stop, I pitched forward until I could smell the dead-skin stench of his hair, terrified I might somehow merge right into his body.

Imitation isn't flattery—it's protection. There's a class of animals called "mimics" who pretend to be other kinds of animals, to avoid becoming the delicious prey they indeed are. The powdery gray owl butterfly bears a convincing owl-eye spot on each wing, guarding it from bird attack. The harmless milk snake imitates venomous copperheads and coral snakes, with bright red-orange bands to warn off predators. Their lies are their hides. Tear a mimic free from her disguise and you'll find only inner flesh, viscera, a heart emptying its last blood into the dirt. She will die, and be eaten.

Unless she learns how to rip off your disguise first.

In the fall of 2002, I was living in the Front Range foothills of the Colorado Rocky Mountains, in a small city that hosted a university and a swarm of tech startups. I met an attorney in a bookstore there because we were both reaching for the same Paul Auster novel. We withdrew, laughed, chatted briefly about the author and books, and then he started telling me about his life. He wasn't complaining, just reporting. "I'm a partner in the kind of law firm I've always dreamed of. But I'm beginning to hate it."

The man looked like a lawyer. He was about twenty years older than me, my height, in a cornflower-blue button-down shirt that matched his eyes so exactly he must have bought it for that purpose. But his hunched shoulders betrayed misery, and his arms flapped at his sides like he had no use for them anymore but didn't know how to shed them. The man said, "Or maybe I'm just sick of it. My job. My life. I don't know if what I'm doing has any meaning anymore. I'm thinking about leaving my law firm. Maybe even leaving the practice of law altogether."

Then he stopped, shocked. "Wait."

"What?"

"I've never told anybody this stuff."

"It's okay," I said.

But he scanned the stacks, unable to meet my gaze, and his voice cracked. "What did you do? What's happening?"

"Don't worry. People tell me secrets all the time."

"*I* don't. I don't even know who you are." He jabbed an index finger in the air between us. "My partners can't know. This is confidential stuff."

"I won't tell anyone." He still looked upset, so I said, "It's not you. It's just my face. It does that. People tell me things. I'm sorry."

"People tell you things like *this*?" The man's expression slowly changed as he regarded me, as if I had suddenly gone on clearance. Then he said, "Come work for me!"

"What?"

"I'm offering you a job." He now looked relaxed, expansive. He leaned back against the books in the B section.

"What kind of job?" I asked. I was afraid he was about to say something dirty.

But instead he said, "You could investigate my lawsuits for me. PI work. Talk to witnesses. Get them to open up."

The idea was amazing, getting paid money for what usually ended up happening anyway. The man told me his name, Grayson. He said, "If you got that stuff out of me, you can get anything out of anyone." Then he named a generous hourly rate, five times what I was earning as a temp for a pharmaceutical company.

At that point in my life I was destitute, despite the fact that I had "made it." I was a thirty-three-year-old fiction writer. The year before I met this man, I'd had a short story published in *The New Yorker*. My collection of stories had come out with a major New York publisher. My book won a prize Toni Morrison had won ten years before.

Wasn't it supposed to get easier once you got published? Instead, I was already forgotten and even more broke than before. I felt cheated by my own fantasies. My apartment was the size and shape of a one-car garage, chalky white and "garden" (basement) level. There was no garden, nor air-conditioning, nor a thermostat. I ate cheap food, which gave me daily stomach cramps. My bed was a nearly clean mattress I had found leaning against a Dumpster.

I was living with my decision to forgo some safe, progressively lucrative career in exchange for any writing time I could snatch. I had been temping for two years. That week, I was doing data entry and wearing a white name tag that said TEMP, although sometimes people called me "the new Linda." It was an upgrade from my last temp job two weeks before, as a receptionist at a large medical practice where they refused to give me a chair because they couldn't spare one from the crowded waiting room. I had to stand for eight hours a day crouched over their black eighteen-line phone to transfer calls, and my back and ego still hurt from it.

That year was the worst of a multiyear drought that plagued five western states. In the summer, sixteen fires had erupted across the state in the space of a few months. The flames were mostly ignited from lightning strikes on dry, beetle-killed lodgepole pines, except for one from a coal-seam fire that had been burning underground since 1910. All the fires killed nine firefighters and burned a total of almost 430,000

acres of forest in one summer, and some fires still burned into that autumn. Grayson's clothes smelled dry-cleaned, but mine reeked of the
mottled, unlaunderable campfire-like smoke, as did the books we held
in our hands. There was no rain. This—Grayson's offer—felt like rain.

I kept a running list of all the jobs I wanted to hold in my lifetime but never believed I could. "Private investigator" was number
two, right after "writer," and before about seventeen other jobs that
included "composer," "food critic," and, for some reason, "cobbler."
Crime excited me in the abstract. I had wanted to be a PI ever since I
read my first Dashiell Hammett book. I wanted to help people and find
things out, not necessarily in that order. I wanted to be the one who
could walk into a room and know what happened there.

I loved secrets, even terrible ones. Especially terrible ones. When
people told me things, I felt happy. The more they didn't want to tell
me that secret, the happier I felt when they did. Secret information was
something I earned at a cost—someone else's cost. I could hoard that
intelligence and never lose it. It was one of the few things in the world
that was entirely mine.

Even if I hadn't wanted the job, I would have taken it anyway. I was
used to accepting any employment offered, regardless of how I felt
about it. Lie to creditors? Sure! Lie about our money-back guarantee?
Sure! Lie about the doctor's nooner whereabouts to his wife as she
jiggles a screaming toddler covered in chicken pox? Sure, absolutely,
you bet!

So I didn't even ask this lawyer about the cases, or what I'd have to
do to extract the confessions he was talking about. It didn't matter. He
wanted me, so I would take the job. But this Grayson person seemed
like a nice guy, so I said, "I have to make this clear. I don't have any
experience as a private investigator."

Grayson grinned. "Perfect," he said.

My first few cases, I had no idea what I was doing. Grayson sent me to
a women's triathlon where a personal injury client had gotten run over
by a bicycle the previous year. His instructions were rushed—for law-

yers, every minute is worth dollars—so I wasn't sure how to find witnesses to talk to. During the race I held up a fluorescent green poster board sign that said DID YOU SEE A BICYCLE ACCIDENT HERE A YEAR AGO? IF SO, PLEASE TALK TO ME!! Nobody talked to me. I got a bad sunburn.

I kept trying. In winter, he assigned me a medical malpractice case, featuring a maternal death. Grayson was again vague, instructing me to "find something on them." I visited the hospital and pretended I was pregnant—no pillow under the shirt, just a big burrito for lunch. I told a nurse, "I may be high-risk. Do pregnant women ever die here?" The nurse extracted me from the group and escorted me to a lilac-smelling charge nurse in pink paisley scrubs who said, "I think another hospital may better suit your needs."

Grayson assigned me to a car accident, another personal injury case. A state trooper showed me accident scene photos, but I couldn't decipher them. "What's that smudge here?" I asked. "Tire tracks," he said. "And this?" "Blood." "And this bump here, where's that?" "That's the median." I pretended to stare hard, to see something that meant anything to me. In my report for Grayson, it was difficult to disguise the fact that I had nothing to say.

Grayson frowned and said, "I don't think I'm making good use of your skill set."

What skill set? I knew my methods were wrong, but I didn't know what the right ones were. I had read enough detective fiction to know a good PI doesn't just find out what happened; she makes things happen. Or he does. Maybe the problem was that I was a woman. If I were a gearhead man, maybe the accident photos would have made sense. If I were a cute man, some woman might have talked to me when I held up the sign at the women's triathlon.

I didn't even have a PI license. Colorado, ever a cowboy state, didn't require licenses for marriages, psychotherapy practices, or private investigators. But every private investigator in every novel I had ever read was an ex-something—an ex-cop, an ex-lawyer, an ex-con. I was an ex-dishwasher, an ex–instructor of poetry. I had also previously worked as an ice cream truck driver, a waitress, an accountant, a shoe saleswoman, a house cleaner, a canvasser, a school bus monitor, a hospital aide, an after-school elementary teacher, a creative writing instructor at the university in town, a pizza cook and delivery person, a security guard, an administrative assistant, a piano player at weddings and funerals, a telemarketer, a data-entry drone, a B&B night manager, a tarot card reader on the street, a cafeteria worker, and a writer of fiction, nonfiction, poetry, technical manuals, marketing materials, book reviews, and even horoscopes for a fashion magazine, all without proper qualifications or any particular talent. But I couldn't seem to pull off this PI job. I had never exactly been a wunderkind, but I had never failed at anything so spectacularly before. I wondered which would disappoint Grayson more—if I quit, or rode this job until the wheels fell off and the poor guy was forced to fire me.

Despite my nonperformance, Grayson was still paying me by the hour, which made me feel bad until he called me into his office. I had been working for him less than six months, and I dreaded the meeting. This job had ended before it had really begun.

Our meeting was postponed because of the weather. Following a season of Chinook winds clocking up to eighty-five miles per hour, the drought temporarily paused with a record-breaking three-day spring blizzard. An upslope snowstorm dumped three and a half feet of snow on the flats and foothills, and between seven and eleven feet in the mountains that crowded our small city. Wind pushed drifts against doors, garages, Dumpsters, or any still structure. All the powder in the air completely obscured the mountains that defined the western perimeter of the city. We might be in any flat place—Nebraska, Kansas. Except for gusts, the city was silent. Cars hulked like sleeping animals, houses wore marshmallow caps, and the roads turned to cold, white silk.

It took four days for the city to clear the sidewalks downtown near Grayson's office, and I had to walk there because my street was still unplowed. Commuters cross-country skied to work even on main artery streets. Few cars drove the roads, but every now and then an SUV towed a whooping skier behind it on a long bungee cord. Walls of melting snow flanked my path so high it felt like I was traversing a maze. With the mountains obscured, everything was strange again, which would have been exciting if I hadn't been about to get canned.

I gave my name at the front desk and Grayson called me into his warm, windowed office. The room was spotless. In contrast to the sloppy weather, Grayson sat at his desk with perfect posture in an immaculate suit. He smiled amiably and gestured for me to sit on a mesh chair so deliberately ugly it must have been expensive. Too late, I noticed that my blouse had a hole in the elbow, so I sat with my hands tucked into my lap, ankles crossed like I was in finishing school. I had never been fired before, and wondered how to sit in a way that would make him regret his decision.

But it turned out Grayson had a new case for me. He rolled his chair forward and consulted his yellow legal pad. "It's rape. College rape, gang rape. That okay with you?"

Involuntarily I shook my head, which I converted into a vigorous nod.

Grayson told me about the client, Simone Baker, raised in a tiny town on the eastern plains. Her mother worked a desk job and her father ran cattle and raised horses. The family chose Grayson to represent them because he had been wearing cowboy boots when they met.

In high school, Simone had been part of the National Honor Society and she taught Sunday school. While attending the university full-time, she worked thirty hours a week, Big Sistered a foster-home teenager, and spent a summer doing refugee relief work overseas. I had never met anyone that uniformly virtuous. I wondered if she was real.

Grayson said, "Over a year ago, on December seventh, 2001, Simone was hosting a girls-only party at her apartment when twenty college football players and recruits unexpectedly showed up at her door. She was drunk, so she went to lie down. At least five and as many as eight of them followed her into the bedroom. Several of them allegedly raped her while the others surrounded the bed as spectators. It was too dark to see well, so she doesn't know who her attackers were."

What a terrible story. I wondered what it was like to not know your attackers—if it was a relief, or if it made everyone on earth feel dangerous.

Grayson said, "We may be able to sue the university under Title IX. You went to school there, right? Is that a conflict of interest for you?" I shook my head. I had gotten my master's degree in English at that university, but all my favorite professors were gone.

Grayson said, "I'm making an argument for a rape culture. We're going after the system, not the individuals. There's no Title IX precedent for a sexual assault lawsuit of this kind. It's new legal ground." Grayson tugged the edges of his smile downward with a thumb and forefinger, trying not to appear proud and excited.

"Isn't Title IX about facilities and money?" I asked.

Grayson relaxed into an educating-the-client stance. "Title IX is a civil rights initiative. It basically means that if a federally funded education program doesn't protect students from discrimination, they risk losing their funding. Simone's trauma and ongoing harassment amount to discrimination. Football players are funded by the university, which is funded by the state and federal governments. As long as the university allows their football players to behave dangerously, women aren't safe there, which means women can't receive the same benefits as men."

That was a new thought: a school was responsible for the safety and equity of its female students. I had been harassed and discriminated against in most schools, jobs, towns, and venues, and I had accepted it long ago as a given. It was unfair, sure, but so was weather.

Grayson said, "This case is different, because we're claiming that it's a system of sexual abuse. My colleague dug up one Title IX precedent, with an elementary school. Sandra Day O'Connor had ruled that you have to show that the school was"—he tried to decipher his own handwriting on the yellow legal pad—"'deliberately indifferent to sexual harassment, of which they have actual knowledge.'" He looked up for emphasis. "That's going to be the hard thing—proving that the school's decision makers knew about it. Because if they did, they'll deny it all over the place."

Excitement displaced my nervousness. I was going to work on

a civil rights case. Me! I wrote down everything Grayson said: *pervasive harassment, school's knowledge, deliberate indifference. Inequality.* The phrase "deliberate indifference" ricocheted around my mind. Could indifference to crime *be* a crime? I had never imagined such a thing.

Grayson said, "I want you to start discreetly gathering evidence. If we file, it'll be much harder once the university mounts their four-dog defense. So keep it quiet."

"What's a four-dog defense?"

Grayson recited, "One, that's not my dog. Two, if it was my dog, he didn't bite you. Three, if my dog bit you, it didn't hurt you. And four, if my dog bit you and hurt you, you provoked him."

I thought for a second. "So they'll argue they're not responsible for the football players. But if they are, the players didn't rape your client. If they did rape her, it didn't hurt her. And if it did hurt her, she asked for it. Is that it?"

Grayson said, "You understand this pretty well."

Of course. I understood perfectly.

I had to turn down this job.

My own sexual assaults had been different from Simone's. I had been a small child, not a college student. I was abused not by multiple peers, but by one adult I now call X. The attacks continued from when I was four until I was about seven, not just one brutal time.

But all differences felt academic now, with this dizzying, whirling feeling in my chest. I knew I should leave. Instead, I pressed my back against the mesh ergonomic chair. I was too light-headed to think of a lie that would transport me out of there. And I wasn't about to tell Grayson one bit of my history, then or ever.

Grayson prattled on about legal crap, but all I could focus on was the can of seltzer water buzzing on his desk. It was surreal to discuss rape in this airy, clean, splinter-less office with blond wood cabinets and wide, tall windows, where women who made more than I did served me tea in mugs designed to perfectly accommodate a human hand. Power bounced off the eggshell-finish walls and throbbed from the light fixtures, and none of that power was for me. I had the familiar feeling of being the wrong person in the wrong place at the wrong time. It was the overture to danger.

Many—most?—of my jobs had been far more dangerous, but typically, physically dangerous, like canvassing door-to-door in Boston's shot-up Roxbury neighborhood, or reading tarot cards on the street late into the night, when the drunks came out. And sometimes the jobs that seemed safest were the most dangerous. When I was eighteen, I took a waitress job at a twenty-four-hour Greek diner just off a highway. Lines grew at my counter while everyone else's tables remained empty. Regulars told me their problems, tipped me five bucks on a sixty-five-cent cup of coffee, and left for their truck cabs or office jobs. They'd reappear a day or a week later to update me on their worries and tragedies. It was like watching dozens of telenovelas at once, and I always felt secure with a counter between them and me.

One night I picked up a night shift as a favor to one of my coworkers, because she wanted to get laid. By three in the morning, the manager and all the post-bar customers had left. Except for the cook sleeping in the kitchen, I was alone in the diner when a pale, blond boy walked in. He was about my age, wearing a black leather jacket, kind of cute. I asked him if he wanted coffee. He told me he had killed his girlfriend.

"Her name was Sharon. She looks like you. Skin like yours. Cheated on me and I killed her with a knife. Stab stab. After we made love. She's in the crawl space under my parents' house in Ohio. She's hot. Beautiful. I love her, I love her so fucking much. Can I have a cheeseburger? I don't have any money." The boy spoke quickly, brow smooth.

"I'm sorry. They won't let me," I said. A familiar terror had already seized my stomach like a cramp. The diner sat on a highway bordering New York and New Jersey. If what he said was true, the boy's dead girlfriend in Ohio was eight hours away.

He heaved a giant boom box onto my counter. "Is your name Sharon? Here, this is about you. I donate this song to you."

"Dedicate," I whispered.

He pressed a button on the boom box with his thumb. A heavy metal song stretched its tinny fingers toward every wall in the diner.

"Do you remember dancing to this?" he asked. The chorus was his girlfriend's name, Sharon, over and over.

"My name isn't Sharon," I tried to say, but he interrupted.

"Sharon, honey, if I don't eat something soon I can't be responsible for what happens."

Our cook was still sleeping in the kitchen, slumped against a blue plastic bin, head deep in his folded arms. What could he do, anyway? He was undocumented, sending money every week to his family in Chiapas. We liked each other fine, but he wouldn't help me. If there was trouble, he would run before the cops came. He would get fired if he left during his shift, and without his job, his six children would starve three thousand miles south. I pulled two slices of white bread from a plastic bag, toasted them, and scraped butter across their surfaces. I carried the plate through the swinging doors that didn't lock and set it on my counter with a soft clink.

The murderer took a few bites of toast, his thin jaw working hard. What if he didn't like it? But he swallowed and said, "That's better. Can I sleep in a booth?" I said yes and he lay down on a cracked red vinyl seat in the corner.

His silver boom box still throbbed on my counter. When I turned off the music, the boy barked a warning "Sharon!" I didn't know if he was calling my name or requesting the song. I pressed the Play button again, letting the tape run to the end. I was terrified he would wake up and I'd be the Sharon he killed, not the Sharon he loved. I quietly paced the restaurant and let both men sleep, the murderer in the booth and the cook in the kitchen. I didn't know if I should hide behind the counter, inside the kitchen, or in plain sight. I didn't even think to leave.

After 5:00 A.M., truck drivers trod into the diner, loudly slapping newspapers and ordering black coffee. I took trembling orders on my green pad and tried to speak softly over the frying bacon in the kitchen, afraid the boy in the booth would wake up. Shortly before the manager arrived, I realized the boy had slipped out, taking his boom box but leaving the cassette tape on my counter for me. Someone had scrawled a curly, girly SHARON in blue ballpoint on the sticker label. The original Sharon might have written it.

Somewhere in Ohio, a girl who looked like me was maybe rotting in a crawl space. Too many years went by before I realized that I should have called the police. That they might have looked in Ohio for Sharon to see if she was okay. That they could have protected me at the diner. That anyone would think either of us was worth saving.

Which was why I knew I shouldn't work Grayson's case, or any other sexual violence case. It was too important, and I wasn't. I didn't protect women, or make justice happen. I was Sharon, I was dead, I was nobody. Unqualified, and too qualified. I understood rape victims and I understood rapists, and I didn't want to understand either, ever again.

But there was Grayson in front of me, a mirage of idealism. He seemed hopeful. He seemed angry. He shone with it, anger at injustice, empathy for this girl, Simone. More than any of it, he seemed to think something could actually be done—that he could be the one to make things better, to change things forever. It struck me like an aftershock:

I would do anything to feel like that.

Grayson wouldn't have served toast to a murderer. He would have found the girl in the crawl space in Ohio. He would have sought justice, maybe even for my terrifying childhood if he knew about it. That's what a lawyer is supposed to be—the person in the room who understands the problem and knows how to solve it. And, wrong or not, he believed I could help him do this great thing.

But it didn't make sense that Grayson was even involved. He wasn't a criminal lawyer. Stalling, I asked, "Why do you have this case? Shouldn't the cops and the district attorney be handling it?"

"Oh, the DA decided not to pursue the case," Grayson said. "They're not trying it in the criminal courts. The DA referred Simone to our law firm instead. Some players did get charged for providing alcohol to minors, the recruits. The recruits weren't charged with anything."

"So if this is a civil suit, it doesn't even matter if we find out who hurt Simone. The bad guys aren't going to jail."

"Oh no," Grayson said. "It matters to us. We need people to prove out our theory about the system. As for whether or not they'll go to jail, sometimes a civil case will prompt a criminal one. It happens." Grayson thrust his arms forward to hike up the sleeves of his suit jacket, as if he were getting ready to begin some kind of manual labor. Grayson was going to make lemonade from lemons because he wanted lemonade. If there were no lemons he'd squeeze whatever he could find—a steak, a stick, a clod of dirt. And it would taste the way he wanted it to.

It was an instant antidote to despair, the idea that I could feel this way, too. I felt better, braver in this tempting game Grayson was inventing in front of me. I asked, "So you want me to find and talk to the suspects? Try to get them to confess?"

Grayson recoiled slightly. "No. Never. Find them, yes, if you can. Identify every suspect you can for me. But you don't talk to perpetrators once we know they committed a crime." I was touched by his protectiveness until he said, "Best not to tip those people off, if we can avoid it. Once they know we're researching them, they'll lawyer up and we won't be able to find out anything."

I wondered how I was supposed to research people if I wasn't allowed to talk with them. "How about the football coaches? Staff?"

"No. Current football players are okay, but current university employees are off-limits."

"Can I talk to Simone?"

"No, you are under no circumstances allowed to talk to our plaintiff. I have the relationship with her."

I modulated my voice low, so it didn't sound like I was complaining. "Who *can* I talk to?"

"Witnesses. Find new witnesses. You can talk to them."

"Until they become important. Then they're yours."

"That's right." I must have looked frustrated because Grayson's voice softened. "I only need you for one thing, Erika, but I really need you for that one thing."

"What thing?"

"There are three kinds of evidence." Grayson held up a thumb and two fingers and started ticking them off. "Physical evidence, which is DNA and rape kits. Bruises, like that. That's not you. Then there's direct evidence. Eyewitness testimonials. People at the party who saw one piece of something that can fit into the argument as a whole—you can find that. That's you. Most definitely you. It's important because it's human. You can pry these people open, get information that can help the case. It's what you're good at," he said, but I wasn't so sure.

"What's the third kind of evidence?" I asked.

"Circumstantial."

"Which doesn't count," I said. I remembered TV shows with lawyers shouting, "Objection! Circumstantial evidence!"

But Grayson said, "Oh yes, it does count. It counts just as much. Circumstantial evidence shows that things *had* to have happened a certain way, even if you don't have physical proof." I must have looked confused, because he said, "Think of it this way: say you're walking through the woods and there's a turtle sitting on a tall tree stump. You know what happened, even if you didn't see someone pick up the turtle and place it on the stump."

"So that's what you do," I said. "You fit the pieces of the past together, so we can know what happened."

"Yes."

These ideas were exciting. "I get people to talk, so you can show how the turtle got on the stump."

"Yes. You gather testimony from victims, witnesses, ex-employees. If they're important, they testify, if they're willing."

"Do they have to be willing?"

"I don't want to subpoena someone hostile if I can avoid it. I need to know they're there to help us, not to destroy what we're building. I need you to make us some friends." Grayson handed me a yellow slip of paper. On it was a phone number in loopy handwriting. "Talk to this woman. My paralegal pulled her name and number from a police report. Her name is Calliope. She's a star university athlete who was at our client's party for a brief time. Maybe she saw something."

It took a long second for me to remind myself of who I was, what I'd been through, and why this case was a terrible idea for me. That's when I could have told this nice man, "I appreciate all you've done for me, but I'm simply not suited for this job." I could have made a new plan, called my temp agency, and accepted another assignment playing with paper clips, pretending I was happy for eight hours a day.

Instead, I stuffed the slip of paper with Calliope's phone number deep into my pocket so I wouldn't lose it. Grayson and I shook hands and I walked out of the expensive office building into the snow, and back into my basement-level life.

Hours later, in the blue glow of evening, I phoned Calliope. She said hello in a clear, young voice. I said, "My name is Erika and I'm a private investigator." The label sounded as good as anything I had ever called myself. "Can we meet?"

I was nervous about meeting Calliope, afraid of failing like before. I decided to come well prepared this time. In advance, I had scoped out a restaurant bar, a regional chain that didn't look like one, downtown but empty. The snow was still melting outside, and fewer people went out in the evenings after the roads began to freeze. The place had few windows and smelled like pizza and wood polish. I often have to strain to be heard in public spaces because my voice is the same pitch as ambient noise, but this place was quiet, with no music or bar sounds. The dim booths were spaced farther apart from each other than usual, allowing for private conversation. I showed up early and watched the door for Calliope.

A young woman walked in; I stood and waved. When she approached, I introduced myself and shook her cold hand.

"How did you know it was me? Because I'm Black?" Calliope asked, sitting.

It was a reasonable question in such a whitewashed city, but I hadn't known anything about what Calliope looked like. "I knew it was you because you were alone," I said. Women that beautiful don't often walk into bars or restaurants unaccompanied. Calliope was about twenty, thin and muscular, with large almond eyes, immaculately cut black hair, chin in a delicate V. She had previously worked as a model and danced in videos for rappers whose names I didn't recognize. She rested a pristine Gucci purse on the table between us, squeaky with newness.

In high school, college, even now, I might have felt jealous of her, or I might have been her best friend. Beautiful women love being friends with me because my plainness makes their beauty stand out more, like backlighting. I grew up with thick glasses that narrowed my face and turned my eyes into brownish peas, so gawky and flat-chested that boys called me "Kansas." Nobody ever gazed at me with his chin propped in his hands. Beautiful women are never safe except around people like me. Everyone else wants them too much, or wants to defeat them to prove their own worth. Calliope began to relax as she regarded me across the table in my plain beige dress.

Still, she said, "I'm not sure I should be talking to you."

"You showed up, didn't you?" I handed my credit card to the server and told Calliope, "At the very least, you get free food and booze." Calliope selected a burger and an amber microbrew; I dittoed her order.

After the server left I asked, "So why shouldn't you talk to me?"

Calliope sighed silently. "After the party where that girl was attacked, the police called and I talked to them. That didn't go so well."

"No?"

"No. My coach kicked me off the team."

"For talking to the police?"

"I don't know. I think so. I went from being a freshman Division I-A starter with a future to sitting on the bench. Then they threw me off the team entirely and revoked my college scholarship." Calliope registered my expression. "Yeah. My coach said, 'You're never playing for this team again.'"

"Did he give you a reason?"

"When I asked why, he started shouting, 'I don't really know how to explain except to say that you never deserved it, and you don't belong here. Why are you crying?' And then he kicked me out." Calliope's face hardened back into her beautiful mask. "The thing is, I didn't even see much at that party."

"What *did* you see?"

She wrinkled her delicate nose. "It was a strange party. Mostly in the hallway, like a long line of people hooking up. Then the players went into the bedroom—I don't remember who. The football player I came with said 'I'm getting out of here. I don't want to be a part of this.' We left. That was it."

She paused.

"Did something else happen?" I asked.

"Well, not too much later we went to Illegal Pete's for burritos and met up with all the guys who stayed and disappeared into the bedroom. One of those recruits, he looked like he'd seen death. Something was definitely wrong. I've never seen anyone look like that." Calliope then sniffed and waved one languid hand. "But I don't know his name."

"Would you recognize him if I could find a picture?"

"Yes. Definitely."

This was something I could write about in my report. Maybe I wouldn't be fired after all. Maybe I could do this PI thing. Maybe I wasn't a fraud.

From my manila file, I pulled out a photo of some of the women at the party and showed it to Calliope. She pointed at our client right away and said, "She was the only one at the party who was nice to me."

"That's the victim," I said.

"*She* was raped?" Calliope asked, upset. "*She* was?"

"Tell me more about that night," I said.

As Calliope talked, part of me stayed separate, watching myself, the way I sometimes did in relationships. I found myself pulling tricks I had learned over decades of desperate socialization, and inventing new techniques right there at the table. I kept my hands always in Calliope's view, and gestured with open palms. I matched her breathing, her posture. I took enough notes to make her feel important, memorizing the rest of what she said so I didn't have to break eye contact for too long. When she was vague I acted bored, only resuming eye contact when she disclosed something interesting. When she leaned back in skepticism, I stuttered so she'd feel sorry for me, and she leaned forward again. I gazed at her like she was the older, wiser one, like each fact she uttered was the most important thing I had ever heard.

You can find out anything if you listen that way.

Was it fake? Did it matter?

Calliope's voice grew thinner and scratchier. "And then after that, you know, the rest of the night was normal. Normal college student stuff." Her words evaporated and she looked away from me. Calliope had abandoned her beer halfway down the glass, and the remainder had lost its carbonation. Her burger stiffened on its plate. She reached for her bag, which was my cue to reach for mine.

I didn't. Something was off. Calliope's long fingers picked at each other. She leaned slightly forward, head tilted away from me, staring at a picture on the wall. She was there, and not there. I recognized that look from a lifetime of receiving confessions. Calliope was straddling a limbo that entwined past memory with current pain.

"But something happened to *you*, Calliope," I said.

Her face contorted, as if she had gotten caught at something shameful. She still clutched her bag. She still didn't look at me.

Outside it had begun to rain. When the door opened, the dank smell of falling rain and melting snow twisted toward us. Calliope had no umbrella or hat, only a thin jacket. She wasn't going anywhere.

Calliope slid her bag back onto the table. She whispered something like, "I'm scared this will get out." Her eyes reddened. She groped in the metal dispenser for a napkin to blow her nose.

I didn't move, didn't speak. I wasn't just going to repeat whatever she told me—I was going to write it up in a memo, as part of a lawsuit for money. Calliope was smart, and she knew all this. But she wanted to tell me something anyway. I had to hope this desire conquered her common sense, as it seemed to do for most people.

"Two of those same players raped *me*," Calliope finally said. "*That night.*"

Calliope was furious, trying not to cry, pressing her lips together until they lost their shape. I didn't want to cry with her, screwing it all up, stealing her emotions for myself. Images of my own threatened to crowd into the room—flesh in my face, suffocating weight, the yellow bars of my headboard as I rattled them in panic. But as I focused on Calliope, those other thoughts slipped backward to the margins of my consciousness. I stared so hard at her shattered face that the room pixelated to black. I tried to tell the girl silently, *Your pain is mine. Your pain is important.*

Minutes passed, minutes of rain. "I've never told anyone before," Calliope finally said. I felt the weight of that phrase for the first time.

But my face was doing things I didn't want it to, tugged in opposite directions by grief and—yes—an elation that felt sociopathic. In the last minute and a half, this case had become a real one, with corroborating evidence and identifiable criminals. This poor girl was as vulnerable as an egg. Her story was something we could all leverage for redemption, justice.

We might actually nail those fuckers.

Then I lost control, and hid my face with my hands. So she wouldn't see me smile.

2

Maybe They Like Me

That night I called Grayson on his cell phone, so excited my teeth chattered. "Slow down," he said. "You're sure she said it was the night of the party? Same guys?"

"Yes. Two players attacked Calliope after the party, after being in the bedroom with Simone. Their names are King Chambers and Zachary Mooney. Two names! Two attacks!" It felt strange to say those words in such a happy voice.

"Wow. That's terrific, kid." This was the first time Grayson called me "kid," and I'd soon learn it meant he was pleased. "Write up a detailed memo ASAP, and then let's meet to talk about next steps. Leave nothing out. Everything may be important, whether you realize it or not."

I stayed up late writing the memo and Grayson stayed up late waiting for it. Writing it down sobered me up, especially the details: how one player pinned Calliope facedown on the bed and allegedly sexually assaulted her while another player entered the room, undressed himself, and touched her. She couldn't see what was happening and thought they would hurt her if she dared say no. They ignored her when she tried. For weeks after the alleged attack she felt afraid to go outside, and drank alone in her room. She took "a bunch" of pills, "not to kill myself, just . . . they were supposed to be my friends." For the first time, I felt comparatively lucky about what had happened to me.

At least I had been spared the bewilderment of having an attacker who had once been kind to me.

I typed up my whole conversation with Calliope nearly verbatim, discovering that I could do that—reconstitute an hour-long conversation from scant notes and memory. I had never tried something on that scale before, but I'd always had good verbal recall. Even when I was small, I was able to point out my mother's hypocrisies by quoting her, and she'd snap, "You should be a lawyer when you grow up." That's how I learned lawyers were supposed to be bad.

But this lawyer couldn't be bad, this man who believed a single sexual assault survivor could hold a Big 12 football team accountable. The next day, Grayson bought me lunch at a Nepalese restaurant. He said, "I think Calliope has a claim herself. Being cut from her scholarship like that is a violation of her educational rights. She could join Simone as a plaintiff."

"You sound excited," I said.

"Well, yeah! The case is growing."

"So you don't want to quit law?"

"Not anymore! This case changes everything. Everything in my life." As seemed to be his nature, Grayson immediately turned the conversation away from himself. "I need you to make Calliope trust me. Best if it's soon."

I nodded, but I wasn't completely sure I trusted him. "Why the rush?"

"As media coverage ramps up, people will change. Some will be more guarded because they don't want to get involved. Some will be more forthcoming because something's actually happening. You'll have to work with both populations to find me information I can use." His knee started bobbing fast, as if he couldn't wait to start jogging. "We're still muddy on what happened that night. Simone was too drunk to remember much, and people's memories might change as they read the news. It just happens that way."

The case had broken for real by now and the news services loved it. Grayson's name dotted all the local newspapers. 9News interviewed him on TV, and Grayson presented well, buttoned and ironed and

unassuming. He had hearing loss in his left ear from his time in the
military, giving him an endearing head-tilt that wooed the interviewers
and made them ask him back again and again. But Grayson was an in-
trovert, and the wear of a public case was starting to show in his face,
now tinted sallow by the mustard walls of the restaurant. He was still
respectful, but impatience undercut his voice in staccato consonants.
His time was worth lots and lots of money, and educating me wasn't
worth anything.

Regardless, he seemed to enjoy bouncing ideas off my face. He
leaned back and squinted at me. "So let's see what we've got. There's
Simone, innocent cowgirl, salt of the earth. Calliope, the star athlete,
a model. And the players and football coaches, the greedy villains." I
was fascinated. Grayson was *casting* the lawsuit, as if it were a film or a
novel. He said, "We have to understand these players and find the dirt.
Maybe there are jealousies we can exploit."

Grayson slid a pair of readers onto his face and spread a printout of
my memo over popadam crumbs. He still believed in paper. He tapped
a scrawl on my Calliope memo, which was now scarred with nearly
illegible handwriting, some of it sideways or upside-down. "This guy
is interesting. 'Huge'?"

"His real name is Eugene. Calliope said he was there the night of
the party. He left when the players started entering the bedroom. Calliope called him a Goody Two-shoes."

"Hm. Perhaps he has a conscience. How huge is Huge?"

"I don't know. He's an offensive lineman. Is that big?"

Grayson gave me a "you're stupid" look. "Maybe it's a bad idea for
you to talk to him."

"Because I don't know football?"

"Because some of these guys are dangerous."

"It's okay," I said.

"What will you do if he tries something?"

Grayson had said "What *will*," not "What *would*." He still wanted
me to do it. I said, "Try what? I'm ten years older than all these guys.
To them, I'm a fossil."

"You're a woman."

"I'm a black belt in karate."

"*You?*"

"Yes." When he folded his arms, I said, "Really, I am."

"But he's at least double your weight. Maybe three times." Grayson pressed his lips together, about to make a decision I probably wouldn't like.

So I said, "He's got a neck, doesn't he?"

Grayson laughed, and so did I. I actually was a black belt, but I was also full of shit. I had a neck, too.

"Really. Knees, neck, eyes," I said, so persuasively I almost convinced myself. "Everyone has weaknesses. I'm not scared."

I knew better. I had studied martial arts for decades—karate, and also two kinds of kung fu, Brazilian jiu-jitsu, and ancient Okinawan weapons (so if anyone attacked me with an oar, hoe, or mill handle, I knew exactly what to do). I had started with judo in high school when I lived in Japan, and I continued with karate as an adult because I liked the strategy of it, the weirdness, the possibility of defending myself, and the constant physical challenge of being so outmatched. I loved being the smallest one in the room and surviving it, coming back the next day, surviving it again. But from all that physical study, I had learned one thing: if a big guy wanted to hurt me, he would hurt me.

It had taken a lot to learn this fact: broken bones, sprained limbs, permanently jacked neck and back, dislocated jaw, concussions, grade 3 contusions, bone bruises, black eyes, and a slight but ever-present tinnitus. Most guys, nice guys, hated fighting with me. Bad men relished it, tried to hide their grins as they hit me. But the most dangerous opponents were completely indifferent, staring through me like I wasn't even there.

Football players also focus on the peripheral view. How could they bear it otherwise, if they looked closely at the person they hurt? In karate, we cultivated the "thousand-mile stare." At that time I was doing a lot of Brazilian jiu-jitsu, which took it a step further—we didn't look at our opponents at all as we tried to submit them with chokes or joint locks. An opponent might glance at your arm or leg, but the best ones stared at the wall and did everything by feel. Some people closed their eyes; sometimes even I did. It's ground-fighting, and you're mashed together so close that no space exists between you. You always know exactly where the other person is. His shoulder grinds into your mouth guard. His chest and belly torque against yours, or his skull jams into your ear. You feel his wet breath in your face, but he doesn't see you. *Look at me*, I would think. *I'll make you look at me.*

I was often the only woman at the school, and people were generally courteous to me. But they still used the word "bitch" without compunction. *Make him your bitch, you're my bitch now, don't be a little bitch.* The instructors said, "If you're not the hammer, you're the nail." I was always the bitch, the nail. I was a boring grappler, much smaller than the hammer, taking no risks, giving nothing.

I almost never won, but it took a long time to make me lose. A big guy once tapped out when he was on top of me in the mount—the winning position—after about twenty minutes of trying to submit me. I sat up, confused. "Why did you tap? You were winning." He said, "Because I'm bored," and stalked away to find someone else to train with.

It relaxed me to live at the bottom of the odds, even though I had near-constant anxiety-indigestion over getting seriously hurt and having to negotiate my paltry self-employed insurance. My motives for training had grown beyond the obvious ones that might have started me out: the idea that if I learned how to fight, nobody would ever be able to hurt me again. Because the more I trained, the less I believed that idea.

The better I got, the fewer good women there were to train with, and I didn't have the speed, athleticism, youth, testosterone, weight, strength, or muscle mass to match the men. And I don't care what anyone says—even slight advantages in those categories are what make people win or lose. So I hid behind the rules. They weren't allowed to do any real-life things to loosen me up: torque back my fingers, punch me, jab me in the eyes. A man half my age and twice my size would try to finish me quickly, but I'd turtle up and hide inside the shell of my body, thinking, *Look at me. Look at me.*

After a few minutes, he'd start to get mad. *Who is this boring bitch, coming into my house? She deserves whatever she gets.* He'd get more aggressive, rougher, using big, dumb moves I would have capitalized on had I been a better fighter. He'd stack me up on my neck and bend my spine in two. Jackhammer me into the mat headfirst. Slam me backward, or jerk an arm or leg to hyperextend it, or tear my hair out with his elbows, knees. Gouge fists into my neck, or jam forearms into my eye socket, nose, mouth, ear. He'd "make me his bitch." The longer I made him wait to win, the more he brought his A game to me, a nothing. Because if he couldn't beat a nothing, he was nothing.

I just had to survive the first five minutes. Then my opponent inevitably started to breathe in gasps. A quiver in his abs, biceps, quads. Small despair leaking into his eyes. *Am I as tough as I thought? She's a woman. Who am I? Am I a man?* Then I could make a move to escape, or very, very rarely, to win. The nail hammers the hammer with tiny, relentless strokes. That was the feeling I lived for, the reason why I did any of this ridiculous stuff. It was worth any amount of pain and patience for the rare high of winning against all odds.

When it was over, my opponent stomped off on wobbly legs, or sometimes asked what I did to win and congratulated me. Most often, he called me lucky.

And I felt too good. It fed this ugly animal in my chest, ravenous in there. *Look at me. Look at me, bitch.*

Calliope had prepped me in advance for my meeting with Huge. She said he wasn't like the other players. "The other guys don't invite him to anything scandalous," she said. "Everyone knows he's super straight. He's the best of them, the nicest guy on the team. A preacher's kid."

I had dressed like a college student for this meeting—T-shirt, jeans, light jacket for a dry spring day—thinking Huge would be more likely to talk to me if he believed I was a peer. I had no idea why he had agreed to meet, but I hoped it was the possibility of a conscience Grayson had spoken of. I needed him to give me a fact, a name, something that would continue the story. I fantasized that Huge would say

"Yeah, the guys were bragging about gang-raping Simone and Calliope in the locker room afterward. Here are their names. Do you want me to testify?"

Huge showed up punctually at a coffee shop he had picked, across the street from the university complex. Huge *was* huge—six foot six and 340 pounds, according to the football roster. His size was startling in person, but I was used to being around big men in martial arts schools, and I had grown up with a poking and jabbing younger brother who suddenly far outgrew me when he turned twelve.

We sat down with our caffeine at a table outside the café, surrounded by traffic noise and students. It was at least ten degrees warmer in the sun than in the shade, and I was only slightly chilly, but Huge's muscles would keep him warm. I said, "So tell me about the party."

Huge said, "First thing you should know, I don't drink or get in trouble. None of those recruits was mine that night—I just went along for fun. They pair me with more straitlaced recruits. You know: straight with straight, wild with wild." He didn't touch his cappuccino.

"What do the wild recruits do with the wild hosts?"

"Well, that weekend, one of the recruits was complaining because 'Ya'll didn't put me on no 'ho's.' He was"—Huge held up a double-jointed thumb—"A. a preacher's son, and"—a forefinger—"B. he played piano for his church. So it was clear ahead of time he was going to come here and act a fool."

I laughed. Departing latte drinkers flashed smiles of recognition Huge's way, and puzzled frowns at me. This man was on TV almost every week during the football season. Huge ignored them with a captivating cool. His body sat dormant in the position of an athlete at rest, repairing every muscle for later punishment. He wasted not an electron of energy on posture, manners, or acknowledgment of who was sitting across from him. I was fascinated. Did he not care I was there? Did he think of me as a person with thoughts and feelings, worth a handshake or a nod? I couldn't stop looking at his monstrous arms. Still baby fat, or pizza fat, or whatever was under that smooth skin of youth, his enormous muscles resting on the carbon steel grate table between us like unvoiced threats.

I asked, "On the night of the attack, how long did you stay at Simone Baker's house?"

"Not long. The party was boring," Huge said, watching traffic. "One of the girls spilled beer on my leather jacket. So I just left when I knew there was going to be group sex."

"How did you know there was going to be, um, group sex?"

"I don't know. A girl said something, maybe."

"Which girl?"

Huge shifted, unwilling to be indelicate. "There were only two things there—alcohol and white girls. And the alcohol was gone. So some of the guys stayed for the girls. Later, the guys said 'It went down.' I didn't hear about the raping incident until Monday. I just thought it was the usual group sex stuff." Huge stuck a finger in his mouth, dislodged something, swallowed it.

"Is group sex a usual thing?"

"I wouldn't know."

"How about sexual assault?"

The lenses in Huge's eyes didn't match each other; the left emitted the soft shine of human tissue, but the right one was glassy from what looked like an early cataract surgery. He said, "Blame it on the alcohol. Also, it depends on what the girl says afterward."

"What do you mean?"

"Sex, a raping incident. It depends on what the girl says afterward."

"So you're saying it might have been sex, but afterward, she says they raped her because . . ."

"She'd get to say she was with a starter. The attention."

"I think the attention mostly sucks, Huge. Simone's getting harassed in and out of school."

"Yeah, well. It didn't work out so good for her."

I wasn't doing so well, either. I had never talked to anyone famous before. We were surrounded by an orb of admiration as thick and sweet as Jell-O, and I struggled to keep my head. Something Calliope had said haunted me: "After the attack, I thought everything from, 'How could they treat me like that?' to 'Maybe they like me.'" Now I suddenly understood. I wanted Huge to like *me*—not in a sexual way, just in a way that would keep me in his orbit. His celebrity was something he wore like skin. I didn't know if it was narcissism or star power, but I wanted to be close to it.

A friend told me he'd once met Muhammad Ali in college with a small group of his classmates. Muhammad Ali told the students, "I'm going to show you how I can levitate." He positioned himself against a wall and did a magic trick, turning sideways and lifting his body with one foot that was blocked from easy view. Everyone laughed, applauded. Next, Muhammad Ali made a quarter disappear and then reappear in his palm. Again, laughter, applause. Ali then pointed at a coffee spoon in the middle of a table and said, "Now I'm going to bend that spoon without touching it." He touched his fingertips to his temples. All ten students stared intently at the spoon on the table for a few seconds until the champ burst out laughing. "Ten Ivy League college boys and y'all believe I'm going to bend a spoon with my mind!"

Reality is pliable around celebrity. As I sat with Huge, I had to fight my instincts to believe whatever he told me, marveling at the strength and pull of his presence. Huge seemed to feel no such influences from me. "I just know it's not the way you say it is," he said.

"Even though you weren't in the bedroom? You don't believe in rape kits?" I actually didn't know whether or not Simone had gotten a rape kit, but Huge was pissing me off.

"That could just be rough sex."

"It's different." I formed an empty circle with a thumb and an index finger. "This is a vagina. Or an anus. Whatever." Huge smirked, but I continued. "The violated orifice. If it's rough sex, both parties are willingly participating, so there's slight damage all around the circle." I traced around it with my other index finger. "But if a victim is unconscious or unwilling, she isn't lifting up her hips to 'help.' Or if it's a guy, he isn't." Huge frowned, puzzled, and I saw I had lost him with the implication that a man could get raped. "Okay, so the friction and the damage gets concentrated along one side, depending on however she's positioned, on her back or her belly. Imagine a clock: there would be tears and stress from ten o'clock to two, or from four o'clock to eight, for example. So the rape kit shows sexual assault, not sex, not even rough sex. It shows nonconsensual sex. Or unconscious sex." I sounded like I knew what I was saying, but I had learned all of this from a TV show. As the logic of my explanation began to settle, Huge's expression changed. His eyes began to flit, like he was shopping for images, dismissing those that didn't fit.

"Who went into the bedroom, Huge?"

"I don't remember."

I had only two names—Calliope's alleged attackers—and wasn't sure I was allowed to use them, but I did anyway. "How about King Chambers?"

"King's cool," Huge said a little too quickly.

"Yeah, but did he go into the bedroom?"

"I don't remember."

I named Calliope's other alleged attacker: "Zachary Mooney?"

"I don't remember."

"Which recruits were asking for sex?"

"I don't remember."

I looked at my steno pad as if I had more names on it, said, "How about—" and then shut my mouth. Huge wasn't a bad person, but had I really expected him to help me? "Make us some friends," Grayson had told me. This was all going to be much harder than I thought.

I dropped my pen with a clatter and leaned away. "Why did you agree to meet with me, Huge?"

Huge smirked again and one dimple appeared on his cheek. "Because you sounded pretty on the phone."

I stifled a laugh in my throat. Huge was flirting with me at a rape investigation. I knew he was just flexing a muscle from boredom and habit, and maybe not even that much of a habit. For some reason, I wondered if he was a virgin. I pretended to be distracted by another man within his view, someone smaller than Huge—everyone in the vicinity was smaller than Huge. I played with the dried-out manzanita in the planter next to me.

Most people are uncomfortable with silence. Huge started to fidget almost immediately. He was trained to fill media time. Huge was more politician than boy, more spokesperson than student. I assumed he had checked with the football head coach before meeting with me. Maybe he was trying to keep himself out of trouble. Or maybe he had been sent to stonewall us, because he was harmless.

After about ten seconds of silence, Huge leaned toward me. "Okay. We're just talking, here, right?"

"Yes," I said. "We're just talking, here," not yet realizing that he'd just given me a useful phrase I'd come to rely on in nearly every future interview.

Huge said, "It's just that we have to stay competitive with other schools. If we don't show the recruits some fun, it would be boring and we wouldn't get anybody. With the girl thing, if it happens, it happens. It was bad choices that led to the raping incident, but those were individual choices. We were just showing them a good time."

"Coaches tell you to show the recruits a good time?" I asked.

"Yeah, the coaches always say that. But they don't look you up and down and give you the eye or anything. If it leads to sex or . . . well, that's not about the team or the school. It's about that host player and that recruit. Just them, only them."

"And the girl," I said.

Huge paused, recalculating in his head.

"Yeah," he finally said. "And the girl."

I got ringworm.

Brazilian jiu-jitsu is a filthy fighting style under normal circumstances, and worse when the weather warmed up. The sport mostly involved some greasy guy grinding into me on a mat until I tapped out. The mat smelled like a decade of bare feet. Whenever my opponent blinked, his sweat dripped into my eyes, splashed against my mouth guard, or slid up my nostrils into my sinuses. Everyone was terrified of staph and MRSA. The gym had no shower, and even after scrubbing my skin with Clorox wet wipes afterward, I left each practice smelling like testosterone, ass-sweat, and fungus spores.

One of those hundreds of sweaty guys worked with tigers—I didn't know if he was a veterinarian or a zookeeper or just a weirdo. Regardless, the tigers had ringworm, which I discovered is not a worm but a fungus. Apparently, this ringworm plagued the jiu-jitsu school, passed from athlete to athlete until it turned into a superparasite. I now understood it had been foolish for me to wear short-sleeved rash guards to "no-gi" (no uniform) practices. The heat-seeking ringworm attacked my armpits and wouldn't go away. I tried over-the-counter creams and prescription antifungal pills. The ringworm just laughed. I tried vinegar, tea tree oil, and bleach. I considered taking a lighter to it. I had been living with it for five months, and as the weather grew warmer, my skin cracked and bled.

Finally, my karate teacher gave me the number of an acupuncturist, a karate and kung fu guy. I knew about him, had seen him on fuzzy videotapes beating people up with a relentlessness that impressed and terrified me. He was from Colorado but had left for graduate school, recently returning home to settle and set up his practice. I knew all his friends but had avoided him for years, calling him "Scary JD" in my head. When people said "JD's in town and coming over—want to grab lunch?" I always said "I'm out of here." I knew Scary JD wouldn't attack me on sight for no reason, but I had trained with enough of these guys to know sucker punches were part of their fun. Some of them, the woman haters, sometimes suddenly overturned me in the street for no reason, on the way to many a post-training burrito. Scary JD was friends with those guys. But my bloody armpits were ruining all my shirts, so I finally called him and made an appointment.

JD's office was in the next town over, shared with a chiropractor who was sitting behind the counter when I arrived, eating Oreos four at a time out of a plastic sleeve. Scary JD came out of a treatment room to greet me. He seemed benign in his lab coat, which flattened his huge shoulders into a slump. The fluorescent lights made his eyes even greener. He led me into a windowless treatment room that stank of skunky burned herbs, and instructed me to sit on a massage table.

The big guy chitchatted in a medical way, asking about my appetite, which I told him about, and my poop, which I refused to tell him about, and also weird questions—did I like salty food or sweet? Feel hot or cold most of the time? What was my job? He did the usual double-take when I told him about my PI work, and he asked about the case while he inspected my eyes and tongue. It felt odd, since I was usually the one who asked the questions.

"Interesting," he said, taking my pulse at my wrist, rolling the vein beneath his calloused fingertips. "Although are you really surprised that the football player stuck with his team? That's the culture for those guys."

"But who's at fault for that culture? The lawyer says it's the university's. Or maybe it's just the individual players who commit those . . . acts because they want to." I found myself avoiding the word "rape" around him.

"You don't think the university's to blame?"

"I don't know if it is or isn't." I was unfamiliar with this college football culture everyone else seemed to know about. For my undergraduate degree, I went to a small college in Iowa with no football scholarships. The football players I met there were physics and economics majors. No one attended games, and lots of students didn't even know we had a football team. I hadn't experienced big college football until moving here, when students wore gold face paint and puzzling foam hats to the Intro to Creative Writing classes I taught while earning my master's degree at the university I was now investigating. "Whoever's to blame, I'm supposed to target the university system," I said.

"Well. Be careful. If you can target the system, the system can target you. So." JD raised his eyebrows and crossed his arms. "You know you're going to have to show me that ringworm, right?"

I was embarrassed. This acupuncture-karate badass was cute—green eyes, a soft reddish-brown goatee, thick, glinty hair, and those big shoulders. I lifted my arms. JD took a peek at my disgusting armpits and winced. "I'm so sorry," he said. I lowered my arms.

JD gave me a white plastic bag of strange-smelling herbs to brew into tea and wipe onto my underarms ("Dip in a new paper towel each time"), pills to swallow, and a paste to smear around my skin. I went home and did the things he told me to do. After five months of suffering, the ringworm was gone in three days, and the sores and scabs repaired themselves in five.

I returned to the office to see JD, at his request. I showed him my armpits, all healed and shiny. We both admired the transformation.

"That tea tasted terrible," I told him.

JD blanched. "What? You *drank* the tea?"

"I wasn't supposed to? It's tea."

"It's poison. For your skin. The instructions were clearly marked. You drank it? *When* did you drink it?" His eyes hardened in fear.

I smiled. "Yeah. I drank the tea, ate the paste, and rolled the pills around my armpits. Ha."

JD sagged, palm pressed against his big chest.

"You're gullible," I said.

JD was quiet for a moment. Then he finally said, "Okay. We're done here. You are not my patient anymore."

"What?"

"If you need medical care, you'll have to seek it from another provider."

Hold it. He was firing me?

"I'm sorry about the tea joke," I said. "It was stupid."

JD gave me an opaque smile. "Oh, no worries, no worries. But this visit is over. Okay?" Awkwardly, he shook my hand, one quick tug.

I couldn't read this guy's face at all, which scared me. I suddenly wanted to cry. JD led me to the door and I trailed him, saying, "I really didn't drink that stuff. I promise."

At the front desk, JD waved off payment. There was nothing to do but leave. There was the door in front of me. I was so confused. I turned around to say goodbye. JD stood there, his fists thrust deep into the pockets of his lab coat.

"So, Erika," he said. "Want to have lunch with me sometime?"

I was going on a date with Scary JD and I had survived my interview with Huge. Either these men were puffballs, or I was invincible.

The case warmed up with the weather. I tried reaching other players by phone, names Huge had accidentally dropped, people Calliope
had mentioned. I had to call them at strange hours. Some of them
were still in school, their lives governed by strict schedules: practice,
training, meals, classes, girlfriends, tutors. On game weekends, the
coaches scheduled their time in five-minute segments.

Players mostly said "Not talking to you" but didn't hang up, and
neither did I. I learned that I could uncover more information by ignoring social cues. It was like physical sparring—if you fall into their
rhythm, you lose, but if you interrupt their rhythm with your own,
you might have a chance. So I asked direct questions they didn't expect:
Do you think it's wrong for a girl to say no? Do you think everyone
wants to have sex with football players?

The best question was "What have you heard?" because they loved
to gossip. They said, "I heard she was a jersey-chaser." "I heard she was
scandalous." [Me: "What does that mean?"] "You know. The kind of
girl that has to have a football player between her legs all the time."
[Me: "Where did you hear that from?" while imagining how such a girl
could walk.] "Nowhere, I guess. That's how they are, though."

Sometimes the silences on the line lasted so long that I asked, "Are
you still there?" Some players spoke with no affect at all, like low-
voiced robots. Some players erupted in fury when they heard a question they didn't like, and then seemed to forget their rage immediately,
friendly again. Most of the players I spoke with seemed confused.

At that time, the *Journal of the American Medical Association* had not
yet conducted their 2017 study of the brains of 202 deceased football
players. They studied people who had played football in high school,
college, and the NFL. They diagnosed chronic traumatic encephalop-
athy (CTE), a degenerative brain disorder, in 21 percent of high school
players and 91 percent of college football players. Among the 111 NFL
players they studied, 110 had the disease, bringing the statistic up to
over 99 percent.

The longer you play, the worse the symptoms, which include aggression, ADHD, cognitive impairment, impulsive behavior, apathy,
confusion, disorientation, dizziness, vertigo, headaches, social/emo-

tional instability, personality changes, sensory processing disorder, speech impediments, balance issues, deafness, erratic/inappropriate/ explosive behavior, pathological jealousy, paranoia, depression, progressive dementia, memory loss, amnesia, strokes, and suicidal ideation. Football players' chances of contracting dementia at any age were between 33 and 85 percent.

But I didn't know any of this back then. I only knew what Calliope had told me: "These guys get hit in the head a lot. A *lot*. They don't always even understand what they're saying or doing. And then they forget immediately, like their brain is quicksand." I wondered what it was like to forget everything—everything bad that had ever happened to you, everything bad you ever did or watched someone else do.

One player spent our conversation repeating that everything was "clean, aboveboard. Just a sports team at a party." After I gave up and said goodbye, he called me back a few moments later and said earnestly, "Erika, I just want you to know something. I've met hundreds of people in college programs. The stuff that happens here, well, that happens everywhere. Everywhere. It's just the general culture of recruiting trips."

"What stuff happens everywhere? What general culture?"

And then he hung up again.

Another said, "I was a recruit, but I decided not to go to school there." When I asked why, he said, "Because of what I seen." "What did you see?" "Nothing. I didn't see *nothing*."

One player said, "I don't know anything about it. I wasn't there. But maybe one girl's discomfort is worth it if, you know, it means winning a championship. Sometimes you have to make a sacrifice for the greater good."

"Who has to make a sacrifice?" I asked. "The girls?"

"If that's what it takes," he said. "This is glory we're talking about."

"Of course," I said, exuding warmth, fearing for humanity. "Can you give me some other examples?"

Most of the players hadn't been at the party, so whenever I reached one who had, it was important. One night I reached a player named Clifford, a recruit who had attended Simone's party but decided instead to attend school in Nebraska. "Nope, nope, nope," he said when I introduced myself. But, again, Clifford didn't hang up on me. None of the players did. I was beginning to think these young men were lonely.

By now, I had learned to split witnesses into two types: yes and no. Yes-witnesses liked being led, so I posed positive questions ("So you were expected to get the recruits drunk?"). With no-witnesses, I framed my questions so I was always wrong, so they could say no, no, no to me, but always in the direction I wanted them to go. I guessed that Clifford was a no-witness and asked, "You don't want to talk about the recruiting weekend?"

"No, I can talk about it. It was a great time. We did normal things, house parties, like that."

"Normal? You didn't hear what happened that night?"

"No, I heard what you heard." With every "no," he warmed up. "I left the party before it went down." There was that phrase again: "It went down."

"How did you know it would go down?"

"That woman said 'Let the fun begin.' The one who invited us into the bedroom."

"Who? Who invited you?"

"I don't know. I thought it was the girl who lived there."

"She didn't invite you. She was asleep."

Clifford sounded impatient. "Listen, I remember going to a party and going to my hotel and going to bed. That's it, that's all. I was a good boy back then."

"Are you a good boy now?"

Silence on the line. Then Clifford rumbled in a low voice, "No. I'm bad now. I'm a bad boy now. A big, bad, bad boy."

A barbed current ran up my spine. Clifford was younger than me, but he sounded like X.

Clifford asked, "This your phone number on my caller ID? What's your address?"

Clifford asked, "What you look like, Erika?"

Clifford asked, "No man at your place? You all alone right now?"

Clifford asked, "Girl?"

I hung up, my hands shaking. I locked my door and windows carefully, as if this world I had built for myself might fracture at the slightest pressure. But that other, lightless world still threatened to force its way back into mine, through any opening—unwanted, unavoidable.

3

Hour of Power

Colorado skipped spring that year and sprinted straight to summer, hot and close. Virga stretched downward from gray clouds, with tapering shafts of rain evaporating before touching ground, looking from a distance like wispy fingers pointing to earth: *Here is where it all happened.* No rain, no hope of rain. The spring blizzard hadn't done enough to replenish the water supply, and we already worried about fires, flash floods, climate change, our dogs' paws, our limp, burned gardens. Temperatures rose to the low hundreds, and overtaxed air conditioners sparked power outages.

The multiyear drought doomed the century-old lodgepole pine forests that dominated Colorado's high country. It was our fault for letting our forests get so unidimensional. Natural cleansing forest fires ordinarily keep a forest in check, killing off diseased growth and making room for saplings, but state policies had suppressed fires for over a hundred years to protect homes and property. So the forest had overgrown, enabled into an ecosystem of preserved deadwood, rot, and weakened trees susceptible to pine beetle.

A pine beetle is only five millimeters long, a dark scarab-looking bug with a gator-skin exterior. But a drive west will show you how mighty those little fuckers are. Every spring, they burrow into old-growth pines, attacking the most ancient lodgepoles and ponderosas. With plentiful snow and rain, a healthy tree can quickly spit out the beetles with sap. But in a drought, it doesn't have enough spit to do it, especially if it's competing with so many other trees for water. The beetle lays its eggs under the bark and injects a blue stain fungus into the sapwood. The fungus blocks water and nutrients from circulating and ousting the eggs.

At this point, the tree suffers a stroke. After surviving several centuries of mountain winters, the lodgepole now dies in months. Its needles burn red and drift to the forest floor. The eggs are safe. The beetles have already moved on.

Millions of acres of ghost trees. Ten thousand new dead trees each day. A dead forest is nowhere you want to be. The central mountains became graveyards, miles of gray lodgepoles stripped naked. Whole forests flamed red and perished in one season. Tree trunks splayed across the ground, piles of enormous pick-up sticks. Live soldiers held up the many dead. The bare trees creaked or growled as their bark chafed against another's, or they clacked in the gusts like wooden wind chimes.

Then came the inevitable fires. The dry needles served as kindling for the parched tree trunks. It took only one lightning strike to ignite what were essentially forests of giant matches. With a real fire, a hot fire, wood and forest floor melted into near-lava. Birds abandoned their nests as their eggs boiled.

Afterward, the land was cleansed of all hope and worry. The worst had already happened. Only charred, limbless stalks still stood, rooted in ash, shocked into silence.

The details about the night of Simone's attack still eluded us, and Grayson had been right about news coverage changing everything. Bucking journalistic convention for rape victims, the newspapers printed Simone's name without her permission. Afraid of retribution from players or rabid fans, Simone asked to attend school anonymously, but the university refused.

Meanwhile, a woman named Ivy joined Simone's case as a second plaintiff. Ivy had been allegedly sexually assaulted by a player at the same time as Simone, in the living room. Grayson was hoping that Calliope would join the case as well. As the survivors increased in number, we started referring to them as "the women," as if they were members of a terrible club nobody wanted to belong to.

When asked to comment on the attack, football head coach Wade Riggs said that there was "no question in my mind that the behavior of the ten young people involved was the result of their own poor decisions under the influence of alcohol." The number made his meaning clear: "ten young people" included Simone and Ivy as well as the eight potential attackers. Coach Riggs had skipped ahead to Defense Dog 4: *My dog bit you because you provoked him*, while also maintaining Defense Dog 1: *That's not my dog.* Peddling doubt, someone began circulating the false rumor that Simone was handing out condoms to the players that night.

I kept lists of people who might have attended the party: names Calliope and Huge had dropped, a few Grayson had mentioned. Grayson wanted me to act as a kind of clearinghouse for information, reserving his own scant time for law and the most important witnesses. He said, "Give me memos. And I want them well written. Make them entertaining. But not fiction," he added.

Just finding these people was difficult, though. All private eyes learn "skip tracing"—finding people ("skips") who have skipped town, gone incognito, or simply moved away. I had grown up on spy movies that implied all you needed was a person's Social Security number to discover their location, workplace, bank balance, best friend's name, and preferred toothpaste. But no matter what information I gathered, I never found the magical database that could split open a person's private life like it was a geode. I imagined I'd have to be able to hack into an FBI database for that kind of information—a skill I didn't have or want. As an alumna of the university, I had access to both college and alumni directories, but few people listed their ever-shifting contact information there. It was the summer of 2003; social media was around, but not yet a part of people's daily lives. College students and recent grads rarely paid for any of the things that left an ID trail on the online people-finder services: mortgages, utilities, landlines, magazine subscriptions.

I quailed at names like Smith, Williams, and Brown, and relied heavily on middle initials. Without context, a nearly unfindable name like Chris Johnson was the worst because it could be either a man or a woman, thereby doubling my work. Women had the annoying habit of marrying and changing their names. I searched everywhere for these people: social media, the county assessor, county clerk and recorder, sex offender registries, and even the Federal Bureau of Prisons directory. Sometimes a phone call to directory assistance yielded better results than I got online, so I tried that often. Staff directories were golden.

After graduation, many students returned home to live while they searched for jobs, and it was hard to break through their parents' protective gauntlets. "Who are you, again? What is this about? Would my son have to go to court? I don't think he's interested in that. No, no." The more protective the parent, the more stubborn I got, but it made me feel jealous of these people whose parents had their backs.

Once I called the father of a graduated player to find out his whereabouts. The boy's father said gently, "I'm so sorry to tell you this, but my son died in a car accident last week." He cried while I gushed apologies, pretending I knew his son so his pain wouldn't be cheapened by the fact that I was just out to get something.

It was best to call people at work, because they were young and usually working crappy jobs—stocking department stores, waitressing, fetching coffee at a local TV station. I'd insist the manager put them on the phone, saying, "It's in connection to a lawsuit." I didn't tell the manager that the employee wasn't in trouble. Inevitably, the potential witness came to the phone and said, "You can't call me at work. Here's my number." I'd spent my whole life working at those jobs where every second of personal time is considered theft, where you're excoriated for getting a non-work phone call or returning three minutes late from your half-hour lunch break. Now I asked over the phone, "*When* can I talk to you tomorrow?" but slowly, to stress them out further. After I got a commitment, I ended with, "Great, and if I can't reach you then, I'll try you again here," pausing in case they had to exchange the number they had given me for a real one.

These tactics generally worked. We added details from all my forced conversations to Simone's testimony, and Grayson and I were able to piece together a picture of a party:

It was supposed to be a girls' night in. A male friend had provided the night's beer, a thirty-pack of Keystone. It took a lot of food and drinks for him to admit as much to me, because he felt guilty and was afraid of getting arrested for providing alcohol to minors. The women played "the hour of power": you drink one shot of beer per minute for sixty minutes, totaling seven and a half beers inside an hour. Of course, they were drunk.

One of the guests, Leah, worked as a tutor for the university's football program. Unbeknownst to Simone, Leah had previously invited a player to bring recruits over. The player believed she had invited them over for sex with the women there. It was the final football recruiting weekend, and the university had just beat Texas to win the Big 12 Conference Championship.

Grayson said that Leah and the player talked by phone at least eight times. By the time her doorbell rang, Simone was intoxicated. Sixteen to twenty large players and recruits muscled their way into the tiny apartment, and Simone didn't know any of them. She was polite, trying to be a good hostess, but the men said things like "I'm a football player, you should suck my dick." The players brought a large bottle of Captain Morgan Spiced Rum, and had already fed the seventeen-year-old recruits several bottles of liquor and plenty of drugs. One recruit spent most of the party puking up Apple Jacks in the sink and on the bathroom floor.

Another group of players arrived shortly thereafter, so there were now thirty people in the small two-bedroom apartment, plus the original guests, Calliope, and a couple of Simone's other friends. Simone asked the players to leave, and a few did. Some players said that Leah ran outside saying, "Come back! It's about to go down!" but she later denied it. Some players returned to the party. Calliope's group left, saying things like, "I'm getting out of here" and "I don't want any part of this."

Simone was already passed out in her bed when a group of players entered the bedroom and locked the door. She awoke to two naked men pulling off her clothes. A group of six to eight large men surrounded her. It was very dark and she couldn't see anything. When she turned her head, someone shoved his penis into her mouth, saying, "I'm a recruit; suck my dick." Another got on top of her and forced himself into her vagina.

Simone said in a deposition, "The players . . . and the recruits just came in and just—they didn't even ask to have sex with me. They just thought it was okay. And they were bigger and there [were] more of them and they just—they could do whatever they wanted to me."

Simone couldn't see who the men were, and didn't know how long it went on, or with how many people. Still intoxicated, she tried to crawl to the top of her bed to escape. Bruises on her arms and knees later indicated that one or more men held her down.

During this time, in the living room, a player groped Ivy. Another player allegedly attacked Leah, the woman who had invited the players without Simone's knowledge. The player allegedly grabbed her by the hair and pushed her head onto his naked penis. Another player masturbated and ejaculated onto the floor. Three other women said they were otherwise sexually harassed: groped, undressed, dragged into the bedroom, harangued for oral sex, and forcibly kissed. All the women kept telling them no. Women left. Other recruits and players emptied cereal boxes onto the kitchen floor and ransacked purses in the living room, stealing money and about six women's cell phones.

At some point the bedroom door was open and the male friend who had supplied the beer saw the men surrounding Simone's bed, but he said he was too scared to do anything. No one else witnessed Simone's attack in the dark. Almost everyone was drunk or high or both.

Simone eventually emerged from the bedroom, and the players and recruits left.

In an alcoholic frenzy, Simone and her friends cleaned the trashed apartment. They washed all the sheets. Simone showered and then sobered up. She contacted her mother, who drove straight over in the middle of the night, comforted her, and helped her clean up the rest of the mess. This was around the same time that Calliope was allegedly sexually assaulted by two of the players who were in Simone's bedroom. The next morning, Simone called the provost of the university. Her third call was to the police, who told her a rape kit would be useless because she had showered. A year later, she hired Grayson.

Of course, I wanted to interview Leah, the party organizer, but Grayson said she was off-limits—he was going to subpoena and depose her. I had to follow lesser leads. One woman, Yvonne, had been in the hallway at the party the whole time, and had seen everything there was to see from that vantage point. She was friendly and agreed to meet.

By this time, I was dating JD a little bit, so I had to work around my schedule with him and my temp jobs to see Yvonne. She showed up at the same bar-restaurant where I had met Calliope, a place that had quickly became my ersatz office. Yvonne was sturdy, shoulders muscular in her turquoise tank top. She had an earthy, maternal voice that contrasted with her transcribed stuttering, guilty chatter from the police report, which was where I had found her name. Still, she was young, and her eagerness reminded me of the way my sister used to act with adults, tripping over herself to help, unsure how she might be useful.

After we sat down, I visibly handed my credit card to the server so Yvonne would order as much food and beer as she wanted. Yvonne said, "I'll tell you whatever I can. Simone is a good friend of mine. This is all such a mess. We had thought we were being safe, staying at home."

I said, "It would have been safe if Simone's friend Leah didn't invite the players over. I don't get that. Why did she do it?"

Yvonne rolled her eyes. "Leah wasn't Simone's friend, more like a friend of a friend. I don't know where Leah got it into her head that we would sleep with those guys. Maybe she does whatever, but Simone doesn't even kiss until like the fourth date. Leah's really mean. She was raped herself a month or two before, so maybe she was still messed up about that."

"Leah was assaulted? By a player?"

"No. Some other guy, older."

Given this information, Leah's role in this party made a strange kind of sense. Maybe she had been trying to normalize her own experience. Or maybe it's every woman for herself.

When I was four, I told my older sister what X was doing to me. We were playing with some small toys, pushing them through hard blue carpet. She was two years older than me, six, and I thought of her as nearly grown up in her yellow-white dress. The world around me felt very big and blurry around the periphery—nobody had diagnosed my nearsightedness yet. I don't remember the words I used to tell my sister about X's abuse. I don't remember her words, either, but I remember what I thought they meant at that time: *Good. If he's doing it to you, he won't do it to me.*

Now, I asked Yvonne, "What do you remember about that night?"

"Well, Simone went into the bedroom to pass out. She's like that; she falls asleep everywhere we go, movies, you name it. And she can't hold her liquor at all. She never could.

"After a while, people went into the bedroom. I went in to see what was happening, but it looked innocent. People were kissing and dancing. Simone was passed out alone on the bed. There were people standing around her, though. It was crowded and really dark, so I couldn't see very well."

"Did you see the players leave?"

"Yeah. King was zipping up his pants as he left, on the phone saying, 'Hey, baby, I love you.'" I wrote that down. Yvonne said, "The football players all kind of left at once, together. When Simone came out of the room, she was wearing boxers and a T-shirt and her hair was everywhere." Yvonne's gaze searched the corners of the room. "She was dazed, like she had just woken up and begun to have a hangover. She had this blank look on her face, like, 'What on earth is happening?' Actually, though, she looks like that a lot of the time. But she kept moving a drinking glass back and forth, back and forth like she was in a trance.

"She went into the bathroom, which was covered in puke, and began cleaning that up. Everyone was like, 'Oh my god,' and started picking up condoms from the bathroom and bedroom. We just cleaned."

"How many condoms?"

"There were nine, but then they found another one later, so it was a total of ten. We threw them out."

"You didn't realize you were destroying evidence?"

"They were gross, and we were still intoxicated. And everyone knows the football players never get charged for anything. But now I don't understand why we didn't think to keep it anyway. The evidence."

I understood, though. Pain defeats logic, and the first instinct is to make it all go away. When I was four, I buried my bloody underwear in the bottom of my trash can and covered it with a whole box of crumpled tissues. The stainless steel garbage can was decorated in yellow smiley faces, and the memory always felt bewildering until I learned the word "irony."

Yvonne's demeanor had changed. She seemed smaller. Maybe I had inadvertently shamed her about the evidence. In a gentler voice, I asked, "Can you give us any names of the men in the bedroom?"

"I can't remember." Yvonne swiped at an eyelid.

"How about during the assault? Did you see anything suspicious?"

"No."

"And you were at the apartment the whole time?"

Yvonne nodded.

I said, "Even if you're afraid you'll get in trouble, you can still tell me whatever's on your mind." I tried Huge's line, "We're just talking, here."

Yvonne nodded again. She reached for her beer. I didn't know what had changed between us, or why, but somehow, I had blown it. We sipped our drinks and sat in silence for a few seconds, separate silences. I glanced at my watch, and Yvonne saw me do it. I reached for the bill and started calculating the tip.

Then Yvonne said in an entirely different voice, "Well, at one point, two players did come out of the bedroom naked."

I looked up. "Naked?"

"Yeah."

"From Simone's bedroom? Where she was unconscious?"

"Yes." Yvonne looked miserable.

My bouncing knee made the beers tremble on the table. "Which two players?"

Yvonne named two new names, Xavier and Frank. I added them to my list, now totaling four. Counting Calliope's alleged attackers, King Chambers and Zachary Mooney, Yvonne had doubled my list of suspects in less than a minute. "They were completely naked?"

"Xavier went into the bathroom, grabbed a towel, knotted it around his neck like a cape, and went back in. Frank wore a towel around his waist."

I asked, "What else did you see?"

"Not much. I covered my eyes."

I had almost missed all this. I wanted to kiss Yvonne, and throw something heavy at her. She had been planning to walk away from our meeting full of her club sandwich and lite beer without thinking to mention two naked men coming from the bedroom where her friend was allegedly raped. "You didn't think that was—"

"Jesus." Yvonne's chin puckered. "I'm a damn psych major, for God's sake. I should have figured it out. How obvious. I should have gone in there to check again. What was I thinking?" She answered her own question, as if I had asked it. "I guess I thought someone would have come and gotten me if anything bad happened. It was so surreal and wrong. I still don't know what happened in that bedroom."

I leaned back in my seat. "What happened was this. Simone was repeatedly sexually assaulted in the dark by an unknown number of large football players and recruits as others surrounded them and held her down so she couldn't escape."

Yvonne looked away at the acrylic menu holder, the family at the next table, the bartender pouring clear liquid from a bottle. Anywhere but at my face. "I didn't know the—the details."

I didn't know why I wanted to make this girl feel bad. She hadn't hurt anyone. But she was there the whole time and did nothing. I said, "Yvonne, it's not your fault. Those players did these things, not you."

"I didn't stop it, though. And the university isn't stopping it now. Football players don't have consequences."

"You blame the university for the attack?"

"I blame everyone, I guess. I blame myself."

I started in again with how it wasn't her fault, but Yvonne waved me off. "That's the problem, right? Everyone looking away and pretending it doesn't happen. The university essentially abandoned Simone. They were supposed to protect her, too, not just their football team. Not just themselves. I know we're legally adults, but really we were just kids."

Yvonne's face turned motherly again. "Hey. Are you okay? You look kind of sick."

I shook my head, but it only made me sway in my seat.

"Are you dizzy or something?"

"No," I said. "Everything's fine."

Ever since I was four, when I got too angry or overwhelmed, I became disoriented with whirling, not in my head but in the center of my chest, right where my heart should be. The feeling started soon after X targeted me, and it never went away, although I could ignore it most of the time. Throughout my childhood, the whirling increased with any strong feeling, angry or sad or scared, or when my mother talked to me, when I went outside, when I was stuck inside, evenings and nighttimes when I was completely trapped. The eddying churned my insides, made me feel like my skin would split and I would spill out. It sometimes accelerated into a downhill, runaway feeling, like I couldn't get my legs under me, the sensation of running and contorting and falling.

I couldn't figure out what to call it, this feeling, until I visited my friend's house when I was about five. In her powder-pink bedroom she had a glass cage with a fuzzy gray pet rat inside, hunched over as if ashamed. It climbed onto a wheel using those strange fleshy feet that looked like four-fingered hands. The rat began running on the wheel until its fur streaked in long lines, tail high, the wheel whirring and slowing. The rat ran nowhere, tripping, gaining ground and then losing it, gaining, losing, eyes fixed.

The erratic pace of the wheel exactly matched the pace of the spinning inside me. I recognized it with my body. That was what I felt inside my chest—a rat running on a wheel until it lost its legs. My rage had a face and a furry body full of dirty things I would later learn to fear: parasites, bacteria, viruses, excrement. These things were inside me, and so was that rat.

In fifth grade we did animal reports in science class, and I chose the naked mole-rat. They are nearly immortal. They live underground in African deserts and can hold their breath for eighteen minutes. To survive underground, the nearly hairless rats have become almost completely cold-blooded, only mammals via technicality, like platypuses.

They die, of course, but not because they age. They die of the same things as any rat—they're killed, they wither from disease or infection, they starve or die of thirst. But they can't get cancer. They don't feel pain, even when immersed in acid. They live by half-lives like radioactive material. Their remaining life spans split by increments, never reaching zero. They're as likely to die at age three as they are at age three hundred. They reproduce forever.

My rat ran on rage, or pain, or maybe some poison unique to me for which there is no name. It ran through my childhood and all the humiliations therein. It grew bigger as I did, strong as Sisyphus. Running, panting through its buckteeth, the wheel always keeping pace. The feeling often buckled me over, but sometimes it felt like relief, the whirring, the running, the stretch and contraction of rat muscle, the wire under calloused paws, the speed at which it—I—went nowhere.

Rat facts:

A rat can survive being flushed down the toilet and will eventually swim back and reemerge from the bowl like a wet phoenix. You can drop a rat from a height of fifty feet and it will still walk away. You can deprive it of sleep for twenty days. A rat can recognize the scent of an unfamiliar poison from rumor alone.

A rat can change its shape entirely, collapsing its skeleton to fit into small holes.

Rats have traveled in space.

Rats dream.

There is one rat per person in the world.

You are never more than ten feet from a rat.

Despite my disillusionment with men, I was still dating JD.

I had never been good at dating. I fell in love way too quickly and inappropriately, admiring the wrong things about the wrong men, like the man who carried his expensive tennis racket everywhere, even in the winter, or the man who could drink (and pay for!) eight or nine Rusty Nails with dinner every night, or the man who counted off ten reasons why I should sleep with him on our first date, or the man who could intelligently discuss Marxist revolutionary politics while high on heroin.

While I was growing up, my mother had pelted me with predictions whenever she got angry: I would never find a man, nobody would ever love me, and nobody would ever marry me. My brother and sister would find happiness, but never me, the rotten kid I was. I rebelled at these "nevers," so maybe they were what gave me the strange idea that dating should be democratic, and all people—narcissists, alcoholics, drug addicts, men destroyed by another woman, men indifferent enough to survive even me—were possibly lovable. They weren't. Neither was I, I learned over and again. All this dating was simultaneously boring and panic-inducing, with side orders of despair and uncomfortable underclothing. But I didn't want to die alone, or die at all, but especially not alone.

I did not understand love, although I had often felt it. I just didn't know how it was supposed to work once you separated the feeling from itself and turned it into action, doing things together. I hardly ever dated anyone until after I graduated from college. Before that, when I truly liked someone, I wouldn't pursue a relationship even if he thought he liked me. I was doing him a favor by saying no. Who would want to get involved with the mess that was me? Even now, I mostly dated people who seemed already broken in some way. We'd spend some time together, he would barely notice me, and we would both emerge intact.

JD was different. He noticed me. He'd ask, "How are you?" when we met up. I'd say brightly, "Fine!" and his face would fall. "What's wrong?" he'd ask. Nobody else I had ever dated had ever been able to read when I was worried or sad unless I told them, sometimes several times, and even then they often didn't care. JD made me feel invaded, but in a good way.

I was already getting attached by the time I met his dog, a boxer mutt waiting patiently for him in his Jeep while JD and I ate dinner one evening. Upon JD's return, the two of them regarded each other, and then JD gave the dog a quick peck on the mouth. And I fell in love.

But we didn't touch or anything. Just dinners, hikes, walks, calls. *What's wrong?* I wondered. Was I repulsive? If so, then why did he feed me over candlelight and ask if I had brothers and sisters and where I went to college? Why did he call to ask for the next date before I had even finished walking away from him, when I could still hear his voice behind me? But no kiss, no touch. Just dinner, dinner, dinner. The impossible was happening: I was beginning to hate dinner.

One night at the end of yet another chaste date, JD walked me to my car and backed away as usual, bidding me good night. Summer was ending; the night air was cool. Exasperated, I let my bag drop to the pavement. "Come here," I said.

"What?" he asked.

He didn't move, so I walked toward him.

"What are you doing?" he asked quickly. In the glow of the streetlight, his face registered fear. He visibly adjusted, face dropping, readying himself. How could such a big man be scared of me? I touched his cheek and kissed him. He kissed me back and wrapped his strong arms around me.

It was great.

As we came out of the clinch, the first thing he said was, "I could lose my license for this." And then he kissed me again.

I was obsessed, on a trail of my own. I needed to know the names of everyone who had been in that bedroom with Simone. My rage had become too generalized, and my whirling spells sometimes burgeoned into panic attacks that lasted anywhere from ten seconds to a half hour. I needed to limit my anger to six or eight strangers. Then I would be okay.

Calliope was my best bet for IDing people. She had been to the party, had been relatively sober, and knew the names of all the players. She knew who had left and who had stayed behind when "it went down." I had been calling her for a couple of weeks to set another meeting with her, but she was packing for a move back to Pennsylvania. She stood me up and then apologized to my voicemail: "I've been depressed and I forgot to set my alarm and oh my god I'm so sorry I'm having trouble keeping things straight." I worried about her state of mind.

On the day of our next meeting at the same bar-restaurant, the air was so dry that my hair clung to my head and everything I touched gave me electric shocks. It was hot outside but too cold in the restaurant, and I shivered on the wooden bench seat. They were remodeling the kitchen, so every now and then something crashed or broke in there, but the place was otherwise quiet because of the early hour. This was my lucky place, and I was beginning to associate the smell of craft beer and french fries with success.

Calliope showed up in a navy shift dress, looking tired and thinner than before. Her bare arms had shrunk, the muscle now dormant. But she was there.

I had come prepared. "I'm going to show you some pictures of players," I said. "What I need to know is who came to the party and who stayed when you left." The Media Guide I had ordered still hadn't arrived from the university—did they know I was working for Grayson?—but I had printed out pictures from the roster on my inkjet printer, so every face had a smeary pink cast to it.

Calliope got very serious and wiped her hands on her napkin. I placed pictures before her, one after the other. "No. No. Yes, he was in the kitchen. No. Yes. He stayed when I left. Not him, I think." Her memory was impeccable. After Yvonne's leads, the names stacked up where I thought they would, placing both Zachary and King in the bedroom group, along with Yvonne's leads and two others I had never heard of before. I wrote down the new names while Calliope flipped through the pages, looking for something on her own.

Then she tapped one face. "There you are," she said softly.

I craned my neck to see who she was looking at. Smooth, unworried brow. Cornrows and a high fade, pencil mustache, no neck.

Calliope said, "That's the recruit I saw at Illegal Pete's after the party, the one who looked like he'd seen death. Something bad happened to him."

"Something in Simone's bedroom? Or was he hungover?"

"No. It was definitely trauma." She gave me an I-know-of-what-I-speak look.

But something was wrong. I hadn't printed out recruit pictures, just pictures of current players. Head football coach Wade Riggs had insisted they pulled the scholarships of any recruits who attended the party. "You saw him that night as a recruit? Not as a player?"

"Yeah, he was a recruit. At the party, a player pointed at this guy and told me, 'Kiss him, he likes you,' and the recruit said, 'Come to my hotel room.' And then later in the night, it's like he's wearing the mask of death."

This player was an incoming freshman at the university. They had waited a year to fund and admit him, as if everyone would forget, and they were right. Everyone had forgotten. "He's not even supposed to be at the university," I said. "Coach Riggs was supposed to pull the scholarships of every recruit at that party."

"Yeah, but nothing got fully revoked, right? Even those player scholarships that were put on hold because of the drinking charges. That was just a semester, and those players still got loans and played football. They didn't sit out a single game. I'm not surprised they still brought those recruits in," Calliope said. "Are you?"

I shook my head. But this was something. Coach Riggs solicited at least one of Simone's possible attackers, brought him to school, and gave him an education paid for out of state taxes. Out of Simone's taxes, and mine. I took notes to pass on to Grayson.

I asked, "Have you heard any rumors about Simone handing out condoms? Because that's false."

"Yeah, that's what they're saying." A nearby table of teenagers flared into sudden laughter, and Calliope shrank from the sound. "Like a girl having condoms makes what they did okay. I said that to King when he called."

"Why did he call you?"

"He was angry that I had talked to the police and told them what I knew about that night. I said, 'I'm not going to lie for you for raping a girl.'"

"Did you use the word 'rape'?"

"Yes, I definitely used the word. He didn't deny it or get defensive. He was just pissed off that I didn't do everything in my power to make the situation look better than it was. He expected that."

"Because he's used to it?"

"They all are." Calliope tapped the oak table with a nail. "My ex-boyfriend was a football player and he got *two* DUIs, but he was allowed to keep driving like nothing ever happened. He could retake any class he failed and the F went away. He said some football players traded season tickets for B grades. Lots of T.A.'s were fans. For every test, teachers gave him the questions in advance. No surprises. Even the 'random' drug tests are handpicked for goody-goodies like Huge. Those guys are there to play football," Calliope said. "School is the *last* thing."

"Does it make them feel like outsiders, do you think?"

Calliope leaned back in the booth, exhaustion leaking from her. Dusk had fallen outside, and the shadows elongated on her beautiful face. "I think being Black makes them feel like outsiders. You always feel like you need to represent. You eat separately—white with white, Black with Black. There's a lot of jealousy. Black athletes take the most shit, probably because we play. And because we're foreigners."

It made me unspeakably sad to hear this all-American girl call her-self a foreigner.

Calliope said, "You know, those people took the best part of me, and I got nothing back but heartache. I'm sitting across from you and telling you, it happened to me, it happened to Simone, and I guarantee you, there will be a next time."

"Is that why you're moving to Pennsylvania? To get away from them?" The server showed up to clear our plates, and Calliope waited until we were alone again before answering.

"I can't sleep," Calliope said, leaning in. "I'm emotional all the time. I'm afraid to go outside and see them. Their sport is to hit each other so hard they can't stand back up. What would they do to me?"

This seemed as good a reason to move as any.

Grayson had left several unanswered messages for Calliope and her mother. I looked at my list. Calliope had confirmed and named seven suspects. She had given us everything, and I had to ask her for more.

I said, "Calliope. Will you please talk to my boss?"

Calliope gathered her bag, gave me a thin hug, and then paused. "I talked it over with my mom. I think I'm going to join the lawsuit."

"You are?" My gut reaction was to tell her no, to go east and re-cover. But this was good for us. Good for me. I said, "You're really brave, Calliope," trying not to imply that she would need to be.

A deep, fragile emotion engulfed her face and then passed. "I know how bad I feel, and I can't imagine how that girl feels. They can't get away with it again. Not this time," Calliope said. "Not with me."

4

The Game

The university town is bordered to the west by rock formations called the Flatirons. They're some of the biggest rocks in the world, several the size and shape of mountain peaks. They're named after the old-timey flat irons women used to heat in a fire, hold by the handle with rags, and smooth over their stinky dresses. Clearly, pioneer women named the Flatirons, because how many men ironed clothes back then? The Flatirons do look like the bottoms of antique irons, or perhaps like something ironed in an upward swipe. The vast triangular rock faces pitch at a fifty-degree angle, each a thousand feet thick, sandstone and conglomerate rock grains glued together by adularia, moonstone. It's why they glow sometimes, reflecting whatever light is aimed at them. They look different every day. In rain they sink into a dark gray, or they pop reddish-brown in sunlight. Sometimes mist flanks the rock faces, Devil's Thumb sticking out to hitchhike. In the summer, the foothills fur up, yellow-brown in the sun. And cracked with white after a snow, the rocks are stern faces, demanding attention.

The biggest five Flatirons are named by number, and a hundred smaller ones stud the foothills: Satan's Slab, the Willie B, the Seal, the Maiden, the Matron. The Third Flatiron is the biggest one of all, rising twelve hundred feet from its base. You can't keep climbers off the rock, as the need to touch beauty is as strong as the need to see it. The eight-pitch route has been climbed in every conceivable way: naked, in roller skates, at night, and somehow without hands.

The Flatirons shelter bears, mountain lions, raptors, bats, and black Abert's squirrels with their tufted ears. Padded forests of ponderosa and lodgepoles, scree fields and sandstone quarries. Elk sedge, clumpy rabbitbrush, wax currant, and goldenrod. I hiked there often, and each time I wondered what had kept me away for so long, even if it was only a week. I had stayed in this small city for the Flatirons. Southern Arapaho Chief Niwot, before his murder at the Sand Creek Massacre in 1864, prophesied the valley's curse: once people saw the beauty of the Flatirons, they would never leave. And their staying would mean the beauty's undoing.

Originally rising from the dust of the eroded Ancestral Rockies, today's Flatirons are about 296 million years old. But since the 1940s, students have climbed the Third Flatiron to paint the university's initials on the rock in glaring white, a fifty-foot-tall billboard. The city repeatedly tried to remove the paint with acid and blowtorches, only for ardent students to strap gallon cans to belts, climb up, and paint it again by moonlight. The city eventually gave up and began covering the white with eight different pigments to blend in with the rock. It didn't work. You can still see the letters if you know where to look.

Calliope joined our case as the third plaintiff, after Simone and Ivy. From that moment on, she was Grayson's territory. Grayson based her claims on the university's post-attack retaliation of revoking her scholarship, and also racial discrimination from her coach and teammates.

For the next few months, I talked to as many people as I could. Each conversation, report, newspaper article, or email from Grayson produced up to five new names, so my list of potential witnesses was now in the triple digits, filled with students, players, athletic liaisons, cheerleaders, trainers, and ex-employees. I was tasked with finding out who might fall on which side of the lawsuit—ours, or the university's. Better yet if I could find more assault survivors, so I asked everyone

I could about the thick rumors that swirled around the football team like cologne.

Grayson's emails made it clear that only results mattered. He wrote, *Here's the plan: first find them, then, through cajolery, flattery, threats, or a combination, somehow persuade them to talk.* But I quickly learned that Grayson was wrong. Cajolery made the players start flirting, flattery made victims mistrust my motives, and threats ended all conversations immediately. What worked with all these witnesses was what worked with everyone else: total devoted attention.

I worked in bars and on the phone, calling from my meager apartment or flip phone between temp jobs and dates with JD, emailing my findings, and sometimes having lunch or an in-office meeting with Grayson whenever I found something good enough to require strategy. I appreciated his guidance on what was still a new job for me, as well as the free meals and snacks. I had no idea how long this job would last, nor when the case would go to court. Grayson kept saying, "The university'll settle soon," but the case still tromped forward, and I was glad.

Grayson was fighting hard to acquire reports of football assaults and harassment from the university's Office of Sexual Harassment and the Office of Judicial Affairs. The university president swore under oath that she knew of no such reports. But I understood that Simone had filed one, and the police, and who knows who else. The honor system that law depended on wasn't working. Given the reputation of lawyers in general, I wondered why it existed in the first place.

Reports and subpoenas were documentary evidence and part of Grayson's problem. The 26(a) disclosures were mine. Well in advance of trial, each side was supposed to trade disclosure documents listing the names, addresses, and phone numbers of the witnesses they had collected. It's the legal version of playing fair and belied a whole decade of 1970s TV shows where the ace lawyer calls a "surprise witness" to the stand. Apparently, surprise witnesses weren't allowed, and both sides have the opportunity to interview each witness in advance. It was part of my job to call the university's witnesses to find out what they knew and what they might say. Grayson regularly asked me for my own disclosure lists with complete contact information, which I provided, looking forward to receiving the same from the other side.

But so many of the university's disclosures were grossly inaccurate. On each document in turn, many names were just plain missing. Names misspelled. Phone numbers wrong. Addresses missing street numbers, addresses missing streets, addresses missing towns and zip codes, or listing the wrong states, like CA instead of CO, ME instead of MA, AR instead of AZ. Defunct addresses, for which I had to mail dozens of empty envelopes with "Return Service Requested" printed on them so I could gather the new forwarding addresses.

There is an enormous difference between trying to find a Christine Davis in New Jersey and a Christopher Davids in New Mexico. Williams and Wilson. Anderson and Andrews. Did the university imagine we'd just give up? Seeing how busy Grayson was, how little he slept or ate and how much coffee he drank (and so much salt, salt on everything to make him thirsty for more of that coffee), how he called me while jogging to work, how frazzled his 2:00 A.M. emails that began in the middle of one sentence and ended in the middle of another—this kind of behavior could be viewed as an effective strategy to confuse the opposition and their beleaguered paralegals. But it only pissed me off and made me try harder.

To decode someone's real name and location from a lie took a skill I had acquired through years of secretarial work, dating, and watching crime television shows: what the storied PI Allan Pinkerton called "powers of combination." Everything is important. Searching through computer images, it helped if I could remember that *this* white, blond bikinied teenager in the beach group photo looked a hell of a lot like *that* white, blond twenty-two-year-old in the staff TGIF photo taken three states away. I learned to triangulate people's locations from road trip pictures, their favorite restaurants from food shots, employment from staff listings and "Employee of the Month" photos.

Coincidences were disguised leads. If I read "Bozeman" somewhere in a one-hundred-page deposition and then heard the town named in a conversation three months later, there was a connection, and I had better remember the deposition and context in time to ask about it before the witness hung up or left. I usually only had one chance to talk to witnesses before they thought better of it and ignored my calls thereafter. Retrospection courts cowardice.

If people were local, I lured them out with the promise of free beer and food, as much as they wanted. I changed my uniform for different witnesses—cheap clothes for players, beige office wear for ex-employees of the university athletic department, something in-between for witnesses. I didn't own any expensive camera or surveillance equipment, or even binoculars. All I needed was a computer, a phone, and a face.

I bought nachos for possible rapists in bars that played "Can't Stop, Won't Stop" over the speakers. I met female strangers at the same bars to ask them about getting harassed or worse by those players—where, when, how long, by whom, what happened after, what happened before? I bought them drinks, pretending to match their inebriation with small sips, wondering if I was playing fair. Alcohol made football players arrogant enough to tell the truth; it made women sad and angry enough to trust me.

I was learning how to read their "tells"—perhaps a face-flash of fear in the eyes and eyebrows, a quick covering of the mouth. Then I'd interrupt to say, voice low with a touch of empathy, "You're afraid of him." I'd nod as if I've never been more sure, and keep nodding with consistency, never releasing the pressure while it all played out on her face—denial, guilt at being caught, realization that she's not going to be able to hide from me or, in some cases, from herself. "Yes," she'd say. "I'm afraid of that guy and here's why." It was like opening a sealed jar with a tight lid. You have to apply heat, push your breasts aside, and lean your weight into it, wondering the whole time if it's stuck for good, until suddenly there's movement, the suction releases, and the lid comes off in your hand.

"I don't know why I'm talking to you," they'd say, and I didn't tell them it was my face. I said, "Maybe you just needed to own your story." Then I asked them to put it in writing and give it to me.

I was seeing JD more and more frequently now, every few days. He wanted to see me daily, but I found myself rationing our time together, sure he'd get sick of me any minute. I wasn't sure why he was dating me, except for the fact that we both did martial arts and his dog liked me. We were so different. I hyperfocused on details, missing everything else, whereas he had the perspective I craved—the wide-angle view on everything from politics to religion to what was wrong with his Jeep when it wouldn't start in the middle of the night. He could instantly read people far better than I could, by scanning their faces or shaking their hands. After we met someone at a party, he'd sometimes lean over to whisper in my ear "Rageaholic," or "Sad," or just, "This guy's an asshole." "You don't know that," I'd say. "You just met him." But he was always right. It made me wonder how he viewed me, what he saw.

We always met in public, often making out in movie theaters or the increasingly cold night streets. He wouldn't let me visit his apartment, and I wondered if he had a secret wife or meth lab or something. He said he was too ashamed to invite me over—his place was small and dumpy, the cheapest he could find, and he was in the middle of moving to a new apartment. But I never cared about that stuff, only him.

JD had graduated from acupuncture school in Oregon the year before I met him. His girlfriend started sleeping with a patient in the last two months before graduation, and she kicked him out of their shared apartment. JD had to live in his car with his dog. After that, he did a residency in Nanjing, and then a postdoc in Lisbon, where he sometimes got paid in sausages and skinned rabbits. Then he came home to Colorado and worked construction in 110-degree heat to earn enough money to open his clinic on the Front Range. He started the clinic with only one thousand dollars, some shitty laser-printed business cards, and a partial lease from an underemployed chiropractor. He was bartending nights to pay the clinic rent while he built up his client base.

My previous boyfriend had been a secret heir to a large fortune, only slumming with me until he had the chance to upgrade. I preferred JD's self-made character, his determination, his incisiveness. His independence fit mine and gave me more flexibility to work the case and follow Grayson's leads when I didn't have to temp. I was now about six months into the case, succeeding more often than I failed. I thought I was finally doing well.

But one morning, Grayson looked up from my memos. He flipped the pages in a disposable way and said, "This is all good," but his "good" contained two faltering pitches on the vowels.

"What's wrong?"

"No, nothing, nothing. You've found some important witnesses for harassment. You've corroborated Simone's sexual assault, and Calliope's, too, all great stuff. We don't have much of a case without it."

"But?"

Grayson dropped the memos on his desk and didn't look at them again. "You're missing the bigger picture. This isn't a simple criminal case. It's a civil rights case, a Title IX case."

I knew the basic differences between criminal cases and civil ones. In criminal cases, the district attorney or prosecutor sues for jail time, and needs to prove the case "beyond a reasonable doubt"—the defendant's guilt is the only logical explanation given the evidence. In civil cases, a private lawyer sues for money, jail is off the table, and the attorney needs to prove the case based on a "preponderance of the evidence"—the claim has to be more likely to be true than not true. Grayson had told me some of this stuff, and I had secretly looked up the rest. But beyond those differences, I had no idea what Grayson was talking about.

He now said, "Criminal cases are against individuals for individual crimes; civil cases are often against organizations, for complex systemic crimes. To argue Title IX, we have to prove what's tantamount to a university conspiracy. We have to prove a culture that discriminates against women by not protecting them."

"But how?"

"Well, that's what we're trying to figure out, right?" His smile tugged down on one side. "This is new territory for me, too. I usually do medical malpractice. But I think we can use some of the same tactics." He thought for a second. "Lawsuits are about stories, sad stories, the kind that make you angry. We still have to create a narrative, but a bigger one, the story of a system. Focus your lens wider, on the program as a whole, how it's run. Recruiting. Football. Find me something on that."

Oh yeah, football, I thought as I left. The part I ignored.

I bought a roll of butcher paper and brought it home. I unrolled the paper and spread it out on the floor. Oriented horizontally, it spanned the length of my apartment. At the top of the butcher paper I wrote: "Prove." Underneath that, at the top left, I wrote:

A. Simone Baker was raped that night.

I drew a vertical line to section off item A, and then drew three more columns to the right. I listed the things Grayson said we had to prove under Title IX:

B. Pervasive harassment of women.
C. Coach Riggs knew about it.
D. University was deliberately indifferent.

I pulled out my steno pads, spreadsheets, witness lists, and memos. I started writing down the names of everyone I had spoken with, listing them on the butcher paper in the appropriate columns. I categorized Yvonne, Huge, the four player suspects, and about ten other students and players, out of all the people I had interviewed. These were the relevant witnesses, the ones who had told me something important. I starred the survivors: Simone, Calliope, and Ivy. The women. In the margins, I listed all the facts and conclusions I knew or had gathered—Grayson's in black, mine in blue. I drew a red square around Calliope's perpetrators and a dotted-line square for the ones I suspected for Simone's attack. I tried to draw arrows between them, showing where information had come from and where it led.

It was a mess, but a clear one. All my information was on the left side of the page. Grayson was right; I had mostly just gathered evidence of items A and B, Simone's attack and the "pervasive harassment" part. The items under C and D, Coach Riggs's knowledge and deliberate indifference, were characterized only by absences—scholarships unrevoked, lack of punishment from the school, alleged crimes left unprosecuted. Can an absence be evidence? I called Grayson.

"No, kid," he said. "The burden of proof is on us. Otherwise, they can just claim incompetence and ignorance." When I was silent, he said, "I mean, Coach Riggs would have to be an idiot not to know what was going on. And yes, of course, he didn't care. But we can't prove that knowledge or indifference at the upper level without a direct tie. Otherwise, they have plausible deniability. People always rely on the incompetent idiot defense—it doesn't hurt them. Look at Iran-Contra. They named an airport after that guy."

I hung up and kicked the butcher paper. It floated, wrinkled, and landed with a puff. It was no good. We only had a skinny third of the case so far, maybe less. Which meant we had nothing.

I taped the butcher paper to my wall. It covered the whole thing, my pictures and windows, a fourth of my one-room apartment. When JD came over to pick me up for a date, he lifted the sheet to look out the window and then let gravity float the paper back down. He frowned, but said nothing.

I have never understood football, although I have tried. My obsessed ex-boyfriend used to insist we drive six hours from our home in Santa Fe to Denver for every Broncos home game. I sat next to him at the topmost brim of the stadium for endless hours each football weekend, either hot or cold, drunk and bored. He had forbidden me to read so I wouldn't embarrass him in front of the other fans. To me, the game just looked like a bunch of orange ants running around grass with paint on it.

Once an older family friend of his felt sorry for me and leaned over.

He said, "Look at it as a collection of personalities. Like, every position has its own culture."

"Culture?"

"Okay, that guy there, he's the kicker. See how nobody talks to him, even on his own team? He's alone, on the outside. Now, the quarterback, that guy, he's the opposite. Everyone talks to him, because he has to make all the decisions for the team. The offense follows him, like soldiers. It's military."

"And the defense?" I asked.

He said, "They're the killers."

For this case, most of the suspects on my list were on the defensive team, headed by Jaden Usher, the defensive backs coach. I needed to understand why so many of these defensive players were so violent. Maybe from there, I could understand football culture as a whole.

A CPI 260 Assessment is a measure of "normal" personality traits that help us coexist with each other. In a Myers-Briggs study, several football teams took the CPI 260 test, and social scientists evaluated the data by position. All the defensive players sank to the bottom of the test, averaging the lowest scores on twenty-three of the twenty-nine measurement scales, including Dominance, Self-control, Responsibility, and Empathy. The director of scouting at one college stated that some scores in the study might be skewed because a great number of student-athletes who graduate college cannot read.

Another study tested college football players against their peers, both nonathletes and athletes from sports such as soccer, basketball, and rugby. Football players scored significantly higher than their athletic and nonathletic peers in measures like narcissism and psychoticism, which is characterized by aggression and antisocial behavior. However, their scores were slightly lower in neuroticism, and significantly lower in the "lie scale." So football players were more likely to be *honest* psychotic narcissists. Or maybe they didn't have a reason to lie, because they weren't going to get in trouble regardless.

Chicken or egg? Were defensive players—and football players in general—chosen because they were rotten eggs, or were they broken by the sport itself? Years later, the questions still bothered me, so I called my friend Steve Almond, a football geek and author of the book *Against Football: One Fan's Reluctant Manifesto*. I asked him, "Why were almost all our perpetrators defensive players? What's with that?"

Steve said, "Offensive players are acculturated to avoid getting hit, but defense is the opposite. Defensive players are taught to deliver big hits and get your man on the ground. Your job is to be aggressive and love contact and hit as hard as you can. If you're a linebacker, for instance, you need to own the middle of the field. There's no written rule that says, 'Hey, hurt the star receiver so badly he has to leave the game.' But if you deliver a big hit and do so, especially if it's a legal hit, that's a good outcome. They're selecting for a personality type that is willing and eager to 'blow people up.' That's what they call it. Empathy is not part of the job description."

"So do you think they come to the team already broken, or does the game break them?"

Steve (like Grayson) told me I was missing the larger point. "The gang assaults you've investigated speak to a kind of brotherhood mentality where 'we do everything together.' Players shower together, eat together, practice and party together. When something goes down, their central loyalty is to their teammates. They're asking 'Will my teammate be all right?' Because if he isn't, he won't be there to protect you. Remember: everyone's running the same risks every game. They're all just one injury away from losing their scholarship, their livelihood, their dream. They're lost boys, kept at an elemental level of morality, a suspended state. And for what? What's the engine? Money. Football is capitalism on steroids."

How much capitalism? The university football budget was about nineteen million dollars per year. Every other athletic program, including men's and women's basketball, lost millions each year. But football supposedly funded them all, with their yearly net profit of five to ten million, if you ignored the massive hidden costs of the stadium, debt service, and facilities.

The income wasn't just ticket sales and concessions, as I had assumed. Grayson told me the big money came from boosters who weren't even alums—football nuts who sat in box seats, drank craft beer, and pledged to build something out of flagstone with their name on it. The football program also got money from radio and TV broadcast rights, licensing, royalties and advertising, corporate sponsorships and apparel deals, NCAA and conference distributions, endowments, youth camps, student fees, alumni donations, and capital campaigns.

The money had a weird racial edge to it. Sports marketing executive Sonny Vaccaro told an interviewer that the NCAA top earners were 90 percent African Americans, all unpaid at this time, ruled over by white coaches with seven-figure salaries. Civil rights historian Taylor Branch wrote that to take a candid look at the college sports situation is "to catch an unmistakable whiff of the plantation." Or maybe it was more like Ralph Ellison's battle royal in *Invisible Man*, where teenage African American boys were forced to box each other blindfolded in a ring while white men surrounded them, cheering and jeering. And why did the kids do it in Ellison's world? For the chance to win a college scholarship.

Alma mater means "nourishing mother," and we expect our university to teach and protect us. In gratitude, we're supposed to pay them back in increments over a lifetime. During grad school, I twice worked two-week phone gigs at the University Foundation, cold-calling alums to harass them for donations. Each donor could decide where their money went, so over and over I had to select the university's football team from a drop-down menu, collecting hundreds of dollars of football pledges each night in a loud room full of twenty other people doing the same. Sometimes I pretended to make a mistake and selected the English Department instead.

Football brought in millions, but it also cost millions. Seven-figure coach salaries, staffing, equipment, game expenses, travel, athletic student aid, recruiting weekends. Medical care for the young men who bashed away at each other every weekend. Most Division I universities pay more for one football player than for a tenured professor's salary.

Also pricey was the immaculate field itself, ensconced in an enormous Coliseum-esque flagstone complex. You could often see the Continental Divide from the squeegeed windowed box seats, and during the city's three-hundred-plus sunny days each year there was always a clear view of the Flatirons. The stadium hosted 53,750 seats and a six-level luxury press box for boosters that cost forty-two million dollars to build and unknown amounts to maintain, just to host home games for three hours on six or seven Saturdays each year.

The building where I earned my master's degree in English literature hadn't been renovated since 1937. Hallways were lit with dim fluorescent lights, bulbs burned out, fixture covers cracked or nonexistent. Shiny yellow-pink ceramic tile paved the walls midway up to the ceiling. It was an interior designed to withstand wartime air raids. The ghosts of old letters permanently scarred dirty classroom chalkboards. To teach the Intro classes that paid my graduate school tuition, I frequently had to beg at the office for chalk, where the secretary insisted on reading to the end of the page in his magazine before lifting his head and asking me to repeat myself. I started buying my own chalk. We had only about a hundred photocopies allotted to us for the semester, but we were allowed to use the fossilized mimeograph machine as much as we wanted, so my handouts were all bluish purple and smelled like antifreeze. The air-conditioning didn't work in the summer and the heater didn't work in the winter. Wasps trawled the corners of the rooms, planning their nests. Once I saw a mouse.

It was clear what the university valued. What would they do to protect it?

Thanks to Grayson, I had just enough money to take a full week off from temp jobs, so one summer day I rode my bike across town to the courthouse to look in their public records. I was public; those records were for me. I emptied my pockets of change and removed my belt and shoes to pass through the weapon detector. The security officer regarded me with disdaining disinterest. I realized that there were two categories of people who went through this line: attorneys and criminals. I was dressed in jeans and a hoodie.

The Clerk & Recorder's Office was in a little courthouse offshoot room that smelled like ancient dust and shed skin. Everything was tinted orange. I waited in a crowded line and finally walked to the window to greet a vexed-looking man with scarred square brown glasses three decades out of style. I said, "I'd like court records on these people, please." I handed over my list of suspects.

The man handed my list back. "Docket or case number and date."

I handed the list to him again. "I don't have them. I just need to know if these people did anything bad."

The man sighed. He dropped my list in my vicinity and neither of us touched it. Then he sighed again. "First, middle, last. Exact DOB." At my blank look, he said, "Date. Of. Birth. And I'll need a date range for the search. I can't look in all records for eternity." Then he stared past my shoulder at the next person in line, and I left.

I returned the next day to the same little orangey brown waiting room, and the same little man was there. When I reached the service window, I handed over my list and said, "Full names, dates of birth, date ranges."

He said, "This is going to cost you. Ten cents a photocopy."

"Can I just look at the records? I don't need copies."

He was much nicer then, and buzzed a door open. He led me inside to a strip of desk finished with scarred gray laminate. "Sit here," he said, and returned with a stack of files so tall that I understood his initial reticence. "Have at it," he said.

Each file was an informational wonderland: photographs, middle names, dates of birth, addresses, cell phone numbers, driver's license numbers, and Social Security numbers that someone had forgotten to redact. Why hadn't I been living in this little room all along? The university's fancy lawyers would never bother to come here to be insulted by a little man in old eyeglasses. I finally felt useful.

Except for that one charge of providing alcohol for minors on the night of Simone's party, players' records didn't list any arrests or court dates during the years each one played for the football team. I looked for the DUIs Calliope had told me about, but they were absent. *Maybe the cops tear up tickets,* I thought.

After the players graduated, however, there were plenty of arrests for those who stayed in town. Drug charges, DUIs, fights, domestic violence. Grayson had told me that when one player hadn't been drafted by the NFL, he told his girlfriend that he didn't want to go anyway. She asked him why not. He bragged that he could have all the money, cars, and women he wanted without going to the NFL. She said that was a chauvinistic thing to say. Enraged, he grabbed her by the hair and smashed her face against the closet floor, beating the back of her head with the other fist until he knocked her out. He ruptured her eardrum, detached her retina, and dislocated her shoulder, leaving the young woman with permanent hearing loss. He received a deferred sentence. The beaten woman was an administrative assistant for the university and she was afraid to go to the police until her boss found her and convinced her. Then her boss transferred her to another department so the athletic department couldn't fire her in retribution for coming forward.

I found a record for a man named Fredrick, another Simone-bedroom suspect, who visited his girlfriend in town after he graduated. He stayed out all night, returning to her place in the morning. She woke up angry and hit him. He swatted her hands. She threw a remote control at his head. He threw a table at her. She threw candles at him. He pushed her onto the sofa. Then he spat in her face three times "to calm her down." The police arrested them both. King Chambers posted his bail. Fredrick received a deferred sentence.

Only one player had arrest records while he was still on the team, probably because Colorado had a mandatory-arrest law for domestic violence. This player beat his wife when she was eight and a half months pregnant, forced her back into their apartment when she tried to escape, hit her in the face with a plunger, held her down on the bed, and cut her hair with scissors. Police charged him with third-degree assault, felony menacing, wiretapping, and false imprisonment. The player admitted his behavior was "immature." He received a deferred sentence because the prosecutor believed his attack was "out of character," but I wondered; it's not as if wiretapping is a crime of passion. And how did the prosecutor know the player's character, anyway? The ability to score touchdowns is not a character attribute. I had caught that court record just in time; if the player avoided arrest for eighteen months, his criminal record would be sealed. How many other records had I missed?

I wondered what's it like to learn you can do anything you want without consequences, and then to unlearn it. To be on TV as a star and then work as a stock boy. To be a college student, and then nothing. I wasn't even sure how fair it was to say that players got a college education out of the deal, if tutors wrote their papers and did their homework. One report on college athletes said that tutoring was designed to keep them eligible, rather than guide them toward a degree. And the degree is supposed to guide us toward our lives.

Many of the university's best football players were pulled from poor neighborhoods and thrust into a school in one of the wealthiest towns in the country. For four years, they were above everything—the law, classes, social rules, other people. Even with tutoring and help, a third of them wouldn't graduate. Two percent got drafted to the NFL, and an even smaller number might actually play on a team, continuing their career of untouchability. Everyone else was severed from the team and the university, with none of the protections they'd rapidly become accustomed to. They fell, like Icarus.

But the rape victims couldn't see into the future. They only knew that at the time of their attack, the players had all the power and support, and they had none. So if nobody's going to help you, why tell anyone? If I searched for a record of what X did to me in a courthouse like this one, I wouldn't find it. I had been taught to keep it to myself.

After initial failed childhood attempts, I had tried to talk to my older sister when I was twenty-two. She went through the trouble to visit me from a thousand miles away, so I took the chance. Through a mess of tears, I blurted out the bare facts—X sexually assaulted me starting when I was four, ending when I was about seven, forced oral sex and rape, I didn't know how many times. I had barely finished my sentence before my sister said, "Well, that certainly never happened to *me*." *Or did it?* I wondered. Her view was that if it didn't happen with her, it couldn't have happened to me. Because X liked her more.

For a child to have evidence of the violence done to her, someone has to care enough to notice it, accept it, and preserve it. I had nothing and no one, but I knew what I knew.

I said, "I don't have to prove this to you. Your opinion doesn't matter. You weren't even there." Stone-faced, she made a "hmph" sound, turned away from me on the sofa, and picked up her book. She was quiet for the rest of our three-day visit, refusing to speak to me entirely on the last day, like she had been stricken mute. She didn't even say goodbye.

A month or two later, she called me. "I've thought about it, and I have to tell you. I just can't believe what you told me. I can't. So I'll understand if you don't want to have anything to do with me anymore."

I thought, *Maybe she's dealing with her own memories*. And I wasn't so sure I was ready to lose my sister yet. So I said, "That's okay. You don't have to believe me. I'm not mad at you."

Then she said something like, if I wasn't mad at her, it was proof that I had to be lying about what happened. Because if it were true and she didn't believe me, I wouldn't be so willing to speak to her now. So she was glad she didn't believe me.

My sister's logic reminded me of the Salem witch trials: if the accused woman floated, she was a witch and must be burned at the stake. If she drowned, she was innocent. Either way, she was dead and you didn't have to worry about her anymore.

After my sister, I didn't talk about *X* for over five years.

Now, in the courthouse records room, I leaned back in my plastic seat and surveyed my steno pad and the stacks of records in front of me. I added those records to what students and players had already told me, and counted eighteen alleged crimes that ranged from DUIs to physical and sexual assault, all over the course of about five years. For each documented case, the accused received suspended sentences, or all the charges were thrown out in court. Some of the crimes that witnesses told me about never appeared in the records at all. No players did any time, no matter whom they hurt or how much.

I had heard that the athletic department often persuaded the police and prosecutors to let them handle crimes "internally." What I couldn't tell was how this was possible, or who arranged this. Was it the football coach, or the athletic director, or the police and prosecutors themselves? Who was drowning the witches?

The current running backs coach, Milo "The Terror" Lehrer, had several prior criminal convictions, none resulting in prison time. The university police department had permanently banned Lehrer from campus ten years prior for an alleged physical assault. "What that means is that he is not allowed to appear on campus," a university police sergeant said. "He does not have a right to appeal." Lehrer had allegedly grabbed a female parking lot attendant by the neck. And then, a few years later, head football coach Wade Riggs effortlessly brought Lehrer back to campus, and the university was paying him a salary.

I finally understood what Grayson had been saying all along. This was what a culture of violence looked like. I wrote Coach Riggs's name on my steno pad, circled it in black, and drew a circumference of arrows pointing to him. I had my bad guy.

5

Comfort Woman

It is not the detective who creates the culture of the crime, like Sherlock Holmes fiddling with his matchbooks, watermarks, Dutch cigarette butts, or the fading scent of white jessamine perfume. The culture of the crime is defined by the culture of the place where the crime is committed. In the "Teikoku Bank Incident" of 1948, a murderer posing as a health inspector convinced twelve employees of a Tokyo bank to drink cyanide in unison, explaining that it was a dysentery vaccine and they were under orders. The employees drank the poison and all died, because one must always follow orders from a health inspector. That's Japan.

Conversely, some crimes create their own cultures. For centuries the Mafiosi got away with blatant extortion because they had designed their culture: snitches get stitches. You'd never see it coming, your children's kidnapping, or your own blunt-force-trauma death as you're closing up your bakery or picking up a delivery from the back-alley entrance.

I couldn't tell which we were dealing with, crimes that created a culture, or a culture that created a crime. I was beginning to think it was the latter, the way Grayson already did. The university was 70 percent white and 1.6 percent Black—Calliope had called herself a "foreigner." An academic coordinator once told *Sports Illustrated*, "If you're a black football player here, you're ethnically a minority because

you're black, socially a minority because you're an athlete, culturally
a minority because you might come from the projects, economically a
minority because you can't afford to drive a BMW, and physically a minority because you're bigger than everybody else." Even Coach Riggs
was white. Out of 124 Division I-A college football head coaches, only
5 were African American, despite the prevalence of African Americans
on most Division I-A teams. All our sexual assault suspects were African American, many from marginalized communities, most led by
defensive backs coach Jaden Usher.

Most other players on the football team were similarly racially
isolated and/or came from similar financial circumstances, but they
didn't break the law or hurt people off the field. So Simone's attackers
made their choices. But so did the university. Perhaps by ghettoizing
these men, isolating them, removing consequences, delivering regular
blunt force trauma to their brains, and teaching them daily to hurt
people, the university was molding an elite group of potential perpetrators for its own financial gain.

A current player named Xavier had visited two years prior, for his
recruiting trip. His player host plied him with drugs, alcohol, and strippers. Xavier was so offended by the recruiting weekend that he turned
down his scholarship entirely. Coach Riggs flew an assistant coach a
thousand miles away to Xavier's home to fix the damage and convince
him to enroll, which he did. And then, after just two years of playing
for the university, Xavier stood naked in Simone's bedroom with her
bathroom towel knotted around his neck like a superhero cape. If his
environment hadn't changed him so dramatically in such a short time,
what did?

There were two sides to the football culture here: one hyperexposed
under stadium lights, and the other one illicit, in bedrooms and hotel
rooms. People cheered for one side and shrugged at the other. *He did
what? Well, price of glory. She shouldn't have been there.* It was the same
attitude I got from guys who sucker punched me in a dojo or did some
dirty trick to win. They gave me the same shoulder-twitching shrugs, as
if saying, *You came into my house. My house, my rules.* The problem was,
I couldn't tell where the women's house was. Men owned everywhere.

So far, I wasn't gathering evidence; I was gathering a feeling. It wasn't that these players were lying, necessarily. They were honest with me, but they used a common language I didn't quite understand, or perhaps they were following a common religion, and like most religions, it was incomprehensible in small snippets. You can't nibble the pill; you must swallow it whole. Until I fully understood every aspect of this culture, I might stumble through the facts—who did what to whom and when—but I would never understand this knotted case or what it meant. What it meant to me.

I began focusing research on football head coach Wade Riggs, scanning online photos and videos as well as Grayson's depositions. Riggs was the way I had pictured him: too-fine brown hair in a politician's cut and fluff blow-dried to look more plentiful than it actually was. Small, pale eyes, a golf tan with white skin circling his eyes where his sunglasses had shaded them. He made no unnecessary movements, no miscalculated gestures. He wore ill-fitting cheap beige sports jackets, yellow ties. He was a frequent mouth-wiper and looked uncomfortable all the time, as if plagued by sports injuries. He smiled with his mouth but not his eyes.

His recruiting practices seemed to be like any other coach's. From February to September, Riggs and the other coaches reviewed between four and five thousand high school players, narrowing the list to sixty-two prospects, and the university spent about $315,000 annually to bring them in. Some players came from academically low-ranking schools where most were on free/reduced lunch, with math proficiency scores as low as one percent. A former athletic director said, "Sure, we recruit in the margin. But that's not to say it's a bad policy. You have to be prepared to support and teach them to develop in the classroom and football and socially."

Their "support" seemed to consist of one seminar. A player told me over the phone, "It's called, uh, something about life. Life Sense. Life Tools. Skills, Life Skills. And a handbook Coach said we were supposed to read." His slight emphasis on "supposed" implied that no one ever did. Coach Riggs also thumbtacked newspaper articles of athletes getting arrested onto a bulletin board in the locker room. They called it the "mother board," because that's what your mother will read if your name is in the paper.

I asked, "Did Riggs teach you about sexual harassment, or train the player hosts for the recruiting weekends?"

"I don't think so. At my other school, though, they made us watch videos on harassment and stuff. They were terrible. One was called 'She Hears You,'" the player scoffed. "But with Coach Riggs, it was about being late to practice. And you can't gamble on games. And you can't embarrass the team."

"What does that mean?"

"Whatever Coach wants it to mean," he said.

The player gave me all the recruiting details. During the fall season, groups of eight to twelve seventeen-year-old recruits visited for forty-eight hours across six weekends. The university paid for their transportation and hotel rooms, and also provided a pretty female student guide or "Ambassador" for the daytime, a player host for the nighttime, daily activities, all meals, and thirty dollars per night of discretionary entertainment money for the hosts. Hosts spent it on alcohol or drugs, since everything else was free. Coaches ordered, "Show them a good time." The university had the twelfth-best record in Division I-A of the NCAA, a conference-leading record in the NFL draft, and had won a national championship and recent trophies from Heisman, Butkus, and Thorpe. Winning, and Coach Riggs's own job, hinged on recruiting success.

At that time, Wade Riggs was the coach to watch, the blood-and-sweat model of American success. I learned from Riggs's memoir that he grew up in a small farming town in the Midwest. He loved football as a child, and wore his football helmet to bed. Riggs had a "miserable time" on his football recruiting trip but played for his home state's university anyway. He got in trouble once for something, but his coach rescued him somehow, and "it was bad enough that I don't want to say any more about it." They temporarily took away his football scholarship. He stayed for his master's in education, playing football there for three years and coaching as a graduate assistant. He considered becoming "a famous shrink" but instead moved here and worked as assistant coach for the university football team. At Riggs's first head coach job at another school, a grand jury indicted four of his players for perjury charges related to gambling on games, but only two pled guilty and received short sentences. Riggs denied responsibility, saying, "What occurred here is a societal issue, not an athletic issue. The stain is on the individuals, not us."

From there, Riggs returned to this university, now as head coach. He brought the team a conference win and four Big 12 North titles. He seemed to possess some mysterious secret that no one else had. I wondered if it was the way he recruited. In his memoir, he talked about how his previous team only got good after he had his own players, the ones he had persuaded to join the team using his own recruiting methods.

Or maybe it was his coaching methods that made him win. In his memoir, their team role models were movie villains like the velociraptors from *Jurassic Park* and the Terminator. His self-image was twinned with winning—when he badly lost a game, he wrote, "It was like I didn't even know who I was." He wrote that others compared him to John the Baptist, and he compared himself to Hernán Cortés, the sadistic conqueror of Mexico. One of his personal affirmations was, "I am and will be in total control."

Riggs's memoir talked about how "relentlessness" was the standard for assignments. He had T-shirts made with a secret acronym that only the coaches and players could know. He told them, "Even your wives can't know. It's so serious that if your wife knows, I've got to kill her or you've got to kill her."

At his prior job, Riggs's team motto was "Expect Victory." Here at the university, he created two. One was "Return to Dominance." The other one was "We Don't Care."

Autumn 2003 was a season of leaks. Someone leaked Calliope's name to the press after she joined the case, but she said, badass, "I never planned to hide."

Someone else leaked information from Grayson's deposition with Beatrice Hull, the district attorney. Hull disclosed that four years and one day before Simone's attack, a high school girl was lured to a hotel for what she thought would be a girls' night out to celebrate her engagement to her high school sweetheart. Instead, players dragged her into their hotel room. Two football recruits weighing approximately 260 and 325 pounds stripped and allegedly raped her, one after the other. Her friends searched the hotel and found her afterward, half naked in the bathroom near the front desk, sobbing.

"Sex is being used as a bartering tool," the DA said in her deposition. After the alleged attack, Hull met with the university's attorneys, the chancellor's aide, and the athletic director to warn them about their football recruiting practices. Hull said a former athletic department official told her that Riggs and the athletic director "decided, after discussing the history, that they would not change anything because they could not afford to lose the competitive edge against universities such as Oklahoma [and] Nebraska."

DA Hull also reported telling the chancellor, "There should be zero tolerance for alcohol, zero tolerance for sexual contact within the context of recruiting the football players." When she believed the athletic director wasn't paying enough attention to the problem, Hull said, "If it happens again, we are going to deal with it very seriously. You are on notice." But with Simone's attack, I didn't think the DA dealt with it "very seriously," or at all. She refused to try the case in criminal court and so it ended up on our for-profit desks.

I was beginning to wonder if Grayson was the source of some of these leaks, the ones that went in our favor. He had to be giving the press something for all the PR and information we received in return. From all the leads he handed me, it sounded like he and the press were in constant barter, trading and feeding each other witnesses and interviews on a quid pro quo basis. Investigative reporters had career contacts we simply didn't have. Most of the leads they gave us were small—rumors, gossip, a photo—but one day, Grayson called me, panting like he had just sprinted to the phone. "I need you to set a meeting with this woman ASAP. Holy frijoles, she is *it*."

Sometimes Grayson had a habit of forgetting to give me details before hanging up, so I rushed in to ask, "She's what?"

"She's a madam. A madam! Like, she employs hookers and rents them out to men. She owns an escort service. You've got to get on this right away."

"You want . . . a sex worker?"

Grayson snorted into the phone so loudly I had to hold it away from my ear. "Not for *me*, Erika! She was servicing the football team! Or at least, her employees were. She saw Coach Riggs's press conference where he said he would never use sex to entice recruits. She came forward to say, 'That's not true—they hired my girls.' The police told her to contact me, and *she did*. Hoo boy. I need to know everything. How it all worked. The money. Most of all, is she for real. Is she credible. And is she sane."

"Did you get her full name?"

"Yes, it's"—paper crinkling sounds—"Daisy Oakley. And she gave us her phone number."

Gave us her phone number! Nobody did that. I wrote down the digits carefully, repeating each one back to Grayson. After I hung up, I started dialing immediately.

Daisy answered the phone right away but then hung up on me three times at the first sound of my voice. On the fourth try, I blathered, "HelloDaisymynameisErikaKrouseGraysongavemeyournumberI'maprivateinvestigatorwantingtotalktoyouaboutSimoneBakerwhowasrapedbycollegefootballrecruitsandplayersandIthinkyouhavesomeinformation?"

Daisy's voice warmed up, deep and full in her throat. "Oh, hi," she said. "Sure, I'll talk with you."

The whole time we chatted, I thought, *I'm talking with a sex worker!* I felt naughty, fetishy, like this was a taboo life experience I was collecting for the thrill of it. But Daisy sounded normal, a little like me, or maybe I sounded like her. She agreed to meet, so I chose a more public spot than where I had met Calliope: a pastel-colored, pie-smelling café with lots of windows, near a busy intersection. I think I was afraid.

On the afternoon of our meeting, I don't know why I recognized

Daisy right away because she looked nothing like a sex worker. She seemed to recognize me back, scooted right into my booth, and smiled as she took off her coat. She was maybe 160 pounds, with a generous lap and comfortable laugh. She was half Asian and in her early thirties, like me. Her hair was startlingly long, thick and black, with overgrown Bettie Page bangs. Daisy had highlighted her eyes with sparkly purple eye shadow. She visibly relaxed when I said lunch was on me. "Good, because I'm broke," she said.

"So why did you call the news station?" I asked after a server in a pink retro uniform took our orders.

Daisy toyed with the cup of crayons on the white paper–topped table, and said, "Because it was all a gosh-darned lie, Coach Riggs saying they had nothing to do with it. They hired my girls. Besides, I'm all about supporting the sistas." In a few beats, she added, "I got busted for my escort business. So maybe you guys can help me out."

My internal buzzer activated. Maybe Grayson's suspicions were correct; maybe she wasn't legit and was just angling for free legal help. "Tell me about yourself," I said. "Where are you from?"

"San Antonio," she said. "But I hated it there. My dad was a prick cop and my mother was a full-gospel Christian. I majored in psychology during college and put myself through school working as a domestic abuse counselor for the women's safe house. I was a milk donor for a crack baby after I had mine. And I was a stripper." She swung her long hair over a shoulder. "You know, it's actually more hostile in the shelters than in the strip clubs."

"Why?"

"In the shelters, you're supposed to be perfect, and in the strip clubs, everyone knows you're not. I knew I was acting out stuff from my family, even while I was stripping."

Daisy told me her grandmother was a comfort woman during World War II. Korean and Chinese women were abducted into the Japanese Imperial Army's *ianfu,* its state-run military brothel system, or lured with promises of nursing jobs. Once enslaved, the women were considered to be "public toilets," there for military use. In the name of reducing battle stress, up to forty soldiers a day raped, beat, and tortured each woman, all day and all night. Not many survived.

Daisy said, "My grandmother gave birth to a baby while she was there, and the soldiers left it outside in the snow to die. My family doesn't talk about it, but they talk about it, if you know what I mean. The brothel marked my grandmother with a tattoo over her heart. She still has it."

At that point, I would have believed anything Daisy said to me. "Is that where you got the idea to become a madam?"

"I don't know if my grandmother was where I came up with the idea to work," Daisy said. "I got pregnant when I was nineteen, and my kid's father wasn't . . . he wasn't involved. My kid's medication was a thousand dollars a month, and the doctors told me I had to either hospitalize my kid or find a way to stay home." She traced a half moon in the paper place mat with a long thumbnail. "The first night I went out on a job, I cried and cried. But I made seven hundred dollars. So, of course, I went out the next night, and the next. And then I thought, these women need a better-organized system, with safeties in place. So I became the boss."

When Daisy talked about sex work, she stopped slouching and her eyes ignited. She became, well, pretty. "It's not always sex," she said. She told me about an Adult Baby client who outfitted his apartment with an adult-size crib and high chair. Daisy played babysitter. "He just wants me to snap gum, talk on my phone, and twirl my pigtails. I ignore him while he toddles around in a giant diaper. I refuse to change that diaper, though," she said. The Adult Baby was a lawyer. "Lawyers are my best clients," Daisy said and waited for me to write that down for my memo to the legal team.

Daisy also had a client she knew only as "Shower Curtain Guy." Shower Curtain Guy liked to sit on a chair in the middle of the room with a shower curtain draped over his naked body. "All he wants me to do is sit on his lap and lick his chest through the shower curtain. I make him buy a new one for each visit."

"Why?"

"Because it's unsanitary."

"No, I mean, why does he want that?"

She shrugged. "It's usually something to do with their parents."

Daisy was educated, articulate, and able to create immediate rapport. She could probably do my job, but I could never do hers. I asked, "How did the football players contact your service?"

"It was always the recruiting coordinator who called us."

She had already told Grayson about the recruiter over the phone. "He was still a university employee?" I asked. She nodded, and I tried to wipe the excitement from my face, so as not to scare her off. This wasn't a player acting out, or some kind of misunderstanding that turned into a solicitation. This was a university employee searching for sex workers for seventeen-year-old boys, recruits. This was that "system" Grayson had sent me to find. Daring to hope, I asked, "How about the head coach, Coach Riggs? Did he ever call?"

Daisy shook her head. "No, just the recruiter. He found us through the phone book—we had lines routed all over the place and classified ads in the *PennySaver*. At first he came across as this great guy, getting tickets to games for my kid. He wanted Black girls or blondes for the recruits—one or the other, always."

"So this was a regular thing? How many recruits?"

"It was probably ten or twelve kids he hired us for. I don't know if he used other escort services, too."

That was way more than I would have anticipated, if I could have anticipated any of this. "High school boys wanted to sleep with older women? Sex workers?"

Daisy poked a slice of cucumber with one tine of her fork, her flawless manicure gleaming. "Most of the time, the kid gave the money to the girls. But in some cases, Tanner would pay me himself and say 'Don't let the kid know this is a working deal.' He wanted the kid to think this kind of thing would happen to him all the time if he came here to play football."

"Tanner, his name was?"

"Tanner Liddell. Mr. Testosterone Guy," she said. "White, a little too aggressive, kind of like a habitual steroid user, a sex addict, lonely. His eyes were probably a color other than blue . . . I'm not good with faces. I could describe his anatomy, though."

"You dated him?"

Daisy's eyebrows shrugged. "If dating means having sex without money exchanging hands, then yes, we dated."

"So you liked him?"

"No." A brusque shake of her head. "He didn't like me, either. He just liked that even though I was bigger, he was able to flip me around. He also liked the mirrors at the hotel—that fed into his ego. He was aggressive but didn't give me bruises or anything. But then he turned into a jerk. He'd call me sometimes twelve times a day. 'Whatcha doin'? Do you miss me?'" She shuddered and retreated into the pink vinyl seat. *Daisy likes her space,* I thought. *Daisy likes to choose.*

Daisy said, "I mean, look at me—I'm a large girl, older. I'm not a babe. Tanner was really muscular and cut, but I prefer a man with meat on his bones. I think I confused him, because I wasn't into him. He didn't get that. He wanted to figure that out." A dimple punctuated her face as she shook her head.

I could see why Tanner liked Daisy, even if she couldn't. Daisy had a guilty-feeling appeal, like the first swallow of a beer, or a puff of secondhand smoke after you've quit. She wasn't conventionally attractive—neither is a chunk of magnetic iron—but she *attracted.*

"How long did you date the recruiter?" I asked.

"That depends on how you define it. My fee was two hundred fifty dollars, but I only charged Tanner a hundred and fifty because he gave us business. Then he gave us so many referrals to recruits that after two months, I just saw him for free."

"What are we looking at as far as total money spent?"

"Well, I saw him about twice a week during that time, plus he hired girls for ten to twelve recruits over two months."

I did quick math on my steno pad. Even with Daisy's discount, Tanner had spent about $5,400 on sex workers in two months—$3,000 for the recruits' "girls" and $2,400 for Daisy's services. That was a lot of cash for a low-ranking university employee. If he didn't limit himself to the recruiting season, he'd spend over $14,000 per year on Daisy alone, which was likely more than half his salary. Or maybe he did limit himself; maybe the recruiting season was his only chance to indulge, if the athletic department paid for it all. "Where did he get all that money, do you think?"

"We don't really ask that kind of thing." Daisy had slipped into present tense again. She sat very still. "Sometimes I feel bad about . . . the work." She was strangely squeamish about her job title. "One kid said he was a virgin. Some of them were scared, and I felt like they didn't ask for it, that they were pressured into doing it." I wondered what it did to a boy, for his first time not to be with someone he loved, but with someone he paid.

"I didn't let my girls go with Tanner's seniors because they're violent with women. I think it's because they've been taking steroids longer. So it was mostly the younger players and recruits. I didn't like to do those jobs myself because I'm not into mommy fantasies," Daisy said firmly, palms pushing something away, activating her jasmine perfume. "Tanner once asked me to see a kid as a favor. He wasn't a football player, just a skinny little white runt, punk-ass kid. He was practically suicidal, scared, failing his classes, and didn't have any family. All we did is talk, and he cried the whole time. We're usually in and out of there in fifteen minutes, twenty minutes max, but I stayed with him for two hours. He gave me a medallion. I still have it for some reason.

"I was a madam, but I'm not a predator. Whenever a girl called and asked for a job, if she had never done this work before, I'd warn her to think it over. I'd say, 'This isn't an escort service where you go to dinner and a movie. This is adult entertainment. And the money is more addictive than any drug.' *You* know what I mean," she said.

But I didn't know. I was poor, and didn't have sex for money. I had never made $250 in fifteen minutes.

Maybe to separate myself, I asked, "Did you feel like you were victimizing them? Your girls?"

"Those women were going to work for someone, whether it was me or someone else. I kept them safer. I had a protocol—they had to call in and answer a series of questions. The code word was 'mercy.' So if a girl checked in and said, 'Mercy, it was hard to find this place,' we knew she was in trouble."

"What kind of trouble?"

Daisy leaned back. "It's not a matter of *if* you get raped in this business. It's a matter of when." I nodded, and then realized what she was telling me.

"You were raped on the job?" I asked.

"Well, yeah," she said immediately, as if it were a stupid question.

"What happened?"

As she described the horrific details, Daisy's face and words disconnected from each other, and her voice, so full of inflection before, now sounded robotic. That mechanical voice was meant to deflect emotion, to protect the listener, but it didn't work. Now, I could only see the attack, the men. Daisy pouring cereal for her kid the next morning. Worst of all was the image of her heading back out to work the next week, or the next night, or ever.

"That's—" I said, and lost my words.

Daisy gave me a double take. Then she laughed. "Look at your face," she said. "Aw. You're so concerned."

When Daisy laughed, I wanted to cry. But Daisy was having a different reaction. As she looked at me, her face transformed into the same canny expression I had seen on Grayson's face when he hired me. She slapped the table lightly.

"Come work for me!" Daisy said.

"As one of your . . . girls?"

"*You* could work," she said. "Look at that sweet little face. Shit! You'd be great at it. You'd be the belle of the ball."

For a dizzy second, I considered it. I needed money, and I had never been the belle of any ball. Then I wondered what was wrong with me.

"Quit," JD said.

He was calling me from Denver's version of Chinatown on South Federal. He was there to restock Chinese "herbs" that were really powdered bugs. Sometimes he called late at night and left weary messages like "I'm so tired and want to go to sleep, but all I can think about is you." He bought me little rubber finger puppets, clusters of dark chocolate with nuts in them, a key chain of a nose where polymer snot dribbled out if you squeezed it, saying, "I use one of these for pediatric patients. I ask, 'Is your nose like this?' and they laugh." When we couldn't see each other, we talked on the phone every day, several times a day, JD about his medical cases, me about the Title IX case and any other gig work I managed to scrounge. But this was the first time he'd tried to tell me what to do.

"No way I'm quitting," I said. "This is the best job I've ever had."

"Seriously? It's all prostitutes, rapists, and lawyers."

I didn't understand his squeamishness. My last temp job was at a place where my boss timed my bathroom breaks and wrote me up for laughing. JD had grown up poor. He'd spent his summers working construction and laying sewer pipe. He knew what luck it was just to have a job that didn't smell bad.

I said, "I don't see the problem. It's only a part-time job, and I don't have to temp as much now."

"At what cost, though?"

"No cost. They're paying *me*—buckets. One hour of PI work pays as much as five or six hours temping. And I'm good at this job."

"Sure, you're good at the job, but is the job good for you? It's making you manic."

"You just don't know me very well. I'm always manic." I liked how protective he sounded, even though it irritated me.

In whatever grocery store he was in, JD sighed over the sound of what could only be someone chopping a roasted animal with a cleaver. "Every day I'm paid to know what's good for people and what's not. And every time you talk about this job, you sound like a drug addict."

"Addicted to *justice*."

He didn't laugh. "Who's looking out for you in all of this?"

"You are, apparently." When he didn't flirt back, I said, "You're jealous because I have a job chasing down bad guys while you're stuck talking to old people about sciatica."

"Don't poke fun," JD said. "Sciatica is a very painful condition. Especially for the elderly."

So maybe JD couldn't appreciate my work, but Grayson, my big-brother-in-arms, did. After my X-rated Daisy memo, he set a meeting at his office. He was seated at his desk, looking important in a full suit, jacket on.

"So?" I asked, ready for praise. "What do you think?"

"It's dynamite. Really important." Grayson rapped his knuckles once on his blond wood desk. "Our first real connection to the university administration, even if it's minor."

"Minor?" I felt my chest deflate. "That's what you wanted, 'university knowledge,' right?"

"Well, it's good! It shows a connection, and it's dynamite press for our case. But Tanner doesn't have enough power. We need to show university knowledge at the higher levels, the decision-making level. Like Coach Riggs, or the athletic director. That would make the case."

"Oh." I had thought the case was practically won with the prostitution angle, but apparently there was more work to do. Which was good, I reminded myself, because it meant I was still employed.

"Deal me in with Daisy," Grayson said. "Next time we'll meet together: you, me, and Daisy. She's got to testify for us. A hooker with a heart of gold. Boy, can I sell that to a jury."

"Unlikely she'd want to testify, though." I plucked a ceramic figurine of a chicken from his desk and played it back and forth in my hands. "She's really afraid of that cop who busted her."

"I can do things," Grayson said obliquely. Do things? "Don't worry. Just set another meeting for the three of us. I'll convince her."

"Okay. I'll need to give it a few days, though, maybe a week. She likes space." Grayson laughed and I said, "I guess it's ironic. But she likes to be the one to decide."

"Well, then you've got to make her think she's deciding to testify for us."

I looked down at Grayson's chicken figurine in my hand and noticed that it was eating a fried drumstick. I set it back down on his dustless desk made from some unfamiliar-looking wood. "How might I do such a thing?"

"I don't know. Then again, I don't know how you've convinced people to say half the stuff they've told you so far."

That was different. Information was for the taking, but I didn't like asking people to do things they didn't want to do. Out his window was a perfect view of the spiky Flatirons, absorbing and reflecting the sun. "Is my job to find stuff out, or to persuade people to join our side?"

"Both. You're my roper." Grayson gave me the lip-pressing smile I had learned meant, *I'm very very very very busy.*

I had to look up what "roper" meant. In a rodeo, it's someone who lassoes little calves and ties them up. In PI work, the roper is the lure, the confidence builder. The roper subtly gets to know the suspect, establishes rapport, becomes friends with him, maybe even lovers sometimes. She's the operative in the field, pretending to be what she's not. The object is trust—to convince the suspect to confess to you, and then to the world. It's a con, but not for money: for justice.

In 1910, Carl Neumeister was a roper hired by a new detective named Raymond C. Schindler, at the famous William J. Burns Detective Agency in New York. It was Schindler's first murder case, commissioned by the victim's parents and the city, to investigate the attack on ten-year-old Marie Smith in Asbury Park. On Marie's way home from school, the child was raped, strangled with her own stockings, and left dead in some bushes near her house. In *To Kill a Mockingbird* fashion, an African American man named "Black Diamond" was awaiting trial for the crime, but Schindler believed he was innocent. Based on timelines alone, Schindler instead suspected a German man named Frank Heidemann.

Schindler had Heidemann tailed to his new digs in Manhattan and discovered he ate at the same little German restaurant three times a day: eight thirty, twelve thirty, and six thirty. This would be the point of contact for the roper, Carl Neumeister, also German. Initially, Schindler didn't even tell Neumeister the details of the crime, so Neumeister wouldn't blow it. Neumeister was just supposed to become Heidemann's friend.

Neumeister showed up at the restaurant a half hour before Heidemann arrived and sat a few tables away, watching Heidemann over
the rim of the *Staats-Zeitung*, a German expat newspaper. Heidemann
made the first contact, and the two quickly became inseparable. They
ate their German food together, took walks, played chess and pinochle,
shopped, and did errands. After a couple of weeks, Heidemann suggested they room together at a boardinghouse.

By now, Neumeister knew about Marie Smith's rape and murder,
so during the first month they lived together, Neumeister tried to extract information by dropping idle comments about Asbury Park, or
telling Heidemann he was shouting strange things in his sleep and
what did they mean? No go. His boss, Schindler, told Neumeister to
try the play-within-a-play technique from *Hamlet*, so Neumeister took
Heidemann to a horror movie where a man brutally kills a little girl
the same age as Marie Smith. Heidemann started shaking, said he felt
ill, and left the theater. But back home, he said nothing to Neumeister.

After two months, all the money from Marie Smith's parents was
spent, and the two investigators were desperate. Schindler and Neumeister staged another play. Neumeister invited Heidemann for a sce-
nic drive through Westchester County. On a lonely road, Neumeister
began arguing with a "stranger," in reality a planted PI. The stranger
pulled a knife. Neumeister drew a revolver and shot him with a blank.
The stranger fell, feigning death and blood. Neumeister and Heidemann roared away in the car, babbling in fear.

The next day, Schindler's newspaper contact printed one copy of
a dummy newspaper with a front-page story reporting that the man
was dead. The police were looking for the murder suspect. They left
the fake paper at Heidemann's door.

Neumeister pretended to panic. He draped his coat over a chair so a
steamship ticket peeked from an inside pocket. When Heidemann saw
the ticket and confronted him, Neumeister confessed he was going
on the lam and returning to Germany to evade capture for murder.
Goodbye forever.

Unable to live without his new—only?—friend, Heidemann begged
Neumeister to take him to Germany, too. Neumeister said, "No. We're

friends now, but friends have disagreements. If we quarrel, you might turn me in."

Heidemann said, "If you had a hold on me like I have on you, would you take me?" Neumeister said, "You couldn't possibly." But Heidemann kept pushing until Neumeister agreed with reluctance.

And then Heidemann confessed everything about Marie Smith: the rape, the murder, the method and location, everything. Once he started confessing, he couldn't stop, leaking details, facts, and sensory impressions for days—long enough for Neumeister to covertly contact the police, and for them to listen to Heidemann's confessions from the next room. Heidemann was arrested and pled guilty, still compulsively confessing right up until the moment of his execution by electrocution.

When people write about this case, they're amazed by Schindler's masterminding, his scriptwriting of the incredible ruse. To create the fiction of the gunshot murder! To use *Hamlet*! To know Heidemann would confess to secure his ticket to Germany with his friend!

But what impresses me is Neumeister, the roper. To befriend a man, to spend every day with him, to listen to him snore at night, to know he killed and could kill you and might, except he loves you. He loves you enough to risk himself rather than separate from you, and maybe you even love him back a little. You pretend to be the friend of a terrible man, and then you betray him.

Heidemann was a pedophile, a rapist, and a murderer. That little girl was only ten. Heidemann deserved prison and worse. I don't support capital punishment, but I can't help but feel happy Heidemann died alone in an electric chair in 1911. I hope it hurt.

But I also imagine the look in Heidemann's eyes as he turned to his best friend and realized the lie of their relationship, the cold and tactical betrayal. I wonder if Neumeister, the roper, regretted it, then or ever—if he considered the cost of such a job, so well done.

6

The Fixers

As my people-finding/getting/manipulating skills grew, I began contacting my mother: tentatively at first, and then more directly. A letter. An email. On my birthday or hers, maybe a phone call. We hadn't seen or spoken to each other in several years, but I now asked her to visit me. "Why?" she asked, as if it were the most ludicrous idea she had ever heard.

I didn't know why I wanted her to come. I only knew that I didn't remember her anymore. I only remembered other people's reactions to her, their awkward pauses and silences. Like whenever my mother had wished aloud to another mother that she had only had two children, while my older sister smiled and my brother and I silently looked at each other. The prolonged silence from my pediatrician when my mother explained why she waited a week to seek medical care for my broken foot, because she didn't want to reschedule an appointment. Another silence when she explained that she sent me to school without crutches. "I wrote her a note for gym class," she said. Then the doctor's slow, wary speech afterward.

Who was my mother? Who was I? I used to parrot her opinions: that you must always seek revenge for every slight or people will take advantage of you, or that having children ruins a woman's life. It didn't help me understand her, or myself, or anyone else. I was perpetually weird, immature, always behind, learning the foreign ways of humans. When a friend told me her father once locked her in a closet, I said, "That's cool." She said, "That's not cool. It's terrible." Oh. It had sounded nice to have a locked door between you and a grown-up.

I had to learn ordinary things by rote, like the fact that people enjoy their families and want to be near them, especially during holidays. People like kids, especially their own. Children want their parents to be there for their achievements. Some parents don't compete with their kids. Some kids didn't get kicked or hit. Some kids didn't grow up frightened all the time.

When I was four, I tried to tell my mother what X was doing to me. She had given birth to my younger brother a few months before; the baby was sleeping somewhere, my sister was at school, the house was quiet, and she was alone. My mother sat in our kitchen, which was green. I don't know what words I used, but I now know they were specific from the relieved and emptied-out way I felt afterward.

My mother leaned back, but not in surprise. It seemed that she already knew. She gave me an assessing, adult look. It's a look I would now describe as lawyerly.

"What do you expect me to do about it, Erika?"

I didn't expect anything. I was four. I just wanted it to stop.

My mother returned to her toast and tea. I walked away and played with my Raggedy Ann doll, beating her flat cotton body with my fists, and then against the wooden floor, and then against a doorknob. Her body only made a pat-pat-pat sound. I finally stopped to study her painted closed-mouth smile, her eyebrows tilted upward in a plea, the triangles of jagged eyelashes below her eyes like black tears. Her blush of shame, her hair on fire. I cried because I had hurt her, and still wanted to hurt her, and she had endured everything from me in silence.

I tried to talk to my mother about the abuse a few more times. When I was sixteen, I didn't get far before she said, "That's it, we're forgetting the past as of right now. I forgive you for everything you've done. And you're going to forgive me." She walked away, refusing to speak about it again.

The last time I tried to bring it up, I called her from my dorm room telephone when I was twenty, but I only squeezed in one sentence about the abuse before my mother interjected, "I don't want to be your mother anymore."

I stood clutching the beige plastic receiver. "What?"

She said, "I'd rather we were just acquaintances from now on."

"Acquaintances?"

"I want to be able to relax around you, and I simply can't do that as your mother." Then she hung up. I held the receiver in my hand until it blared loud beeps at me.

I looked around my dorm room, the rust-brown carpet, the anemic overhead light, the irrelevant posters I had hung on the wall. Was I an orphan now? Did I still have a brother and a sister if my mother wasn't my mother? I didn't dare call them to ask.

As hurt as I was, part of me felt hope. Somewhere under the apathy, my mother must have cared about me enough to feel discomfort, to make me stop talking. She just didn't care enough to listen.

But maybe she had changed since then, or would change if I could change her. Maybe we could start over. If my mother and I could just spend time in the same room together, maybe it would be like a chemical reaction, both of us transforming into something that might heal us.

"But you're so *normal*," people always say on the rare occasions I mention that I had a rough childhood. I studied normalcy. I made friends and imitated them. Normal people had mothers, mothers they saw, mothers they loved and who loved them. I didn't want JD to know what a solitary freak I was. My mother said no, no, she wouldn't be visiting me. But I didn't give up. I had learned how to be a normal human in reverse. I would teach it to my mother.

It was the late fall of 2003, and university football ticket sales had gone up, not down. The case was news, and the backlash was stronger than the lash. The biggest resistance came not from players, but from women. That baffled Grayson, but made strange sense to me, after my mother's stalwart support of X my whole life. The ones to fear in

James Bond movies were always the henchmen—Jaws and his metal teeth, Nick Nack, the Three Blind Mice, Pussy Galore, Oddjob with his machete hat—more than the actual villains. Henchmen will shrug away their consciences and go to the greatest lengths, because unlike the villains, they're not acting out of greed. They're acting out of love.

I called cheerleaders who said, "Wade Riggs is a great man and a great leader. I don't know why you're persecuting him. I love the football team." Maybe they did love the football team, or maybe they were playing ball themselves, acting like the cool girl who won't make trouble, who plays up to the power base so she won't get hurt herself.

The university hosted an "Ambassador" program, in which attractive female students acted as campus tour guides for football recruits to convince them to enroll. I had seen a picture of the Ambassadors: thin, smiling blondes. Nobody chubby, and few brunettes even. One Ambassador agreed to speak to me by phone, "even though what you're doing is wrong."

I asked the Ambassador, "Do any of you spend time with the recruits at night?"

"Sometimes, but it's not like it was set up that way. I mean, sometimes I had dinner with the coaches, too, you know."

"You went out to dinner with the football coaches?"

"It's not like that." But she refused to say what it was like, or answer any more of my questions after that. She only said, "It's a great university and it deserves better," and hung up.

I wasn't sure it was such a great university. Once in my master's program, a tenured professor spontaneously skipped the first two months of my class to stay on vacation in Mexico. Another took a nap on the table while graduate students conducted the workshop over his sleeping body. I myself had taught classes there, knowing nothing, pitying the undergraduates who were paying to learn from a master's candidate just a few years older than they were.

One windy day, I called King's ex-girlfriend. Her name was Vicky Beanblossom, a relief to look up. I could find a Beanblossom anywhere, and especially in the place where she lived, a small town that thinks it's big. My Broncos-loving ex-boyfriend was from there, as was

JD. He'd called it "really cowboy, racist, conservative, full of big box stores, Mormons, Republicans, and mountain-biking tourists." Vicky Beanblossom had been dating King at the time of the party, when he allegedly assaulted Calliope. I hoped Vicky would be fueled to tell us what she knew.

But she wasn't the gold mine of vengeance I had hoped for. When I called her, the first thing she said was, "First of all, I don't agree with what that girl is doing."

"Simone?"

"Me and King basically broke up over that party, after he went into the bedroom with her." Vicky said that when she confronted him about the party, King cried and cried, but wouldn't admit to anything. She didn't want him to touch her anymore. "His family saw him changing. He used to be honest. He never used to drink. But now he was getting tickets for drinking."

I hadn't found any records like that in my courthouse search. "What happened to the charges?"

"Someone in the university always took care of them. They all had some cop's business card in their wallets. They were supposed to call him if they got in trouble."

"Who?" This was like Calliope's ex-boyfriend with the DUIs. I started to get excited. "Which cop?"

"I don't know the name. It was just one of their endless perks. I mean, King got a free college education. But there was no way he could have gone to college if not for football. He wouldn't have gotten in anywhere on earth." Vicky told me that King had tutors for every class, and when a paper was due, the tutor wrote it. When he went out to eat, strangers picked up his tab. And King made money from hosting recruits—eighty dollars each. I interrupted. "I thought it was supposed to be thirty."

"King got eighty." Vicky was smacking her mouth, eating something chewy. "You know, I think his bad character started with his own recruiting trip. When King came back from that, he got really serious and protective of me. Something bad happened over there. He came straight to my house at one in the morning and said, 'I don't want you to go to a big university and turn into that.' Paranoid, asking me, 'Did you drink while I was gone, did you hook up with guys?'"

Vicky paused and said, "Not to be racist"—I braced myself—"but where we grew up, everyone was white and he was the only Black guy. He changed once he was hanging out with the football team. I think he was learning how to be Black," she concluded.

"Learning how to be . . . Black?"

Vicky said that King's biological father was African American and had played football for the university and then for the NFL, but King didn't meet him until college. "King got adopted by a white family, and he grew up white after eighth grade."

"Grew up white?"

"King was the only Black guy in town, and he acted like we did. But around those football players . . . I know the football and basketball teams teased him, called him 'whitewashed.' Maybe he thought that was how he should act. Black and stuff."

After hanging up, I had to regroup. Were bigots going to be our witnesses? All the players and recruits we suspected were Black. Was the lawsuit itself racist, even if Simone and Grayson weren't? At that moment, it was looking increasingly like *To Kill a Mockingbird*: white girls suing Black men for sexual assault. Of course, unlike in Harper Lee's book, this attack wasn't made up. And not all of the women were white; Calliope was Black, and some suspected survivors who refused to talk to me had Latinx surnames. But it was getting more complicated than simple good and bad, victim and predator.

I called an ex-student named Lance, who had briefly attended the party at Simone's but left before the assault. While searching for his contact information, I came across an old campus newspaper article where he was quoted as saying he had no interest in Black Awareness Month events because they had nothing to do with him as a white man. In another article, when questioned about the campus women's rifle association, Lance said, "Women should be at home cooking the food, not outside shooting it."

Lance had a thick East Coast Italian-American accent and worked as a day trader. "I can talk to you because the market's high and I can't make any money at this second," he said when I called. "I'm not friends with Simone or anyone from Colorado anymore because I'm in New Jersey now. I believe Simone, I believe that happened to her, but not for any reasons you'd want me to say in court."

"What are your reasons—"

"Because I've known enough Black people and I know what they're like. And I've known enough athletes and I know what *they're* like. So you put the two together . . . but you can't tell that to a naive college girl, she wouldn't understand," he said.

For a long time after I hung up, I sat in a self-made oil slick of doubt and confusion. These witnesses—*our* witnesses—had done the impossible. They made me feel sorry for the bad guys.

JD and I were in deeper territory now. I wasn't seeing anyone else and neither was he. I recognized this feeling—falling in love—but I didn't recognize the man I was falling in love with. He was mysterious to me. He could push over dead trees and carry a sofa bed up a stairway by himself, but he was also sweet to dogs and children, sweet to me. He could break people and he could also heal them. He knew how everything was made, and romanticized nothing but me. Once when I was admiring a Hiroshige woodblock print of workers roofing a house, he pointed and said, "That's not how you shingle a roof. You go from bottom up, not top down," and I fell for him all over again. I saw design and color, but he saw bullshit. He knew about meridians and *chi* and lots of stuff I had trouble believing, except for the fact that he once took away my migraine by holding my head in his hands.

He was inside my head, too. One night we were kissing on the floor and I thought, *I love you*. He said, "Me, too." I said, "What?" He blushed and said, "Nothing."

I couldn't figure out why he liked me. JD was not broken. He was him. I had dread-induced panic attacks the minute he left for work, or went anywhere without me. He had introduced me to a new reality where I had something to lose.

JD and I drove three hours to Glenwood Springs, in his Jeep Wran-

gler that had a glorified tarp for a roof and sides. Autumn in the mountains is essentially winter, so our fingers and feet were numb by the
time we arrived and jumped in the hot springs. We clung to each other
in the steaming water like snow monkeys.

After too long in the hot springs and too much wine in a restaurant
with red-and-white-checked tablecloths, JD and I kissed with chilly
noses. To warm up, we ducked into what looked like the stairway entry for a dim, narrow walk-up apartment building with no buzzer. We
made out on the stairs, laughing and warm again. I said it out loud this
time, in the dark: "I love you."

JD said, "I love you, too." Then, "Why is there a TV up there?"

We glanced up the stairs. On the second floor were a TV, sofa,
chairs, and a bookcase filled with books. We weren't inside an apartment building. We had inadvertently broken into a row house, a house
people lived in.

"Shit," we said in unison and burst out the door. We ran two blocks
to the Jeep, revved up, and hit the eastbound highway within minutes.
About ten miles into the darkness, when no flashing lights appeared
behind us, we relaxed and smiled at each other. We felt like we had
gotten away with something.

"The ticket fixer is a weight room trainer they call Duke, Duke Dumond," Grayson told me over the phone. "I deposed a university detective, and that's the name he gave me. Duke acts as the team's liaison
with the cops, one cop in particular. Named Officer Peppar, with an *a*."

"Peppar, honestly?" I asked, scribbling. Peppar, Duke, Beanblossom, King—the names in this case made it sound like an allegory.

"Peppar's a city cop, not university police. The university police
seem honest, but the city cops . . . The university detective said Peppar
interferes with investigations. He gathers players and coaches them on
what to say before the university police have a chance to arrive. Peppar
privately met with Simone's attackers before they talked to the university police, to help the players and recruits coordinate their stories."

"Isn't that illegal?"

Grayson paused. "They called it 'improper,' but not illegal. Either way, the press will love it. Sunlight is the best disinfectant. Talk to some players and see if this is a regular thing, Duke and Peppar working together. How it works."

"The system," I said, proud to finally understand.

I heard a grin in his voice. "Yeah. The system."

Current football teammates had stopped talking to us that autumn, probably under orders, so I researched and called random ex-players from old rosters until one picked up. His name was Eli. The first thing he did was parrot what everyone was saying these days: "I think what you're doing to the team is terrible."

"Noted. Let's just talk about football, then. How much time did you spend in the weight room?"

"Four or five days a week for two hours a day."

"In addition to football practice, or instead of?"

"In addition. We spent six days a week practicing on the field for two hours. And one or two hours a day in meetings to go over game plans."

"That's like a job."

"The best job."

I did quick math on my steno pad. "So, about thirty-plus hours a week? I thought it was twenty."

"That's the NCAA rule. But you don't win that way. And you couldn't complain about it or Coach Riggs made you wear the pink jersey."

"Pink jersey?"

"Yeah. Coach Riggs got three jerseys made in pink. The three weakest players had to practice in the pink jerseys instead of regular ones."

"Why?" I asked, but I already knew the answer.

"To motivate you not to be a pu—not to be weak." Eli sighed. "Listen, I don't know why this is such a big deal. Football players work really hard, and need to blow off steam. We shouldn't be punished for it."

"But you don't get punished, right? You have someone who helps out when you're in trouble, I hear. Someone in the weight room?"

Eli's voice cleared, matter-of-fact. "Oh, that's Duke."

I walked over to my butcher paper and drew a star next to Duke's name. "You trained with Duke Dumond?"

"We all did. He's a good guy."

"And he had a way to fix tickets and stuff?" When Eli hesitated, I said, "We're just talking, here. I know how it works." I used another one of the phrases the players said all the time: "That's just how it is, right?"

Eli said, "Well, sure. Yeah. People got in trouble all the time and went to Duke when they needed help. There's nothing wrong with that."

"Of course not."

"Nobody paid attention to it. He just wanted to help out the team. It was a nice thing to do."

"Above and beyond."

"Yeah."

"Not illegal."

"No! How could it be illegal? He's working *with* the cops."

I frowned out my smile, which I was afraid he would hear in my voice. "That's right. Which cops, do you know? Officer Peppar? Was Peppar paid for this?"

"Peppar got to watch games from the sidelines. At away games, too."

"Why would he travel with the team?" He wouldn't have jurisdiction outside the city.

"Coach Riggs flew him out to work as team security."

"Private security? Like moonlighting on his police job?"

"I think it was some extra money, perks and stuff. The cops were just fans, you know. Loyal. Protecting us. We need our players out on the field. If we don't win, everyone suffers."

"Everyone?"

"We do, and they do. The State of Colorado suffers."

In some places that was true, like flat Nebraska, its college football identity wrapped around the state like a red hand-knit scarf. But our small city was better known for tourism and tech startups. Far more locals owned skis than a football, and it seemed like every other person was originally from California. On university game days, more people in town were concerned about the traffic than the score.

But Eli would never believe that. I picked at a frayed piece of carpet. "Eli, can I ask you something, just you and me? Off the record." There was no record, but people knew the phrase from TV and it made them relax. "Not as an investigator. I just want to understand."

"Sure. Shoot."

"What's more important? Justice or winning?"

When Eli finally spoke, a soft, breathy laugh cushioned his words. "Well, lady PI, you should know. Why can't they be the same thing?"

John "Duke" Dumond, the strength and conditioning coach, was a thick ex–weight lifter with silver hair and black eyebrows. He wore a signature uniform every day: black golf shirt, black pants, and black Killer Loop sunglasses, tiny on his giant, square face. Duke had a criminal record from a past training job, charged for his connection to a scheme to sell 97,000 doses of steroids and prescription drugs to athletes at three universities. More than thirty former or present football players at his university had been using steroids. Duke pled guilty to one count of distributing, received a suspended sentence from the courts, and did no time. A few years later, he was hired here.

Calliope told me, "Duke did absolutely nothing, but he owned that weight room. They loved him, and everything went through him. Some said he used to be a prison guard. The big rumor was that he once dead-lifted a car. I don't know anything about ticket-fixing, but I'll tell you that his role with the players was *personal,* not anything else. It was like he was a godfather."

Football was Duke's main athletic concern; female athletes were distractions. A cheerleader told me Duke instituted a dress code for the female cheerleaders and dancers: they had to wear T-shirts and long shorts, but no tank tops, sports bras, or short shorts. Women also weren't allowed to wear any T-shirts that hung longer than their shorts, so the players wouldn't be able to fantasize that they were naked underneath their shirts. The men had no dress code, other than the fact that nobody, male or female, was allowed to wear red in the weight room for fear of upsetting the football players. Red was the team color for the University of Nebraska, their football rival.

Grayson told me over the phone, "Duke allowed student offenders to work off their community service hours in his weight room. And you'll never guess where he lives." He waited, as if I would actually guess.

"Um, a house?"

Grayson named the one home everyone in town knew: "The Ramsey house."

The information felt like a steel ball dropped inside my head, ricocheting and sparking stray connections. "How can he even afford it?"

Grayson's suit coat whooshed as he shrugged over the phone. "I set a deposition," he said.

Back in 1996, a six-year-old beauty pageant queen named JonBenet Ramsey was murdered in her home in this city, igniting a wildfire of national press. Even now, locals remember the facts: the child died of blunt force trauma to the head and strangulation from a garrote around her neck. Her attacker sexually assaulted her before murdering her. The father found the child's corpse in the basement of the house.

Some people suspected the parents of the murder, based on evidence around the points of ingress, and also their strange behavior, such as hanging up on 911 and immediately using past tense to refer to their daughter. Others said that slight trace DNA on the child's underwear pointed to an outside intruder. Current DA Beatrice Hull had served as the chief of the Sexual Assault Unit during this case. Nobody has ever been prosecuted for JonBenet Ramsey's murder.

Beatrice Hull later became the DA who also refused to prosecute the football players or recruits who had assaulted Simone. Who was this DA? I studied Hull's picture online. A straight bob, hair dyed ash blond, a German-looking face that looked like it had been squished. Her broad, rectangular body seemed designed for suits. She looked like a mother. JD glanced over my shoulder at her photo, pointed at the two rage lines between her eyebrows, and diagnosed, "Liver problem."

The next day, I brushed fallen maple leaves from the seat of my bike and puffed across town to Upper Chautauqua, a treed neighborhood as posh, plush, and foreboding as it sounded. It was what Raymond Chandler would have called "a nice neighborhood to have bad habits in." The streets were quiet, weighted down with money, the Flatirons knifing far above the roofs of the multimillion-dollar homes. In this neighborhood, the Ramsey house was a fifteen-room, 7,250-square-foot Tudor mansion in an ornately patterned brown brick and stone masonry, with three floors, 104 windows, seven bedrooms, and eight bathrooms, in the top percentile priciest real estate market in the United States.

The Ramseys seemed to still co-own this house with their lawyer, and Duke Dumond was in negotiations to buy it from them. That made no sense. Duke had only a university strength coach salary. He grew up poor in Mississippi, pulling menial jobs and joining the military to earn his education; an inheritance was unlikely. I searched for assets and found no real estate under his name nor his wife's. I needed context and inside knowledge.

One of my friends knew a former prosecutor for the district attorney's office named Beckett. He had been a prosecutor during the era when football players actually got arrested and convicted for their crimes, two coaches ago. That coach started recruiting tougher players and the team went "from woeful to bowlful," as *Sports Illustrated* said. During Beckett's tenure as a prosecutor, twenty-four players were arrested in three years, for alleged murder, rape, serial sexual assault, physical assault, menacing, breaking and entering, criminal trespass, disorderly conduct, theft, biting, drunk driving, stabbing a mattress during a fight, and illegally skinning a rabbit.

But it was more complex than simple thuggery; one of those fights arose when Milo "The Terror" Lehrer was called "little [n-word]" by a bar patron. He ended up receiving a deferred sentence for charges of disorderly conduct and fighting in public. The same year, another player also received a deferred sentence for a charge of third-degree assault, for hitting a woman after she called him a racial slur.

Now, under DA Hull, it seemed that nobody was ever prosecuted for anything, based on what felt like excuses on her part. Grayson was investigating Duke Dumond; I was going to ask that former prosecutor about DA Hull. But I was a little worried. I didn't want to lose my job with Grayson. I had the feeling that loyalty was the quality in me that Grayson valued the most, and I knew he wouldn't approve. We only had this case in the first place because DA Hull had recommended Grayson to Simone. He and Hull were friends, and she had agreed to testify for us. She was a star witness. He owed her.

But I didn't owe her anything. She didn't even know I existed.

Beckett agreed to meet me and showed up on time at a sports bar downtown. He had asked me to find a booth in the far corner of the bar; when he arrived, he chose the seat facing away from the other patrons so his voice wouldn't project into the room. He wore the lawyer's requisite uniform of a blue long-sleeved shirt, and was either warm-blooded or worked nearby enough to forgo his jacket. There was a disconnect between the top and bottom halves of his face— eyes warm and lively, mouth grim. From his clothes to the stoop of his shoulders, he had a look I was now beginning to associate with attorneys: that of a person used to doing what he has to do so he can do what he wants to do.

Perhaps from professional habit, he immediately beat me to the questions: "You work with Grayson?"

"You know him?" I asked. Beckett nodded. A microsneer. "You don't like him," I said.

"No, I don't," he said immediately, eagerly, or maybe he was just surprised. "He's your friend?"

"He's my friend." At least, I thought so. No one had ever done more for me than Grayson, by employing me so improbably and so well.

Beckett and I surveyed each other, the lines drawn.

We ordered. Perhaps predictably, Beckett was a "no-witness," so I tried to phrase my questions accordingly: "You don't believe there's a connection with all these unprosecuted cases?"

Beckett said, as if I had a voice recorder running (I didn't), "I don't know anything about that. I don't know how much help I'm going to be to you. I'm only going to say that I question Beatrice Hull's judgment."

"Is bad judgment why she used the 'third party consent' argument to justify not pursuing criminal charges against the players?" I asked.

"What's that?"

As Hull had explained to Grayson in her deposition, her reasons for avoiding this case had changed over time. At first she said she couldn't prosecute because it was too dark for Simone to see her attackers. Then, once the recruits were identified, Hull said it wouldn't be fair to prosecute them and not the unidentified players, because the recruits had been pressured into sex.

Once the recruits *and* players were in the process of being identified, DA Hull then used an argument she called "third party consent." She claimed that since Simone's friend Leah had invited the players to the party, the players expected sex and therefore couldn't be tried for sexual assault. Hull argued that the players had been given consent for sex by Leah, the "third party," so it might be viewed by a jury as permission for consensual sex and not sexual assault. I tried to explain this to Beckett the best I could, despite the fact that I didn't fully understand it myself.

I said, "The internet says third party consent is an argument some attorneys use for illegal trespass. Like, someone points to a house and says, 'There's a party in there, go right in' when there's no party. It was invented to justify unlawful entry into buildings." I couldn't resist adding, "And, now, women."

Beckett covered his face with his palms for almost ten seconds, not speaking. When he dropped his hands, he said, "I've never heard of such a thing. The only one who gives consent to have sex with me is *me*." It was satisfying to see a gut reaction like this from a man, a good man. Beckett wiggled the gold ring on his left hand. A server wafted by, drenched in the same perfume my mother used to wear.

"This is why I'm meeting with you," I said. "Beatrice Hull makes this excuse to avoid investigating football players, even though the university police said the evidence against the partygoers was overwhelming. And just with my limited searching ability, I've counted eighteen alleged crimes by these players in this time period, ranging from sexual and physical assault to DUIs and petty theft. Nothing was ever prosecuted."

"These were documented arrests?" Beckett asked.

"Some anecdotally, some with court records."

"Police records?"

"I couldn't get those." The city police were stingy with their records. They insisted I provide them with police report numbers, but how would anyone know those? Instead, I gave them all the other information they asked for—dates of birth, dates of arrest, full names and middle initials, and Social Security numbers. They always said they couldn't find anything, no matter how many times I reapplied.

I couldn't figure out the police. Were they letting the players off, or profiling them, or both? Officer Peppar seemed to be protecting the players, but other police officers must have acted differently. In the late 1980s, the NAACP had accused the city police department of profiling the mostly African American football team. One campus detective had admitted, "At the first home football game of every season, a couple of detectives drop by the stadium and pick up a few programs. Saves you time. Instead of having a victim go through the mug book, you just take out your program and say, 'Is he in here?'"

I now told Beckett, "On the police level, we know a strength coach named Duke Dumond somehow covered up violations with the help of a police officer named Peppar, who probably did it for perks. What we don't know is why Duke did it. Because he's a coach, and coaches did that kind of thing? Equally puzzling is why the DA refused to prosecute any of the football players for these tickets." Pushing my luck, I said, "And there's this weird Ramsey connection, with Duke living at the Ramsey house and DA Hull refusing to prosecute in both cases." While Beckett ate, I tore off a piece of paper and tried to diagram these specious associations.

Beckett dismissed the Ramsey angle as cockamamie, which it was, but it was still weird. I tried another "no" question. "So none of this is connected?"

Beckett paused. "No, with that many alleged crimes dismissed . . . I don't know. When I worked in the DA's office before Hull, nobody ever approached me or tried to influence me while I was prosecuting football players. But one football player was a serial rapist, and that case . . ." Beckett again covered his face with his hands. His half-eaten hamburger chilled in front of him, its pink middle belly-up.

"You look so sad," I said.

Beckett's big hands dropped to his plate. Worrying a french fry in a swirl of ketchup, he described a university football linebacker who serially raped eight women two decades before, mostly by home invasion. He was nicknamed the "Duct Tape Rapist" because he covered the women's eyes or mouths with silver duct tape. The police thoroughly botched the investigation, from omitting fingerprints to losing the perpetrator's pubic hairs, which had been carefully combed from each victim in each of the eight rape kits and preserved on slides. The physical evidence was gone, just gone.

Internal Affairs interviewed every police officer and everyone said no, they didn't know where the evidence went. Then, in the middle of the night, someone dropped all the pubic hair slides into the evidence locker. Only police officers would have had access to the evidence locker in a police station at night.

"Do you think the cop hid that evidence on purpose?" I asked, forgetting to frame my question in the negative to support the answer I wanted. Beckett seemed to hate leading questions.

"No," Beckett said (of course). "I think it just ended up in someone's squad car on delivery back from the Colorado Bureau of Investigation. Someone probably forgot to file it. Bad police work cuts both ways."

I tapped my drawing again. "But eighteen alleged crimes and no trials—"

Beckett interrupted, "Be careful of your assumptions. Because the truth might just be that the police department *sucks*."

I laughed and crumpled up my pathetic diagram.

Everyone blamed everyone else. The survivors blamed the perpetrators, understandably. The perpetrators blamed the women. Coach

Riggs blamed the perpetrators *and* the women, but not himself. Grayson blamed Coach Riggs and the university. The other players blamed the system but didn't think it was so bad. Beckett blamed the cops. I didn't know whom the cops blamed.

Beckett leaned forward, paternally. "Okay, I'm going to tell you a story that says everything you need to know about the city police department. So, my colleague's wife asked him to defend this woman who did her nails." Beckett rolled his eyes. "The nail lady ran a red light and was going to lose her license. My colleague said okay, but there was no defense, I mean, she did it.

"This lawyer's secretary looked a lot like his client, so on trial day he said, 'You're coming to court with me.' Before they got there, he made his client carry his secretary's papers and notebooks. When they were in the hallway waiting for their turn, he made a show of talking to his secretary, but really he was talking out of the corner of his mouth to his client. He told his client, 'You have one job: to sit at the end of the table and take notes.' He told his secretary, 'Sit next to me on my right. You have two jobs: look at the arresting officer when he's talking, and look down at the table when he looks at you.'

I said, "He did *not*."

Beckett raised his voice, as if I hadn't already guessed the punch line. "The judge asked, 'Do you see the person you ticketed here today?' The police officer looked where he was supposed to look and said, 'Yes, I see her there.' The judge asked the officer to point to the offender; he pointed right at the lawyer's secretary and said, 'That's her in the pink sweater.' The lawyer nodded, and the officer sat down and relaxed. And then my colleague got a motion to dismiss the case, based on the fact that the cop had identified the wrong defendant." Beckett leaned back and to the side, like a pitcher winding up. "So what does that tell you?"

"That your colleague is brilliant."

"No. You're missing the point." I was always missing the point. "To make that trick work, what important fact did the lawyer have to know about this police department?"

When I didn't answer, Beckett clasped his hands and smiled. *"That they lie."*

Beckett was right that the police were in the habit of, if not lying, presenting guesses as absolute facts under oath. Beckett said if a police officer couldn't remember a face, he'd secretly ask a prosecutor to point out the defendant, or the officer would look up the defendant's driver's license photo and study it directly before the trial. Then, on the stand, the police officer would say with certainty, "Yes, that's her right there," and point at the person he didn't remember. It was nearly impossible for a cop to remember all those random strangers' faces between tickets and arraignments, but cops can't exactly say to judges, "Come on. I spent thirty seconds with this guy and I've written fifty tickets since then." They can't say, "I'm about sixty-five percent certain that person there is the one I arrested," or even "I'm ninety-five percent sure." No, a cop has to speak with absolute certainty about a guess, or potentially lose the case, and, eventually, the job.

I did the same thing every time I expressed sympathy for sociopaths or said "You can trust me." Beckett's colleague and Grayson and most lawyers, really, were paid to lie by omission, to advocate for someone and hide whatever blemishes marred their image. This is what made us good at our jobs; we caught lies because we lied, too.

The first documented private investigator in history, Eugène François Vidocq, began his career as a professional liar. Vidocq was born in 1775 in northern France. He began committing crimes at age thirteen and was imprisoned countless times before he even grew up. Vidocq was a con artist, a forger, a thief, a pirate, an army deserter, a fighter, a fence, and a fugitive. He kept escaping prison and getting caught and escaping again, once in a stolen nun's habit, once in women's clothes, once by jumping through the window into the river Scarpe.

After a while, his only crime was that of repeatedly escaping his punishment. Vidocq was in prison so much he ended up making a living as a prison informant, strategically lying and manipulating information so he was never suspected (and thus immediately killed) by the other prisoners. Once released, Vidocq's informant job turned into a position with the French police force as the founder of the Brigade de la Sûreté, a plainclothes police unit. In 1817 alone, he was responsible for 811 arrests.

Vidocq eventually opened the first-ever private detective agency in history, Le bureau des renseignements. He ran his agency for fifteen years and hired former criminals as his operatives. He was so good at disguising himself that one ex-convict even enlisted him in a plot to catch and "kill Vidocq." In deep disguise, Vidocq waited with his tormentor in the dark outside his own apartment, acting equally shocked when Vidocq never showed.

Vidocq was the first criminologist to work in disguise and undercover, to use ballistics, and to solve crimes by using cast impressions of shoe prints. He developed the first-ever forensic laboratory. He invented a filing system for criminals, including anthropometric measurements of body dimensions—a version of the facial recognition system used by mobile phones today. Vidocq had a photographic memory for faces, even through disguises, and he and his operatives regularly visited prisons to memorize inmates' faces for future detection.

Vidocq hired female private investigators, including a woman known only as "Annette," the first documented female PI in history. They worked cases in the street by using a code of hand signals Vidocq had invented. He used his contacts and knowledge of criminal methods and hideouts to solve cases based on intelligence and known criminal modus operandi.

Above all, Vidocq was a charmer, brilliant at establishing rapport. When Vidocq arrested someone, sometimes he didn't bring the criminal to jail right away. Instead, he took him to dinner and tied him to a chair. They chatted. That's where Vidocq elicited his confessions, and also recruited informants and operatives to join him after their release. He understood them; he was one of them. Vidocq had accumulated a wide variety of tools and disguises in his job, but it wasn't the variety that led to his successes. Instead, it was one simple principle that helped him understand each crime, and thereby solve case after case:

It takes one to know one.

7

Follow the Money

The deeper I sank into my work, the more I wanted to see my mother. It seemed like all the people in the case—survivors, players, witnesses—were in constant contact with their mothers. When I asked to meet with these twenty- or twenty-two-year-olds, they always said, "Let me talk to my mom first." They relied on parents for help, advice, comfort, perspective, advocacy. I knew my mother wouldn't give me those things, but I still felt a blistering need to see her, to understand her denial of me. Maybe it would help me understand my work, I thought. Maybe it would help me finally understand myself.

That autumn I again invited her to come see me. She was ready for my request this time, because she countered with, "I'll bring X."

I actually stepped backward, as if X were about to vaporize out of the phone and materialize in my yellow kitchen. Without realizing it, I had reached for the handle of the knife drawer.

The last time I had seen X was over ten years before. After avoiding home for a few years after college, I missed my mother and my brother and sister. So I said I wanted to visit for occasional holidays under the condition that X agreed to never touch me. I said, "If he touches me even once, he'll never see me again." All these negotiations took place over the phone through my mother, who asked no questions but said it was fine, we were all in agreement. No touching.

So I visited a few times. All was okay until the last time, a decade ago. On that visit, I was jumpy because the normally unaffectionate X had made motions to reach for me a couple of times—once when I arrived, and again leaving a restaurant. I had backed away, hands up, and he had retreated. On that visit, I mostly visited friends, dragged my brother out with me, or hid in my room, until it was finally time to go to the airport. My mother took me, and X drove. I couldn't wait to leave.

Inside the airport, I hugged my mother goodbye and did my usual wave to X. But he stepped forward and grabbed me.

Maybe he figured I wouldn't do anything with so many people around. But I struggled against him, and he struggled toward me, grabbing me tighter, trying to hug me, or maybe he just wanted to show me that he *could* hug me if he wanted to. It didn't take long, but it felt long. I shoved him hard, my second time ever doing that in my life, and broke his grip. X recoiled, stumbling backward.

X said, "You're so cruel. So cruel," as I said, "You promised!" My mother's gaze was on him, only on him.

I fled for the plane and spent the flight looking out the window and crying behind my sunglasses. As the plane finally landed in Colorado, white peaks slicing the horizon, I vowed to myself, *No matter what, I will never be in the same room as X again.*

Since then, that vow has been the most solid thing about me, more core than any belief I've ever held. I have lost friends and missed weddings and funerals to keep this promise to myself. I felt like if I ever broke it, I might kill myself.

So now, standing in my kitchen, I said to my mother, "No, he can't come. He's not invited. He will not come. Just you."

She said, "Then I don't want to come."

"But you visit friends alone," I said. "You just flew to England without him."

"That's different," she said. "That's friends."

"Don't you want to see me at all?"

"I don't need to," she said. "I see your brother. I see your sister."

"But I'm your kid, too."

"You can visit me. You can come by when he's not around."

I wasn't crazy about the thought of clandestine visits to see my mother. Besides, I couldn't afford a hotel. "I'm your daughter," I said.

"What would I even tell him?"

"Tell him you're visiting your daughter."

She wafted out of the conversation with an unconvincing, "We'll see."

She was punishing me for those years I wouldn't come back home during college and afterward. But she didn't see that I was already punished. It's hard to have nowhere to go. I was kicked out of the dorms every winter and spring break in school, so I had to scrounge a couch somewhere, rent from strangers, or go home with a friend whose family was so sweet to me that I could tell they didn't want me around. Once I spent four weeks in Iowa at Christmastime, when it was so cold that the radio station threatened us with death if we ventured outside. I spent the school break hiding in a bedroom from the three large, strange men I rented from, while they drank in the living room right outside my door that didn't lock, lit their farts, and watched very loud porn.

JD started hovering once he heard panic in my voice. After I hung up, he asked, "Why do you even want her to visit you?"

"Your mom visits you."

"That's different, you know that," he said. He meant that his mom and her partner were nice. "Does this have something to do with the case?"

"No. Yes. I don't know. I'm just trying to understand her."

"You're not looking for understanding," JD said. "You already understand her. I understand her, and I've never met her. You're trying to change her mind."

"Is that bad?"

His green eyes softened with his voice. "No, baby. I just don't think she's going to help you."

"Maybe I can help her," I said.

"That's not your job." He didn't say what he was probably thinking: *And you're not qualified.*

A month later, I called my mother again. I decided to ask one last time and then drop it forever. Before she had a chance to start talking, I said, "I want to see you before you die. Don't you want to see me before you die?"

She didn't answer. She said a muted goodbye and hung up.

In a couple of weeks, my mother called me back. She would visit me for three days. I could expect her in the spring.

The case was warm but not hot. The third column on my butcher paper, "Coach Riggs knew about it," was still blank, although Tanner Liddell was now all over the news as the recruiting coordinator who enlisted sex services for football recruits. A university ex-employee told me that Tanner probably made $21,000 per year. That wasn't enough money to live in that town, let alone hire sex workers.

I found and called Tanner Liddell's ex-boss, now working in the private sector. Like everyone else, the first thing he said over the phone was, "What you're doing to the team is criminal." By now, I wondered if they had all somehow been coached to open with that line.

"Hey, I'm just doing my job," I said, my by now standard response. It usually warmed them up somewhat. People who worked in college athletics were used to compromising their integrity for their jobs, as they imagined I was doing now. I said, "I'm interested in your experience."

His voice was clipped, thin. "My experience was that Coach Riggs was the most upstanding human being I ever worked for. It's not in his nature for this stuff to happen. The press is giving him a raw deal, dragging him through the mud. It's not fair."

I made murmuring sounds, neither approving nor disapproving. "I know you supervised Tanner. When you worked with him, you had no idea what he was doing? None at all?"

"Tanner screwed up. That was all on him. I don't know what Tanner was thinking, hiring hookers. Any rational human being would know that's not okay."

"So did you know about it?"

"No."

In the background, I heard the sneaker squeaks and echoes of a racquetball court. I said, "Okay, I just need confirmation on how much you were allowed to spend on a weekend. I know the recruits' basic needs were paid for, food and lodging, but I'm wondering about any extras. I've gotten different answers," I said, but of course, I had no idea. I made my face as nonchalant as possible, even though he couldn't see me. Even on the phone, people somehow sense when you roll your eyes or make faces.

He said, "Oh, if I knew I had a big weekend, I could take out as much as I wanted. No drugs or alcohol, though."

"Of course not." *They paid the player hosts to buy that*, I thought. "How much might a weekend cost?"

"Well, the weekend of the Nebraska game, the year we won the Big Twelve championship, I think we spent about eight thousand dollars."

"In one weekend?"

"That was for seventeen recruits and hosts."

"Spent on . . ."

"Dinner and entertainment."

The math physically hurt my brain as I calculated on my steno pad. "So, about five hundred dollars per recruit in forty-eight hours, besides their food and lodging expenses? Because I understand those are paid for out of a different fund."

"Some weekends it went up to twenty thousand dollars, but there would be more people. The weekend after, I had seven or eight kids— that was the rape weekend—and we spent a lot of money that weekend, but probably less than the weekend of the Nebraska game." He had just called it the "rape weekend." So he wasn't denying it, then. I wrote, *Possibly sympathetic, despite himself.* I asked, "And where did the money come from?"

"Oh, it was in the budget. There was tremendous oversight. Secretaries and such. Receipts."

I wondered if Daisy wrote out receipts for her customers. "How did you spend five hundred dollars per recruit in forty-eight hours with no alcohol?"

"They eat a lot."

"But don't they eat their meals with the team, for free?"

"We usually went out to dinner once."

"Each recruit eats five hundred dollars' worth of dinner?" Wait, he had said "dinner and entertainment." "What kind of entertainment?" When he was still silent, I couldn't resist adding, "Strippers?"

He actually growled at me. Then he said, "I think we're done here," and hung up.

All the money was so weird. Thirty-dollar stipends for player hosts that somehow ballooned into eighty. Five hundred dollars for a single alcohol-free dinner. Tanner Liddell's sex expenses versus his modest salary. Duke Dumond in negotiations for the multimillion-dollar Ramsey mansion, presumably on a strength coach's wage.

We already knew that the player stipend paid for alcohol and drugs. And a person could only eat so much dinner. So that left only one thing.

How much was the university spending on sex?

If anyone knew about the commerce of sex, it was Daisy. She agreed to meet me for lunch at the same café as before. I was trying to reconcile Daisy's need for space with Grayson's request for an introduction, so Grayson planned to wait and join our meal midway through. He wanted to convince Daisy to testify for us, but first he wanted me to ask her about a tip we had received about a striptease service called In the Buff. The strip club owner bragged openly to *Playboy* about servicing the university football team on recruiting visits, saying, "It's a tradition handed down from player to player to player." Coach Riggs said he didn't want players taking recruits to strip clubs, but "it's not illegal. Anybody who went to a strip club did not break a university rule." Grayson planned to depose the strip club owner under oath, but he wanted me to ask Daisy about him so he could prep.

By now, I was fully obnoxious. I began thinking of myself as a whistleblower, a bastion of truth, basking in the power of my newfound skills. I said things to my friends just to provoke them into confessions.

"Your problem is you want to fail," or "You don't love your husband anymore." They did confess. Then they started avoiding me, all except for JD. By the time I met with Daisy, I was beginning to feel a little lonely.

Daisy was late for our lunch, and I worried she would bail or forget. I was relieved when she finally arrived, grinning when she spotted my wave. She sat across from me in the booth, emitting a puff of outside cold that quickly dispersed. She shed her too-thin winter coat, revealing a snug purple dress and long rhinestone earrings that dangled next to her impeccable makeup. She was dressed for nighttime, not lunch, but I was the one who felt inappropriately dressed in my gray pants and white button-down blouse. "You look amazing," I said.

"I have a thing afterward." Daisy looked up and ordered a chimichanga and a hot chocolate with extra marshmallows and whipped cream. "Men like my fat," she told the skinny server, who laughed and squeezed her arm.

As we chatted I was reminded of how conversationally responsive Daisy was. Wherever I led, she followed, and it took only seconds to comfortably bring her around to the case. "Did you remember any of those names?" I asked. The meeting before, I had requested names of the "girls" who slept with football recruits, and she said she had to think about whether or not to disclose them.

Daisy said, "I guess I can talk about them. I mean, they did what they did, right? I don't sleep with seventeen-year-old boys."

"But they did." *And you took money for it*, I thought.

"Well, Trudy was okay with it. She was the main one who slept with the recruits, although there were more girls I don't remember."

"Trudy?"

Daisy hesitated for less than a second, then gave me her last name. "She was an RN at a hospital. Lots of my girls were nurses, nurturing types, you know. Trudy was a petite bleached blonde from Illinois. Her hair looked like a used Q-tip. She was flat, with breasts like empty pita pockets." Daisy was happily reciting now—this was clearly a bar story. "Trudy was the only person I've ever met who was a true-blue nymphomaniac. She had sex with everyone she could. She picked up a guy at a bus stop and had sex with him in her car. She would grab my phone, look through it for male numbers, dial them, and say, 'Hi, who's this?' She did stuff like bring guys to my house and have loud sex with them with my kid in the next room, so I had to kick her out."

"That's understandable."

"Well, maybe you understand, but she didn't. Trudy *hated* rejection. Sometimes she would show up at a client's door and he wouldn't like her, so he'd slam his door in her face. That happens in this business; you have to have a tough hide. We have a cancellation fee, but nobody pays it." Daisy waved one beautiful hand. "Anyhoo, when Trudy got turned away, she'd be brokenhearted. She would cry and wouldn't leave my house. One time she was crying and saying she should just go back to her kids, or back home to Illinois, so I said it was a good idea. She got upset at that, but I had to cut her off. I felt bad about it, but she was out of control, a scattered mess. She didn't do drugs, though; she was just made that way. Working for me wasn't helping her."

Did working for Daisy ever help anyone?

Daisy said, "In the month of October, Trudy made close to twenty thousand dollars, and blew it on clothes and a car. After I fired her, the car company called me to verify employment, but I wouldn't, because she no longer worked for me. That made her mad. I think she was the person who reported me to the Broomfield police."

So this was why Daisy was willing to tell me Trudy's name. "Wouldn't that get her in trouble, too? Talking to the police?"

Daisy adopted the patient expression people reserve for children and the hopelessly naive. "Trudy was having an *affair* with a cop. He was obviously married, but Trudy didn't believe it. I sometimes got weird calls for Trudy, probably from the cop's wife."

"Is that why you hung up on me the first few times I called?" I asked. "You thought I was the cop's wife?"

Daisy rearranged her place mat. "Whenever a strange woman calls, you know it isn't good."

"What do you know about a striptease service called In the Buff?" I consulted my steno pad to make sure I got the name right. "I guess they send strippers around to private parties, bachelor parties, like that?"

"I know the owner of In the Buff," Daisy said. "I used to hire his girls for private parties we threw for clients."

"Why don't you use him anymore?" By now, we had both abandoned the pretense that her sex work career was in the past.

"Because I find the owner offensive. He would say, 'What do you want? Big tits, little tits? You want a chink?' He's the kind of guy who slaps women's asses all the time."

I had already researched the service. Their website featured pictures of nearly naked "playmates" fondling each other against a black background, or posing in silhouette with heads thrown back, lips parted in exhale, breasts and butts out so far their bodies turned into switchbacks. The women had taglines like, "Teasing you . . . Pleasing you . . . That's all I want to do with you . . ." or "I work well with anyone and like to be naked with other girls." Some even used extended metaphors: "I'm a sweet, luscious treat! Book me for a yummy time!" They promised to "show everyone a good time." The girls were breast-augmented, tan and shiny, laxative-addict thin. They intimidated me, but I wasn't sure why.

Daisy said, "At In the Buff, you know that stripping is the least of what they do, right?"

"They sleep with clients?"

Daisy wiggled in the booth, getting comfortable, and leaned forward. "Their tamest show goes like this: they balance a lifesaver on the tip of the guy's nose and bump it into his mouth with their private parts. They do whipped-cream races, where they draw lines of whipped cream from their feet to their breasts, and two guys race up their bodies to lick it off. And they offer nipple shots—this is where they could really get in trouble, serving alcohol to minors—where they pour whiskey off their breasts and the guys drink it off their nipples. They never card anyone."

I scribbled madly, also glancing around the restaurant, trying to gauge whether or not the family with two young daughters at the table next to us could hear anything we were saying.

Daisy said, "They do something they call a 'mango butter body rub' where they strip the guy down to his underwear and rub mango butter all over him, every inch inside his underwear until he comes. They get creative, too—it's not always the same. One time, a dancer brought lollipops to a party and the men lined up to stick them inside her. But it was really quick, like, not even for a second."

I said, "Sounds like a good way to contract a yeast infection."

"Oh, they put condoms on the lollipops first."

A condom on a lollipop. "How much does it all cost?"

Daisy detailed the price list: a flat fee for the "playmate" to attend the party, plus tips to dance, and the extra services. The prices varied according to the wealth of the clients, but it was generally five to ten dollars for each nipple shot; the host had to provide the liquor but the dancers poured. Thirty to forty dollars for mango butter body rubs. Ten to twenty for whipped-cream races, "which is pretty much oral sex," Daisy said. "And for an extra fifty bucks, those girls'll go into a room with anyone. I think you had to pay a full hundred for sexual intercourse, though."

I dropped my pen. This was way out of the gray. "It's straight-up prostitution," I said.

Daisy's face animated. "I *know*! Somehow they're legal, but I got arrested."

Grayson arrived shortly before we finished our food, wearing a suit and the blue shirt he favored. He slid into the booth next to me and said, "I'm sorry I'm late. I had a meeting." I introduced them, and the mood instantly changed from intimate to businesslike. Daisy took in his face, his tie, the way he glanced at the menu and said, "Coffee, just coffee" to our server. He took a quick scan of my illegible, incomplete notes, and told Daisy, "We'd like you to testify for the case."

Daisy stopped chewing for a moment, then she swallowed the wad inside her mouth whole. She bristled and stiffened, rising two inches in her seat, all my rapport work eradicated with one sentence from Grayson. I wanted to take off my shoe and beat him with it.

Daisy said, "The Broomfield cop who arrested me said not to get involved, that it would be bad for me. I told him Erika said you'd keep my involvement private and he said, 'Well, that's a nice story.'" This was such an about-face from our earlier conversation. Daisy was negotiating. Grayson was a man, and men were the people you negotiate with to get what you want. What that was, I didn't know.

Grayson said, "We have the power to keep you private."

Daisy's painted eyelashes flickered. "You didn't keep the victim private." That was true. Simone was in all the newspapers, personified as the college student trying to ruin the institution of football as we knew it. Daisy's face was closed but polite. She kept her own counsel. She kept her own reality.

"Let's take about ten steps back—" Grayson said, but Daisy interrupted.

"And that cop wouldn't even give me my own police report. He said if I come forward as a witness, Broomfield may reopen the case against me and charge me. I can't give my parents any ammunition to try to take my kid away."

"I talked to the DA and she talked to Broomfield. Nobody wants to do what you're saying," Grayson said. "And nobody is allowed to deny you your police report."

"He seemed concerned about me, which was really nice for a police officer."

"Daisy," I said. "You know he's not looking out for you, right? You know he's protecting the players. Not you."

"I've just got to be honest," Daisy said. "I wish I kept my mouth shut. I feel like I just screwed up my life by coming forward." Daisy gazed out the window at the cars sliding by, the women gliding along the sidewalks, gloved hands facing palm-up to catch flakes of snow. To warm up, a middle-aged man with a long beard did solitary yoga at a bus stop, warrior pose.

"Daisy, it's okay," I said, and her gaze snapped back to mine. "Whatever you said, you can unsay. We're just talking, here. You have the power here, over us. We're the ones asking for the favor. We're the ones buying you lunch."

Grayson started to speak, then glanced at me and took a sip of coffee instead. We sat in a silence bordering on misery. Daisy and I chewed our chimichangas.

Daisy turned to Grayson suddenly and said, "I know right from wrong."

I felt his posture harden next to me. "I'm sure you do," he said.

Daisy's lower teeth flashed in a quick grimace. "One time a guy called wanting a child, a young, young girl." She paused, and I dreaded what might come next. Daisy said, "That happened a lot, actually, but this time I could tell the guy was going to keep calling until he found one. So I took all his information, his address and phone number, and then I said, 'Sir, this is Detective So-and-so. We'll be sending a black-and-white car to your house. Do you have clothes on, sir? Well, you'd better put some on. Are you aware it's a crime to sleep with children . . .' and so on. I made him cry." She lifted her chin. "What I do isn't always bad."

"Of course not," I said. Her sudden mood changes dizzied me. "That must have been weird for you, though."

Her gaze settled on me and her shoulders lowered. "Oh, we got all kinds of requests. One guy wanted me to pretend I was dead."

"Like, a corpse?" I asked. She nodded. Grayson stared doggedly at his coffee, eyebrows raised, but I couldn't help but laugh. That was a casting fail; Daisy was anything but dead.

She finally smiled and leaned in toward me, tasted her lips, and lowered her voice. "The money was great, but it was so *uncomfortable*. I had to strip down, get in a bathtub full of cold water and then drain it. He wanted me freezing cold. The heat was on, like, zero. Then he dry-humped me—or, I should say, damp-humped me—in the wet tub while I had to lie perfectly still. It took me ages to warm up afterward. I blew the car heater for like a half hour. I guess if you're a rich CEO, vanilla sex isn't exciting enough."

Rich CEO. While she told the story, I had caught Daisy's chameleon-esque face-flash—a stranger's cheek, lip, and jaw layered over her face like a scrim. For a second, she wore the guy's face as clearly as if she were doing an impression; most people do this when they talk about someone else. I now recognized the CEO's frozen face on Daisy's usually elastic one. I thought I had seen this CEO on TV or in the newspapers. He was well known in the community, very pale for Colorado, and spoke through a rictus, barely moving his mouth. He was diminutive and mild, often dressed in black. It could fit.

"I think I know who you're talking about," I said.

"Right," she said.

I did my party trick, naming the man I had recognized on Daisy's face. He ran a local company that went international.

Daisy was too shocked to lie. "That's him! How did you know? Wait. Did he make you act dead, too?" Grayson turned in the booth to stare at me.

I laughed. "No. I never met the guy." The man used to appear on commercials stroking the company mascot, a glossy Irish Setter.

"You're psychic!" Daisy said.

I shook my head and laughed. I didn't think she'd believe me if I tried to explain.

Daisy flexed her fingers, and then relaxed. "Okay. I'll do it," she said.

"You'll testify for the case?" Grayson asked.

"If you can protect me, I'll help you. But you have to help me."

"I know a very good lawyer who might take you on pro bono," Grayson said quickly, his legs half out of the booth. He clearly wanted out of there as soon as possible. "I'll set you up. Right now." The two of them shook on it, Daisy's manicured hand resting in Grayson's rough one. Then Daisy left for her "appointment" and oxygen returned to the planet.

Grayson paid and then almost limped out the door and into the cold air. He said, "Man. I think I need a nap."

"You seemed a little off. Are you okay?"

Grayson asked, "What, she doesn't wear you out?"

On the contrary, I was almost skipping next to him in the street. Daisy was food to me. She was easily the most fascinating person I had ever met. When she was around, that whirling feeling left my chest and instead swirled in the open air around her. I caught Grayson up on the finer details of what he had missed—In the Buff and Q-tip-pita-pocket Trudy, the recruits' call girl.

He said, "Great. Write it up. You've got the Midas touch."

But the story of King Midas is actually a sad one. Midas touched his daughter and she turned into a gold statue. He tried to eat and drink but all turned to metal. His gift left him starving and alone.

Grayson frowned and pressed the Walk button three more times than necessary. "You know Daisy thinks she's your friend, right?"

"What? No, she doesn't."

"She does. Be careful with that if you talk to her again. I won't be there to put the brakes on."

Good, I thought. "Why won't you be there?"

"You were better off before I showed up. She didn't want to open up to me."

"That's because you matter," I said. "You're a lawyer. You're a man. A potential client." Grayson glared at me. I softened it with, "That's how she might imagine you. You're her avenue to legal representation. She has to worry about what you think of her." Grayson's chest grew broader as we walked, and I felt jealous of his masculinity, his assurance of his value in the world. His feet unconsciously beat out a rhythm on the broken pavement: *I matter, I matter.*

I asked, "So with Daisy and In the Buff, are we close?"

"Closer," Grayson said. "Coach Riggs will claim the recruiter acted alone. He'll hang Tanner and Tanner'll be too scared to fight him. Same with In the Buff, unless we can prove that Coach Riggs paid directly. And he probably didn't. The players probably paid, with someone else's money."

"It's the same university," I grumbled.

"Doesn't matter. The legal precedent's already been set. We need to be able to prove Coach Riggs's knowledge." He dug his fists into his coat pockets. "This is good stuff, though. Juries will like it."

"Who should I follow up with?"

"The recruiter's still mine. Same with the owner of In the Buff." As agreed—once they were important, they were off-limits. I really wanted to talk to the strip club owner, though; I had never been inside a place like that. Grayson said, "You can talk with Daisy's employee, the one who had sex with recruits."

"The used-Q-tip-pita-pocket."

Grayson's smile had hard edges.

"You sure you're okay?" I asked.

"Yeah." He tossed his head to shift hair out of his eyes. "We're just, um. We're getting death threats."

"What?"

"My wife and I. Not our first time. They're nothing."

"From who? What are they saying?"

"Anonymous phone calls. Lay off the football team or we'll kill you, like that. Drunk stuff, dumb fans. Nothing to worry about." His face was tight. "I'm not worried. You shouldn't be, either. But tell me if you get the same."

"Why would I get death threats?"

"If this thing gets much bigger . . ." Glancing at my face, he said, "It won't, anyway. The university will settle soon." He always said that.

When we reached Grayson's car, he suddenly turned to me and grinned. "So how did you guess his name, anyway?"

"Whose name?"

"Daisy's client, the necrophiliac. That was a hell of a trick. How did you know it was him?" His cold, ungloved hand rested on the handle of his car door and he twisted his wrist to glance at his watch. There wasn't enough time to explain, if I even could.

"I'm a good guesser," I said.

I'm not that good a guesser.

In Malcolm Gladwell's book *Blink* he describes how our minds are able to form instant, correct intuitions, a method he calls "thin slicing." The idea is that the mind draws on a wealth of connections to make conclusions that are actually more accurate than those made after hours, weeks, even months of research. It feels more like recognition than deduction—from the gut, not from the head.

Sometimes, rarely, I can "thin-slice" facts from microexpressions, microgestures skipping across a face or body, as impossibly as a rock skips over water. I might deduce names from the slight pucker of a lip, a flash of W (*Her name is Wendy? Wanda?*). Maybe a person leans right, as if pulled by a weak magnet, and I can guess a place (*She's on the East Coast?*). Most interesting to me are what I call "face flashes." A witness might think of someone, and for a millisecond, her face takes on the dominant features of the person she's trying to conceal. The phantom of the absent face flashes over hers to briefly expose itself, and then it disappears, as fast as a camera shutter. It's why when you quote someone you know well, you imitate his accent, look like him, almost become him for a second as your mirror neurons fire. If someone is paying attention, she'll see you transform, momentarily, into someone else.

It's called the "Chameleon Effect," and almost everyone does it. We mimic facial expressions, mannerisms, postures, and behaviors without even knowing we're doing it, imitating each other "in the mind's muscles," as one psychologist phrased it. Married couples actually do begin to look alike, even developing similar facial lines from a lifetime of mimicking each other's expressions. Adult children catch their own parental impersonations, to their dismay: "I look just like my mother" or "I sound just like my dad." People born deaf even subconsciously and accurately copy the regional accents of people they're lip-reading, accents they've never heard before. Primate see, primate do. Studies show that the more empathetic you are, the better a mimic you are.

When Daisy talked about that CEO, for just a moment, her face froze into an uncharacteristic immobility. She shrank ever so slightly in her frame, and her gestures became more muted and limp. Daisy was probably a practiced character actor from her job, so maybe her subconscious impersonation was even more pronounced. I had seen footage of this CEO with this frozen face and these languid gestures, and must have remembered them in combination. Other factors may have contributed on a subconscious level: his relative fame, the deathlike all-black imagery in his company's packaging, and the size of the community relative to the smaller number of big fish. But still, I guessed one rich entrepreneur's identity in a hundred-thousand-person city filled with rich entrepreneurs. I still pull off a guessing trick like this once or twice a year, with accuracy. What I've never quite understood is how.

In my college philosophy class I studied Plato's theory of Forms, which argued that we all carry prebirth memories of perfect templates for everything that exists. Dogs embody a Dog template, so the image of any dog we meet—whether Pomeranian or Great Dane—wanders around our brains until it locks onto the Dog template. We can then understand and store the image accordingly in our minds. Dog.

When I was four and the abuse began, my mind fell apart, and all the Forms disintegrated. It was as if every neurological connection had been cut, all the brain cells flung into the air, landing in new combinations. Nothing had a container anymore, or maybe it was that the label had nothing to do with the box.

Harvard professor Elaine Scarry said torture "unmakes" the victim's world, destroying all ordinary meaning. Torture facilities in the Philippines, Syria, and Greece used domestic furniture to hurt people—smash a head with a refrigerator door, break a hand with a filing cabinet. Weaponized, the refrigerator is no longer a refrigerator; the filing cabinet is no longer a filing cabinet. Objects lose their meaning, and with them, meaning loses meaning. Scarry said it's why our Holocaust awareness particularly attaches to domestic objects: ovens, showers, lampshades, soap. Home is no longer home. The world is unmade.

At four, after X began abusing me, I remember asking my mother, "What is a pear?" She said, "It's a fruit you eat." I said, "No! What is a *pear*? Or a shoe? What is it?" I started crying as my mother described a pear—green skin, white flesh, tasted sweet. A shoe—you put your foot in it and walk on the ground. She grew more and more frantic as I cried and screamed until she was screaming, too: "What do you *want*, Erika? What's wrong with you?" Everything was wrong with me. I could no longer believe in the category of the thing, or in the words that signified the category. And without them, I learned right then, nothing meant anything.

So maybe—this is guessing—I built new categories of my own, so

much smaller and more specific than Dog, Pear, Shoe. Anger begins
with eyes sharpening and changing shape, lines cutting into the center of a flushing face, eyebrows curling, lower jaw jutting. A different
kind of pause while molecules congeal, a gathering before a blow. The
pause is your last chance to run, but it doesn't last long enough for you
to turn your back and try. That's the Anger Form.

Perhaps even the most minute actions and thoughts have their own
forms. Centillions of forms. This is how someone looks when she's
trying to say "Toyota." This is how someone looks when he's pretending he likes brussels sprouts. This is how someone sounds when she
wishes she loved you. Every experience a Form, every Form a meaning, and every meaning can be stitched onto other meanings, into predictions that just might keep us safe from each other.

Maybe we all do this. Maybe what makes me different is the re-
trieval. Talking to someone, I sometimes recognize a Form and know
something specific about that person before my conscious mind
catches up. The Guilty Form. The Hungry Form. The Secret Form. I
say, *You're thinking of a secret right now.* The Contempt Form. *You don't
like me.* The Rapist Form. *You hurt someone. You raped her.*

It's a talent, perhaps. But it's not a talent that comes from being
smart, or good, or even generally observant. It comes from being
broken.

Trauma breaks your brain—makes it atrophy forever. The damage is
not metaphorical but physical. The most severely affected tissue is the
left superior parietal lobule, associated with memory, language, and
the ability to orient oneself in the world. The lobule shrinks. Trauma
also shrinks the right superior frontal gyrus (the part associated with
self-awareness and laughter), the right lingual gyrus (vision, dreaming,
word recognition), right middle occipital gyrus (vision, hallucinations,
and object recognition), and left middle frontal gyrus (language processing, executive function, and emotion regulation).

The first time I saw PET scans of trauma-damaged brains on my computer, I felt sick. So many vacant expanses that should glow red, yellow, green. The traumatized brains looked like maps of flooded land, suspended under black water. I thought, *I am less. I will never be whole, with my shrunken brain. I won't be able to remember, see, laugh, feel, or dream well. I won't understand myself or the world. I will always know I could have been more than I am.*

I knew I was different. I rarely dreamed. Important events receded from my memory while small details plastered themselves like bright stickers onto the forefront of my consciousness. The most terrible scenes of my early childhood remain in Technicolor, and I can remember and retrieve whole conversations for days afterward. But I cannot remember last week, and sometimes an entire year will disappear from my mind except for random particles, like flung sand. I live word to word. It's as if the regular roads are missing from my mental map and I'm left with the ill-advised pathways and riverbeds and frayed rope bridges other people refuse to traverse. Sentences deconstruct and construct themselves in the air, forming and destroying meaning. I snag on exceptions and miss the obvious. I'm only good at a very few things—like this job—and I'm terrible at everything else. I act like I'm normal, but I know inside that I'm not.

Brain function is no more than energy, electrical impulses firing across synapses to create connections. And in physics, the law of conservation of energy states that energy cannot be destroyed nor created, only redistributed and transformed. So where did that lost brain capacity go?

In my college linguistics class, I studied a feral child given the alias "Genie." Genie's parents treated her as if she were an actual dog. The Dog Form. For the first thirteen and a half years of her life, her father kept her chained to a potty chair all day and night and fed her from a dog dish; Genie was only allowed to bark, not speak.

I wonder if I'll ever really understand that last sentence I wrote.

If she made any noise, Genie's father beat her with fists and wood planks. Genie's mother was nearly blind and did not challenge her husband. By the time the police discovered and freed Genie, she couldn't speak any words. Her cognitive impairment seemed permanent, which is how neuroscientists learned that if a child is silenced for the beginning part of her life, it physically damages her brain. Genie's development was arrested at the age of silence. Upon rescue at age thirteen, she had the social maturity of a thirteen-month-old, and she scored far below average for most linguistic and cognitive tests.

Except for one kind. Genie was a genius at a very specific kind of observation: gestalt perception.

Gestalt perception is a way of deriving meaning from our experiences by creating a whole that exceeds the sum of the parts. Given a series of incomplete shapes and colors, we might fill in the blank spaces to perceive a whole face, an object, or motion—for example, Jesus' face in a slice of toast, or a cloud formation that resembles a dragon. When good police officers accurately gestalt a situation, it's called instinct—drawing their gun before they consciously realize the person before them is armed and desperate. We complete the circuit in our minds, filling in the details we don't directly perceive, knowing more than we actually know.

Once the teenage Genie learned a basic vocabulary, scientists administered gestalt tests to discern the extent of her cognitive impairment. Genie scored at the ceiling of the tests, two standard deviations above a typical adult. Not only was Genie good, she was fast. On a speed gestalt test, she scored in the 95th percentile for a "normal" adult.

On a test asking Genie to gestalt faces and facial expressions, she scored the highest-ever recorded performance to date, for any child or adult of all mental abilities.

Chained by the ankles and wrists to her potty seat, Genie's days and nights were composed of silence and only small details—the passage of light across a room, the shape of a crack, maybe one or two minutes of her mother's face as she escaped her husband to blindly shovel spoonfuls of pablum into Genie's mouth. Genie had nothing to look at but her potty chair, a crib that she was only rarely allowed to sleep in (chained), the walls, the door, and window curtains in a lacy floral pattern for a girl who had never seen a flower. Her parents' facial expressions revealed whether she would eat or drink or neither, if they would abuse her or neglect her, if she would live or die.

Denied stimuli, Genie's innate intelligence roamed around her brain, looking for a place to land. Without language to develop it, her left hemisphere stagnated and shrank. So her genius lodged firmly in her right hemisphere, creating a lexicon of shapes and colors, able to synthesize wholes from the barest fragments of life she was given. This one astonishing talent cut through those dark waters of her brain like a current. Genie could observe objects and people better than anyone else *because* she was broken.

X taught me the mechanics of danger. When violence struck, it was sudden and complete. Only the birds would be able to sense it was coming. I had to learn to read the surface of the earth like a bird could. Any stimulus—the flicker of X's lip, the kettle clanging against a stove burner, the temperature rising one degree—could combine with other elements to create a butterfly effect of disaster. To stay safe, I needed to categorize and control it all, to live snugly inside the chaos of that butterfly effect, senses alive. I needed to be close enough to the disaster to perceive exactly what was happening, when, where, with whom, and how.

The easiest way to do that, of course, is to become the butterfly.

8

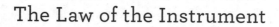

The Law of the Instrument

A guy named Ernie broke my nose.

At the Brazilian jiu-jitsu academy, Ernie had me in the "mount," the classic bully position, with me on my back and Ernie straddling my hips. I usually lost from this position, unable to escape a heavier opponent, especially one who was better than me, like Ernie. It was an after-class practice and a few people were resting on the mat and watching us.

Ernie was about seventy pounds heavier than me and enjoying it, yanking me around while I wriggled underneath him, stuck. Sometimes surviving a dickish opponent gave me a high that couldn't be bought anywhere else. So I hung in, body tight and elbows wedged against my hips until I finally inched onto my side to lever myself free. Bored and frustrated, Ernie tried to force my elbows up by kneeing them hard, but his aim was off and he kneed me too high. I tried to block him with my forearm, but his knee was slippery with sweat and I wasn't strong enough anyway.

Something in my face cracked. I tapped rapidly on Ernie's back, the signal to stop, but Ernie had already frozen at the sound. Adrenaline made the pain pass quickly. I said, "It's okay, I'm good. Let's go."

"I don't know," a training friend said. "Your nose looks weird." Men circled around me. I took a quick swipe to see if I was bleeding, and everyone winced.

"Now your nose is facing sideways," my friend said.

Ernie said, "Damn. That's the second nose I broke this month." He turned to my friend and asked, "Wanna train?" My friend said no, so Ernie asked one man after another until he found someone young and invincible enough to say yes, with a quick glance at my swelling face. *Fucking Ernie*, I thought. I knew injuries were more or less inevitable here, but I still felt stupid and ashamed for getting hurt, weak. I used the office phone to call JD and a doctor.

By now, JD and I were living together. My lease had ended and before I even started apartment hunting, he sweetly suggested we share. "It's too soon," I had protested. We had been dating for less than a year. When JD didn't follow me down the trail of doubt, I packed my stuff and he helped me move into his place. I wanted to be with him all the time.

I had introduced JD to the jiu-jitsu academy, and he now trained there regularly, too, usually on different days from me, sometimes with Ernie. So that night, Ernie called JD and apologized to him. Not to me. "Are we okay, you and me?" Ernie asked. JD asked Ernie if he wanted to talk to me, to apologize to me, and Ernie said, "No, I'm good," and hung up. "Fucking Ernie," JD said, but it didn't help. I guess JD was still Scary JD, and I was . . . nothing to worry about.

My broken face looked weird—my nose swelled up and swung side to side at the slightest pressure. "Stop touching it," JD said, but I did anyway, fascinated by the mirror. Black bruising pooled under my eyes. My luck, that night I came down with a head cold. "Fucking Ernie," I kept saying, sneezing, my nose dripping, plugged, and pulsing with pain. JD gave me terrible-tasting Chinese herbs to reduce the swelling. I spent the night trying to fall asleep with frozen vegetables on my face.

My nose looked twisted so I saw an orthopedic surgeon and asked him to fix it. He said, "I'd have to stick a kind of butter knife tool up your nose. Do you want me to do that?"

I asked, "Should I want you to do that?" My face throbbed.

The doctor shrugged and said, "It won't be straight without surgery anyway. You're not a model or anything, are you?" He had already turned to his computer to type in his notes.

"No," I said. "I'm not a model."

He said over his shoulder, "Unless you need your face so you can work, I'd advise against the surgery."

"Is there anyone who doesn't need a face so they can work?" I wasn't a vain person. But I did need my face.

He swiveled around to scrutinize my nose again and said patiently, "You can walk. You can move your arms and legs. You're not in terrible pain. Unless it leads to breathing problems, a nose break is more of a cosmetic issue." *Give me big bones,* I could hear him thinking. *Give me hips and femurs and orthopedic saws. Not a nose and a butter knife.* The doctor wrote me an antibiotics prescription for what had quickly developed into a sinus infection.

Grayson winced when he saw my swollen face and said, "I think you'd better lay off in-person work for a while." He was right. How could I talk to women while looking like a domestic abuse victim? People glared at JD in the grocery store when we went together. My temp job cut my front-desk gig short and requested a new temp.

I still cold-called witnesses by phone, but couldn't follow up with anything in person. My face was no longer my asset, the blank slate that everyone wanted to write on. Now it was something people felt sorry for. Anyone I managed to interest in the case, I had to immediately hand off to Grayson before I could develop them, court them, or even find out the full extent of what they knew. And I was denied access to their faces and what they told me.

In the three weeks it took me to heal, I got scooped by my own team.

Grayson found out about another football recruiting party that took place two weeks before Simone's, at a hotel two towns south. A trainer named Olive was allegedly sexually assaulted at the party, and subsequently sexually harassed by some of the same players who were at Simone's party.

Olive didn't tell anyone about her alleged attack for two months.

Zachary Mooney had allegedly videotaped a sexual encounter—possibly Olive's—at a hotel. The players were showing the video to recruits, like an informal recruiting tape. Jaden Usher, the defensive backs coach, confiscated the video. Usher later led Olive to the steam room and allegedly sexually assaulted her. Four days later, Olive's boss fired Olive from the training program without giving a reason or letting her explain.

I was way on the outside of this important find, which was much closer to item C on my butcher paper list, *Coach Riggs knew about it.* A positions coach was much higher than a recruiting coordinator, and Jaden Usher was directly under Coach Riggs. Maybe I could find a way to prove that this knowledge flowed upward if I weren't confined to the sidelines. Grayson asked me to skip-trace Olive; I finally found her, but I wasn't allowed to interview her. She was too important for me.

I realized I was competing against my own team. Grayson had laid it out for me early—my role was to find the diamonds in the rock and then hand them off to the cartel. This was a big diamond, maybe the biggest so far, and it didn't come from me. I was only as useful as the last big thing I found out. I knew we were all on the same side. But I needed to step things up or I might make myself redundant.

In college I had worked at a startup pizza place and my boss used to joke, "We lose money on every pizza but we make it up in volume." I was losing money on every pizza. I had run dry on leads, and Grayson was too busy himself to send me new ones or remember me once my face was broken. So during that cold month, I dissected my old notes and emails, and even resorted to the dry legal documents Grayson had sent to me over the past year.

His job had seemed so glamorous—flying to cities, grilling people under oath, a court reporter tapping in every word—until I read those depositions. Each was 100 to 350 pages long, and maybe one half of one sentence was interesting. It might take ten pages for someone to answer a question about who was standing where. Another ten to figure out who paid at a restaurant, with a credit card or cash, how much cash, whose name was on the credit card, what kind of tip they left. Thousands of boring pages of dissembling, vagueness, repeated pronouns, and statements immediately self-contradicted and negated. Long lines of questioning, and affidavits that Grayson used to build a legal argument strand by strand. Names, connections, dates, procedures, and meticulous narrative on the order in which a person navigated a room, or met up with friends, or orchestrated an administrative career.

I couldn't follow the way Grayson drew order from this bloat of information that spanned so many thousands of pages. It seemed impossible. Most cases everywhere else had one or two suspects, one crime, one victim, one thing to prove. But our case had unlimited suspects, unlimited alleged crimes of all kinds, unlimited victims, and multiple roads to prove what amounted to a conspiracy that implicated hundreds of people. Every oddity was a clue to another oddity until they meticulously added up to a system—a culture—of crime.

After this deep dive into the paper vortex, I saw Grayson differently. He was someone who could scan thousands of pages of drudgery to glean a legal argument, a network of truth that binds one seemingly meaningless detail to another. He knew what to look for and found it, a penny in a junkyard, a four-leaf clover in a prairie. He examined every leaf of every tree, learning how it uniquely impacted the forest. Looking up from the bewildering stacks of paper, I realized Grayson was a legal genius. No other mind could have stitched such a case together.

Which meant that if he weren't so damn busy, he wouldn't need me at all.

My paper chase made me want to belong to this case more than ever, and it also showed me how unimportant I already was. I felt small in comparison to Grayson, and then small for feeling small. After all, he had earned this case with his education and entire career. Grayson was taking the professional risks and getting the death threats, while I just asked rude questions over the phone.

Grayson had all the tools I lacked. He had visibility on TV stations as people watched from home and said, "I need to talk to that guy." And if *he* wanted to talk to someone, he always had the threat of a subpoena in his back pocket, a gun made of paper and anxiety.

If I were a lawyer, I'd have the same. If I were a reporter, I could offer publicity, maybe TV coverage or names in print. If I were a cop, I'd arrest them, sweat them in an interrogation room. If I were FBI,

I'd threaten federal prison. If I were CIA, I'd pay them money. But as a PI, I could promise only greasy nachos and bottomless beers, if they were of legal age or the bartender didn't care.

I did have one small advantage: the sentence "I'm a private investigator." Those were words nobody had heard before in real life. I used them whenever I could. They made people feel important, thrown into some larger arena, like a character in a detective novel or a noir movie. They agreed to meet with me to make the story real, with themselves at the center of it. They wanted to be the woman in the red dress and big hat, or the man at the bar on his fifth whiskey, paid for by me.

But it was a paltry trick, a one trick pony trick. Even before my broken nose, I had stagnated all year, relying too much on my now-broken face. According to Abraham Maslow's Law of the Instrument, if all you have is a hammer, everything looks like a nail. Through this job, I had become that hammer, that instrument. The Law of the Inferior, Broken Instrument. And Grayson, multitool Grayson and his team were finding screws of all sizes and shapes—shinier, more durable, better able to do the job of binding this case together into some kind of shape. I would never be able to reinvent myself in time to keep my job. I was just a hammer.

I needed bigger nails.

My nose was healing and the black eyes just looked like I'd had a bad night, but reentry into the case still felt impossible. I searched my lost and broken leads, one "if only" after another, straight out of *The Wizard of Oz*. If this player only had a brain. If that university employee only had a heart. If this or that witness only had some courage. Trudy, the sex worker Daisy used to service recruits, yielded nothing—she refused to talk about it. She had moved on with her life and said her husband didn't know about her past. I called her back twelve times, leaving messages on her voicemail that were discreet enough to imply that I could stop being discreet anytime I wanted to. She still never called me back, and I ended up feeling exactly like what I had turned into—a bully.

I had to bring Grayson something. I was like an addict milking the dregs of her previous high. I felt desperate, jittery. My teeth itched.

I decided to hit my list of players again. Just because I had asked them all my questions didn't mean they had given me all their answers. I would just ask again and again until I got better answers. Hammer hammer hammer. And I may not be smarter than Grayson, but I was smarter than those players, who didn't know how to lie about the truth because they didn't even know what they knew.

One night from the apartment JD and I now shared, I called a player named Gabriel. He hadn't been at the party so he was low on my list of priorities, and I had initially given up after leaving a few unreturned messages. Gabriel was a senior at the university, a lineman on the offensive team, so he didn't socialize much with the defensive backs. He had been friends with Simone and her friend Yvonne. Rumor was that Gabriel was injured and didn't like Coach Riggs. He came from a small soybean, barley, and potato farm in North Dakota run by his single mom.

I studied his picture in the football Media Guide. Gabriel's eyes bore a shocked expression, cheeks splotched, as if someone had just told him bad news before clicking the shutter. His black hair was cropped, and he wore a blue suit jacket and a gold tie. His neck was wider than his head, and by the stiff way he posed, both looked like they hurt.

On the phone I introduced myself and had to repeat the introduction another two times before Gabriel said, "Oh, okay, okay. Yeah. I know who you are. You work for that reporter Yvonne talked about."

"Lawyer."

"That's what I said."

I found myself puffing out my chest, matching the brusque texture of his voice, tough as a beef shank. "We need to talk about Simone's party."

"Okay," Gabriel said obediently. It always amazed me how docile some of the players could be when you told them what to do. But you could never tell them what to think, and Gabriel said, "No way that stuff happened."

"Were you there?" I asked.

"No. I wasn't there. But plenty of girls would have sex with football players. Jersey chasers. They just need to be with football players all the time."

"Like Leah? The woman who invited the players to the party?"

"Yeah. Like her, but they're everywhere. Players don't need to rape anyone."

"So if a player couldn't get sex, he'd *need* to rape someone. But since there's so much sex available . . ."

"They don't need to. And I don't think any of them would."

"Why not?"

"Because we have an image to keep up. Football is noble. The American sport."

"Baseball's the national sport."

"No. Football."

I waited, but that seemed to be the extent of his argument. "Gabriel, I read a *New York Times* article that said male college athletes are responsible for twenty percent of all campus sexual violence, even though they're only three percent of the college population."

"That's New York."

"They surveyed across the country. That's the average for everywhere."

"Well, that's only twenty percent, then."

"It's one in five rapes."

Anger ignited Gabriel's voice. "No, it's not!"

I wasn't sure what I was missing. "Twenty percent. One in five."

"One in five? No way! One in five? Where did you get that number?"

"Twenty goes into one hundred five times."

Gabriel's voice began to cool as quickly as it flared. "Well. That's your opinion." Then, "I don't like any of this. I know what people are saying about that party, and you're saying something different. I wasn't even there. You're not going to get what you want from me."

"What *are* people saying about that party?"

"They're saying it went down, yeah, but it was just sex. There was lots of sex all the time. Before I came, under the last coach, there were ten or fifteen players who pulled a train on one secretary in the football office."

"Pulled a train?" Unfortunately, the image spoke for itself. I took rapid notes, although I knew Grayson only wanted dirt on Coach Riggs. "Who was the secretary?"

"I don't remember."

"The players?"

"I don't remember."

"Was it consensual?"

"Yeah! They weren't minors or anything. They were players, not recruits."

"I mean, consensual for the *secretary*."

"Oh."

I tried one more time. "Gabriel, did the secretary really want ten or fifteen guys to have sex with her in a row?"

"Yeah. I mean, I don't know. What's that sound?"

I was pretending to beat myself over the head with the phone receiver. I recovered the mouthpiece and apologized.

I kept asking Gabriel why, why, why he thought these things happened. Why, Gabriel, why? Gabriel said, "That's just how football players are. You're physical, you're tough. You party a lot. If you're not that way, you're not a football player."

"And you can do whatever you want."

"Yeah, sure, they do think they can get away with stuff, probably a little because they're allowed, and a little because they're just that way."

"Why do you say 'they,' Gabriel? You're a football player, too."

"Not anymore. That's why I'm even talking to you." Gabriel's voice thinned to a whine. "I hurt my back and Coach Riggs made me play anyway. Now I have nerve damage and the doctor says I'll never play football again. Never!"

He complained about his back while I doodled on my printed-out photo of Gabriel, drawing buckteeth, donkey ears, and curlicues around his ears. This conversation was over. He wasn't going to help us—at least, not willingly. When Gabriel started to run out of words, I said, "Well, I sure do appreciate your time, Gabriel."

Gabriel took a deep breath.

Nearly every witness told me something important right before goodbye. It happened after we'd gone through the markers of a nearly completed conversation: clipped, hale-and-hearty voices raised in volume to a near-bark, repeated thank-yous and well wishes. The witness was off the hook. There would be no subpoenas for court. It was the last time he'd talk to a private investigator, or (maybe) anyone working on something that's so much larger and dramatic in scope than his own life. He passed whatever test he had set for himself and could now relax and leak whatever still lurked—doubts, contradictions, reversals—because it was his last chance to talk to someone who would listen to him the way I would.

So now, Gabriel said in an entirely different-sounding voice, as if someone else had just picked up the phone, "You know, it's good that this stuff is coming out. I'm glad, actually."

I sat up slowly on my futon couch. "You are?"

I could almost hear him trying to think, or remember, or feel. "There was a rumor that a coach beat his wife so bad she had a miscarriage."

"What coach? When?" I asked, scribbling.

"I don't remember. I also know two girls raped by players. One attack was really bad. Her name was Simone Baker."

I was confused for a moment until I realized that Gabriel had forgotten who I was or why I had called him. I said softly, "Yes. I work for Simone." So Gabriel did believe Simone was raped after all, even though he had said earlier in our conversation that there was "no way that stuff happened." I envied him the ability to believe two opposite things to be true at the same time.

"And Riley, of course," Gabriel said.

Riley?

"Who?" I asked.

"You know Riley. Hawkins."

"I don't know Riley." Then I lied, "But I know all about it, of

course." I scrawled "Riley Hawkins" in giant letters across my steno
pad. I could hardly talk without my throat constricting, chugging
over the words: "Terrible, what happened to"—was Riley a man or a
woman?—"what happened there."

Gabriel said, "Yeah. She was real upset." I drew a female symbol
next to Riley's name. He said, "She only ever told my roommate and
me about it." If Riley only told two people, didn't Gabriel wonder how
I could possibly know about it?

Apparently not. He said, "I don't really believe Abner would do
something like that. But I don't think Riley would make that up. She's
not a liar."

I wrote "Abner" without asking for a last name. How many Abners
could there be on one team? "What did Riley tell you? Any details?"

"Yeah. That Abner raped her."

"And . . . okay, so did you talk to Coach Riggs about it?"

"I wanted to, but Riley said not to. She was working there."

"Where?"

"For the athletic department, as a trainer."

"Riley was a trainer when Abner assaulted her?"

"It was last year."

I was writing so fast that the ballpoint bored through the paper in
my steno pad. I glanced around our apartment, our camping teapot
on the stove, tin foil peeling from the burner pans, the grime-tipped
polyester carpet. It was its same grubby self, but everything looked
different. Riley was an employee at the university when she was allegedly attacked. What if Coach Riggs knew? This could be the missing link, the smoking gun, all the clichés. I saw Riley in my head, a
gun-shaped girl, pointing everywhere, pulling the trigger and ripping
a hole through the face of this case.

Gabriel's thick voice congealed thicker. "I really like Riley. And that
was really uncool of Abner."

"You're right, Gabriel. It's very uncool to rape someone."

The line whooshed as Gabriel breathed in, out. "Sometimes I think
I should have said something to Coach Riggs. We're supposed to tell
him everything. Like parents." Gabriel's voice, as it filtered through

that dense neck and those meaty vocal cords, no longer sounded stu-pid. It just sounded young. "I didn't say anything because I wanted to, you know, respect Riley." He paused. "Was that the right thing to do?"

Gabriel didn't realize the weapon he had just given to me. He would graduate that May. After his mediocre college football career, he would return to his mom's farm. He'd think only about soybeans and hundreds of potatoes with their bulging eyes buried underground, in hot fields where he could sit atop vibrating machinery all day and rest his brain.

"Yeah, honey," I told him. "You did real good."

9

Gun-Shaped Girl

It took a while to find Riley, and even longer to convince her to meet with me. Riley first wanted to ask for guidance from her father back in Delaware, where she was from. Then she switched the appointment three times. The delays were okay with me because they gave my face time to heal and return to a crooked version of normal. My nose never straightened and I now snored, but luckily, JD could sleep through anything.

I had low faith that Riley would actually show up at the eventually-agreed-upon meeting place she had chosen. The Sink was a bar near the university with ripped Christmas-green booths and only treble in their speakers. The floor smelled like stale beer and the walls smelled like rancid grease. The Sink served aggressively mediocre pizza and they were also known for their "Sinkburger." It seemed like college students had endless appetites for anything that sounded disgusting. Riley had set our rescheduled meeting for midafternoon, and she was late. I waited for her by the door, because I didn't want to eat that food if she didn't show.

Twenty minutes after the hour, a young woman slid inside the doorway and blinked, almost as if she hadn't expected to come inside but now here she was. "Riley?" I asked. She nodded her greeting and held out cold, limp fingers for me to shake. Riley was very tall, a study in contrasts with dark hair and eyebrows, and very white skin. She had deep center-cheek dimples, which I didn't discover until an hour later because she didn't smile. She looked muscular, a little like a trim weight lifter, except it was hard to tell under her baggy T-shirt and jacket. She acted smooth and calm, but her shirt trembled.

I let Riley pick where she sat—the last booth, near the back door. She perched near the booth's opening, as if about to leave. She kept her jacket on and crossed her arms in fists under her armpits. She met my eye only in quick, assessing glances.

I started as I usually did, by asking her if she had any questions for me before we began. "Yes," she said. "How can I be sure you are who you say you are?"

I felt sad that she was able to think this way at so young an age. I picked Grayson's business card out of my wallet, the one he had first given me when he hired me in the bookstore. "We can call him right now and you can talk to him," I said. "Will that work?" I pulled out my flip phone, but she waved her hand and said, "That's okay."

"I work for victims," I said. "Survivors. The women." I brought up the names she had heard from the news (Simone Baker, Calliope) so she knew I was legit, and refused to give other names ("Her identity is protected") so she knew I was discreet. Still, Riley said nothing. She looked so uncomfortable that it physically hurt for me to say, "We're here because Abner raped you."

Once the words were in the air, Riley's discomfort seemed to dissolve and she rose an inch in her seat. She leaned forward and spoke quietly, even though we were alone in the restaurant. I wondered if she had chosen the time—3:00 P.M.—out of convenience, or because she knew nobody would be there to hear our conversation.

"First of all, I'm not going to press charges," she said. "I don't want my life ruined."

"I understand. We're just talking, here."

"But I'll come forward if he hurts someone else."

She seemed to want me to think she was a moral person, so I said, "You seem like a moral person." Again, she relaxed a millimeter. I asked, "What happened?"

Riley told me the facts, simply and unemotionally. I listened and took notes, although I got dizzy and had to stop for a second when I learned that her attack had lasted about forty-five minutes. She had only been nineteen at the time. I refrained from expressing sympathy, because when I did, Riley retreated in her seat. She ended with, "I immediately went to the hospital and got a rape kit. I had physical injuries from forcible sex. I filed a police report. I'm still paying off the rape kit."

I didn't know survivors had to pay for their own rape kits. "That must be hard, now that you don't have your training job anymore."

"I didn't quit the job. I'm still there."

This set me back a second. "You're *still* working as a trainer for the athletic department?"

Riley said, "Yes. I'm still training the football team."

My first instinct was to order her to quit, which was absurd. I had just met the woman. Instead, I asked, "Do you think Coach Riggs ever suspected what happened to you?"

Riley's brow lifted. "Oh, he knew."

"How could you tell? From the way he acted around you?"

"No. He knew about it because I told him."

When I regained my voice, it came out in a rusty wheeze. "Coach Riggs."

"Yes."

"You told football head coach Wade Riggs that one of his players raped you."

"Yes."

It was everything I could do to stop myself from calling Grayson and telling him to drop everything and run to the Sink. "You said it to his face? In a direct conversation?"

Riley's eyes sharpened, but her voice stayed low and measured. "Well, I sure didn't want to. I only wanted my boss to know. I trusted him. But he knew Wade Riggs for like twenty years. So I guess Coach Riggs's friendship trumped my trust, especially because Riggs has all the power."

Riley's boss was the same person who fired Olive after she was allegedly assaulted at a hotel recruiting party and again by assistant coach Jaden Usher afterward. Grayson had said Riley's boss was Coach Riggs's "eyes and ears," reporting anything to Riggs that he overheard in the locker rooms.

Riley said, "So after I told my boss, the next thing I know, I'm called into this meeting three days after everything happened. It was my boss, the assistant athletic director, and Coach Riggs. All sitting there, waiting for me."

"You were ambushed."

"It felt like that."

"You were the only woman in the room? You didn't have an advocate?"

"No. I was unprepared. I didn't know what was going to happen until it was already happening. Again."

"This is amazing," I said. Grayson had already deposed Coach Riggs. "Wade Riggs denied knowledge of any other sexual assaults. He said there wasn't one incident he knew of in his entire time as head coach. He denied it under oath."

Anger brightened Riley's eyes but not her voice. "That's one hundred percent wrong. They made me explain what had happened, how I felt about it, and what I intended to do. I hadn't even told my parents yet at that point."

"They forced you to talk?"

"They kept me in there for an hour. Coach Riggs said, 'I want you to be calm and tell us what happened.' That pissed me off—*be calm*—so I did tell him, just to spite him. Then I told him the police were already involved. That shut him up for a second. After that, he kept asking if I intended to press charges.

"I said at the time that I wasn't in a state to make decisions. I was still in shock. So Riggs said, 'If you decide to press charges, you should know that everything in your life will change.'"

I said, "That's a threat."

Riley thought for a second. "He didn't use a threatening voice, but he didn't sound like he was looking out for me, either. I asked what kind of repercussions *he* would get and Riggs said, 'I'm not his father. I'm his coach. I'm not going to ground him from practice or suspend him. That's not my place.'"

Riley said, "That made me really upset. The thing is, Riggs *is* a father figure. He acts like their father. They come to him for everything. They confide in him, trust him. That is his place to do something. I mean, if players miss training or don't do all their lifts, or even don't put their equipment away, the coaches run the players after practice until they vomit. It's called 'running pukes.' They punish *that*. Not that I wanted them to make *him* puke, but all he had to do was run extra laps. Why couldn't they make him sit out a game, one game? Granted, he has to live with this for the rest of his life." Riley's pronouns confused me until I realized she wouldn't—or couldn't—say Abner's name.

"Some people have no problem living with what they've done," I said.

"Yeah. I don't know. When the DA talked to him, he confessed to it."

"Abner?" This was novel, an alleged rapist who confessed to rape. "But you didn't want to press charges with the DA?"

"No. I still don't."

I wondered if this DA would have moved forward if Riley had wanted to press charges, even with a full confession and a rape kit. "Do you think Abner told Riggs the same thing? That he raped you?"

"They didn't say, but I do think that, because Riggs and the other men offered to get a letter of apology from him. They said, 'Best we can do is that.'"

"Do you have the letter?"

"Yeah. I have it. He wasn't asking for forgiveness, but he said he was truly sorry for anything he did, and he didn't know if writing would help me or not. It was pretty vague." Riley tapped her finger on a spoon. "I don't know if he wrote it himself or if someone wrote it for him. I think Riggs edited it, at least."

"Did you meet with Riggs again?"

"Yeah, the next week sometime, after the cops went to my house and *his*. I was upset, but all Riggs wanted to know was if I was going to press charges. He asked if I had any evidence. I didn't tell him anything because the DA told me that I didn't have to."

"You didn't have to meet with Riggs at all."

"Except my job, you know. I wanted to keep my job. So Riggs asked if I was going to be in the training program still. I said yes. He said, 'You don't think that's going to be hard for you?'"

"Again, a nonthreat threat."

"He wasn't firing me, exactly. Not like what happened with Olive. He seemed worried that if I stayed in the training room, I'd get more pissed off and want to press charges. I remember thinking that he was more worried about himself than me, even though I was the one who went through . . . all that. But Coach Riggs was the one pissing me off. I said, 'If you had a daughter, you'd think differently about this whole thing.'"

"Good for you."

"I'm so mad. Just so mad." Again, the anger was in her face but not her voice. I wondered how she did that.

"Did you feel intimidated by Coach Riggs?"

"Oh, yeah, absolutely. That's why I never pressed charges. Coach Riggs said he would back his player one hundred percent. I felt like I was getting punished more than *he* was. I'd have to take on the whole team if I continued forward." Riley's face compressed. "And there are other reasons."

"Like what?"

She hunched a little. "Well, because I didn't feel like it was his personality to rape someone, really."

This caught me. "If it wasn't Abner's personality, why would he hurt you?"

"Because they can." Abner had become general—not a "he" but a "they." Riley said, "I hear the players in the training room say stuff like 'I tried to pick up this girl and she wouldn't go with me. I told her, I'm a football player! What's wrong with you?' They're given everything they want and they think girls are part of that package."

The server cleared our plates. Riley swept stray crumbs from the table into her palm and deposited them into her jacket pocket. When we were alone again, she said, low, "I don't want my life to change. Everyone would know about me, talk about me, and look at me like that. I'd lose my job. I'd be like Calliope—I'd have to leave town. *He* has so much more power than me. And so does Coach Riggs—much, much more. Riggs could ruin my life. I'm premed—I want to do orthopedics back home in Delaware. Working as a trainer means incredible experience for me in my field, and the football team is the elite job in the training room. It's an honor."

"Is the honor worth the cost?" My question felt familiar. I suddenly remembered that JD had asked me a similar question when I started working this case.

Riley said, "I'm a strong person. I decided that I could do this. I did have to work with *him* last summer. But mostly, I didn't want the rape and the team to have control over my life and my future. I didn't run away. I stayed. At first I felt pretty vulnerable. But now it's empowering."

When I was six, I tried to run away from home. I packed a pair of yellow shorts, pants, T-shirts, socks, an apple, peanut butter, and a loaf of bread, which I figured would last me weeks. I was rarely thirsty, so I didn't worry about water, but I chose four stuffed animals and my favorite book. I knew runaways were supposed to carry a bandanna full of stuff tied to the end of a stick. I couldn't fit everything in a bandanna so I used my knitted blue baby blanket, but the weight bent the stick and the apple kept falling out and bruising on the floor.

Carrying a laundry basket past my bedroom door, my mother asked what I was doing. I said, "I'm running away, Mommy."

My mother's face didn't change. She didn't drop the laundry basket, take my blanket away, or tell me to go clean something or eat something. She just said, "If you run away, you better make sure it's forever. Because once you leave, you can never come back home again."

She went downstairs with her laundry basket. I stared at my blanket and my stick. I thought about it for what felt like a long time.

Then I put everything away—the clothes in their drawers, the loaf of bread on the kitchen counter, peanut butter in the cabinet, bruised apple in the garbage can, baby blanket folded on my bed. I didn't run away. I stayed. And it wasn't empowering.

But Riley wasn't six, and she wasn't me. She sat with her hands in her pockets under the table; I said she was amazing, and she gave a brief nod. I studied her still form. Maybe this was what coping looked like—silence. Yes, Riley was undeniably strong, from the firm line of her chin to the biceps distending the sleeves of the jacket she had never taken off. Her life had betrayed her but she was still talking to me at the Sink. I looked for empowerment, too, in the lift of her chin or the quick shift of her shoulders, but it wasn't there. Just her strength, overpowered by an emotion so powerful, I smelled it on her skin. Fear.

Grayson looked up from my memo on Riley and gave me a slow smile.

"Did I do it?" I asked. "Is this what we need?" I flipped back to my initial notes from him, which I had stapled into every succeeding steno pad—by now I was buying them in bulk. I counted off Grayson's three Title IX requirements on my fingers. "'Pervasive harassment' is Abner raping Riley, right? 'School's knowledge' is the meeting with Wade Riggs and those other jerks. 'Deliberate indifference' is Riggs telling Riley he's going to back his player, grilling her about pressing charges, and warning her that it would change her life." I lowered my steno pad. "That's worse than indifference. It's intimidation."

"Also perjury. Coach Riggs swore under oath that he knew nothing of any assaults." Grayson stared deeply at a painting next to his desk that I loved—cerulean blues melting into purples, expensive-looking. He said, "Riley checks every box, all the way up to Coach Riggs. This is huge. I hope you realize how huge this is."

For the first time since I broke my nose, that jittery, underemployed feeling began to slow inside me. If nothing else, Riley's story justified my job, and I was useful again. She was the definition of credible—she was risking everything she cared about to give us her story.

Grayson squinted at me. "Don't relax. I see you relaxing. You can't. It's not done. You need to get Riley to talk to me, get her to testify. Or none of this means anything. It's just a rumor."

I said, "I don't think she'll do it voluntarily. You'll have to call her in."

"Why won't she do it voluntarily?"

"The exposure. She said she'd only come forward if Abner sexually assaulted someone else. She's terrified of being exposed like Simone and Calliope."

Grayson said, "Well, get her unterrified. We can keep her name out of the press."

"She says 'They'll still know it's me.' She's still worried about what Riggs and the players think. She's still in that world. And she doesn't want her name anywhere, not on legal documents, nothing."

Grayson pressed his palms together in a prayerlike gesture under his chin and said slowly, "You can tell Riley that I can probably make her nearly anonymous in court. I did it for Olive. It involves layers and layers of affidavits, with different pieces of information in different places. It's like the formula for Coke—nobody knows all the information at one time. It's working so far."

I didn't know how to convince someone she should feel safe using the words "probably," "nearly," and "so far." "Why don't you just subpoena her?"

Grayson gazed at his hands, which were trembling from too little sleep and too much coffee. "I promised not to do that."

I rolled my eyes. "Oh, come on. You haven't even met her yet."

Light from the window sank into the deep wells under Grayson's eyes; they darkened each time I saw him. "I promised myself I wouldn't subpoena any victims without their consent," he said.

"What?" I asked.

Grayson half smiled, avoiding my gaze. "My colleagues think I'm crazy. But I just can't do it."

He would rather lose it all than hurt one survivor. Tears stuck in the back of my throat, mortifying me. You can't cry at work.

That teary, mushy part of me wanted to hug him. And a much nastier part of me wanted to slap him out of his stupid idealism so we could win.

It was 2004, the in-between season again. Other places would call it early spring, but on the Front Range we called it "weather"—either storms or winds. We were still in a drought. Even at high altitude, snow clustered only in the triangular shadows of pine trees. Chinooks took over—dry, warm winds that rushed over the western Rockies at vast speeds to the valley below. The region is famous for them, and the university town is ranked in the top ten of the nation's windiest cities (Chicago is fiftieth). At the city's elevation, a mile high, the cold, dense air clustering near the rivers quickly heats up during the day, whisking west to the nearby mountains and then blowing back down at night. Air warms through adiabatic heating as it falls, molecules compressing from the increased air pressure from above, becoming agitated and unstable. Chinook gales can be fifty-plus degrees warmer than the air they replace, and hurricane force, over a hundred miles per hour sometimes. Chinook means "snow-eater," and the winds can evaporate and lift a foot of snow every day. They wake the trees too early in winter and the pines begin to photosynthesize before the ground thaws enough to feed them water. Pine beetles move in, and then the lodgepole needles flame red, die, and burn at the first strike of lightning.

I've seen Chinooks bend metal sign poles into sloppy Ls on east-west street signs. The winds have blown up my dress, torn down my gutter, and almost pushed my car off the road. When the wind forces itself through the seams of windows, it sounds like the shriek in your head when you finally clear a plugged ear. Buildings shake and sway. I'd touch trembling walls and wonder who built them, if they had been in a good mood that day, what beams or supports they might have forgotten. Lying next to a sleeping JD, I'd fret about getting crushed or decapitated in bed.

You can sometimes forecast a Chinook from its silky föhn cloud rippling and arching over the landscape like a manta ray. They're beautiful killers. Once, a Chinook sent a tree branch through a car window, fatally impaling a physicist. After a four-day Chinook, one employee lost his mind and shot his coworkers at the local ski resort. Chinooks blow down trailers and snap utility poles, erode crops. They blow out windows and unroof buildings—not just shingles but also the wood. They flip grounded airplanes, collapse water tanks, uproot trees, and sandblast windows, scarring them opaque. Front Range Chinooks average a million dollars or more of damage each year. They've been measured up to 140 miles per hour before taking out the equipment used to measure them.

We love these murderers because they're ours. We love them despite everything we know about them and their bad reputations, how they trick us into thinking bad ideas are good ones. Like, let's get a gun and shoot up that ski resort! Let's have an affair! Let's buy a house in the mountains and just see what happens!

JD and I bought a house in the mountains.

Why not? It was cheaper because it was rural, twice as big and nice as anything we could get in the city. It seemed almost affordable, and JD and I were employed and in love. I told my mother about it when I called—we were now speaking about once a month—and she unexpectedly insisted on giving us almost one-third of our down payment. I refused twice, saying, "X will never be welcome here," and each time she answered, "I'm well aware. It's my money and this is what I want to do with it. No strings attached."

JD said, "Let's not. It's not worth it." But I had grown up with my mother's yearly story of how her sullen father had refused to accept or open even Christmas gifts, how hurtful it is to refuse a present. "You can't give back a gift," she always said. And wasn't this what mothers were supposed to do, help their kids, give them things? I thanked her profusely. We used her money when it arrived the night before closing, pooled our money for the other two-thirds-plus of the down payment, and signed the mortgage papers.

It was a tall, narrow house with three floors, a rectangle set on end.

We lived at an elevation of about 8,500 feet, just outside a mountain village-town that had one grocery store, one pizza place, no doctor, and seven marijuana dispensaries. The town was mostly known for its "frozen dead guy." In the early 1990s, a Norwegian immigrant named Trygve Bauge hoped to start a cryonics facility about a half mile up our dirt road, so he flash-froze his dead grandfather and secretly stored him in a Tuff Shed. When Trygve got deported, Grandpa began to melt, and the town learned about the body. They wanted to bury it, but Trygve's mother accused the town of trying to murder her father's corpse. Then she got deported as well, and the town was stuck with a melting dead man. They eventually decided to host an annual winter festival called "Frozen Dead Guy Days," with coffin races and polar bear plunges. For authenticity, they voted to keep Grandpa frozen in his Tuff Shed. Every two weeks, a truck carrying 1,600 pounds of dry ice thundered past our house to restock, and we'd wave. I half wondered if I chose the town for that story alone, because the winters were frighteningly cold.

The first time our skinny house swayed in a hundred-mile-per-hour wind, JD and I silently looked at each other in bed: *What have we gotten ourselves into?* Pebbly dirt pelted our windows even on the third floor. But every morning we had three-story views of the Continental Divide, craggy peaks whose names we never learned.

We negotiated our house's temperamental heater, the black mold in the attic, the roof that pissed water when it rained, and the paint-scarred, dog-peed-upon teal carpet circa 1980. The rooms still bore evidence of rage from previous owners: doorjambs kicked in, drywall patched. The Chinooks unmoored the house, shaking loose connections and breaking everything inside, which was how I learned that JD could fix anything—appliances, heaters, thermostats, and anything else requiring wood, metal parts, wires, or all three.

Our trees were heavy with woodpeckers, magpies, and crows. JD frequently threw chicken and even turkey carcasses off the balcony into our yard for the small red foxes, and every bone was always gone by morning. Lodgepole pines studded the ground, naked on the western, windward side, branches ripped off or stunted from the wind. I

waded among wild roses and strawberries, cow parsnip, and incorrigi-
ble quaking aspens that sprouted on our leach field like stalks of grass.
The pitched roofs made our bedroom feel like a treehouse. "This is
the nicest house I've ever lived in," JD said, and his delight delighted
me double. I had always thought JD was a relaxed person, but he now
seemed to release lingering tensions that had buzzed in his chest, arms,
legs. Even I began to quiet down, speak more slowly, sleep more fully.

We were 2,900 feet higher than the university, 17 miles away.
Both JD and I still worked in the city, and the drive was forty minutes
through the canyon, more in bad weather. During good weather, it
was the kind of drive people took on weekends just for fun, the road
flanked by high gray canyon walls, the river tripping beside us. The
road headed upward for most of the drive, and then rounded off at a
large reservoir. Every time the vista opened up, that rage rat running
in my chest slowed, sometimes even paused a beat. When I arrived
home in the summertime, I'd unroll my windows to smell the town,
the wet or dusty dirt alive with pine needles, animal droppings, dead
bugs, and aspen leaves. In the winter, the town smelled like snow.

We were at the right age to live somewhere difficult. We had energy, and each other. I thought we were finally where we belonged,
close to life itself, but safe from it.

Before I had the chance to convince Riley to testify for us, the police
released her report to the papers. Her name was redacted per journalistic convention, but I was scared the anonymous exposure would
make her nervous and she'd shut us down. Luckily for her, a day later
she was upstaged in the news by a female college football player named
Nina who came forward and told *Sports Illustrated* that she had been
raped by a teammate at the same university we were investigating.

A few years ago, Nina had been a walk-on kicker, and the only female football player on the team. On her first day on the field, five players surrounded her and called her "bitch," "cunt," and "slut." During
huddles, players would grope her crotch, or they'd shove her against
the lockers to grab her breasts "to see how those shoulder pads fit on

your tits," then warning, "don't you dare tell anyone about this." The quarterback whipped footballs at her head, using it for target practice. Players showed her their penises at least five times during the season, and one rubbed his erection against her from behind.

Players regularly threatened Nina with sexual violence, and then it happened—a teammate allegedly raped her. She tried to stop him, but he outweighed her by a hundred pounds. Like Riley's alleged attacker, this player had been a friend. Once she was able to escape, Nina ran to her truck and backed it into a pole. She had been a virgin. She reported the alleged assault to DA Beatrice Hull but decided not to press charges when Hull told her it was unlikely her attacker would receive anything more than house arrest.

Nina was too scared of retribution from the player to go to the police or to Coach Riggs. She dropped out of the university in her sophomore year and underwent depression and insomnia for two years. When Simone's case broke, it brought the nightmare back for Nina, who realized she would never heal until she told her own story, so she gave *Sports Illustrated* an exclusive interview.

When asked to respond to Nina's allegations, Coach Riggs first emailed the athletic director to ask, "How aggressive should I be regarding Nina, sexual conquests by her, etc.?" Then he chose a different approach. Riggs told the press, "It was obvious Nina was not very good. She was awful. You know what guys do? They respect your ability. You can be ninety years old, but if you can go out and play, they'll respect you. Nina was not only a girl, she was terrible. Okay? There's no other way to say it."

Obvious shock and outrage aside, I doubted very much that Nina was "terrible." She had walked on to her position on the team. She was the first woman in history to play Division I-A, and the first to dress for a bowl game. I couldn't imagine Coach Riggs giving her those opportunities out of some obligation toward gender equity.

After her experiences here, Nina eventually enrolled in another university and had the courage to walk on to another Division I-A team, one that tolerated no sexual harassment as a matter of principle. Nina could just concentrate on school and football, not survival. She became the first female college football player to score at a Division I-A school, and she scored twice. Her jersey now hangs in the College Football Hall of Fame.

But Coach Riggs insisted, "Basically, we were doing her a favor." He stated unequivocally that there had been no reported harassment, "Absolutely not." Nina's team nickname was "Cunt," as in, "Cunt, go pick up that ball." Riggs said that the nickname wasn't sexual harassment because that kind of language is normal to use on a football field. The university president—who was female—backed Riggs up during her deposition with a more drawn-out version of the following, edited from the transcript:

Q: When a player calls [Nina] a cunt, is that sexual harassment?

University president: I am not a lawyer, sir.

Q: Are you telling us that you think a person has to be a lawyer to figure out whether or not particular conduct constitutes harassment?

Attorney for the university president: I'd ask you please to lower your voice. It's not appropriate to yell at the witness.

Q: That wasn't yelling.

University president: It's very difficult for me to make a judgment when I wasn't there, when I don't know what was actually said.

Q: Don't you agree with me that that word is a filthy, vile, offensive word?

University president: I think it is a swear word.

Q: So you will not agree with me; that's what you're saying?

University president: It is all in the context of what—of how it is used and when it is used.

Q: Can you—can you indicate to me any polite context in which that word would be used?

University president: Yes. I've actually heard it used as a term of endearment.

Q: Oh.

The university president later claimed she had been thinking of *The Canterbury Tales*, by Chaucer.

Nina received hate mail and death threats from fans after coming forward, but her story seemed to tip the balance of our case in the public eye. She was a *football player* and this happened to her. Coach Riggs was temporarily suspended with pay, which sounded to me like a paid vacation. He told Larry King that he expected to be reinstated. It was the third year of his five-year, eight-million-dollar contract. Our state's conservative governor had demanded a public accounting, saying, "Women are not recruiting tools." He appointed Attorney General Ken Salazar, later Barack Obama's secretary of the interior, as special prosecutor for a future investigation.

For half of March, *Doonesbury* comics lampooned our case. (Grayson crowed, "You know you're doing something right if you're in *Doonesbury*.") At *Doonesbury*'s fictional Walden University, a woman was assaulted at a recruiting party. Boopsie, the acting football coach while the coach was serving in the army, called out our university by name, saying, "We should learn from their mistakes, not blame the wider culture or insist everybody does it." I wished we had our own Boopsie, or anyone at all in the university to stand up for what was right. But there was an immediate cost to her advocacy: when Boopsie decided to shut down the football program to launch an investigation, the Walden president fired her with a puppetlike "zip it" gesture.

In the following week's comics, two *Doonesbury* football players explained the situation on cartoon TV. They sounded so similar to the players I'd been interviewing, I wondered if my email had been hacked. "Look, those recruits are trying to choose a school—they need to know who's got the top sex parties, okay?" the cartoon players said. "And no one forces these girls to be part of the recruiting process. The fact is, players are campus gods . . . and not too many chicks say no to us." A reporter asked what they did when a woman did say no. The players answered, "Well, usually it's too noisy to hear her. The parties are crazy loud."

This was the first time I ever heard of football recruiting sex parties mentioned in a comic strip. Grayson was almost manic with delight. He looked better, now that he was on television so frequently and spontaneously. He was doing something with his skin, facials perhaps, or maybe he was finally sleeping more. His nails were perfect, especially compared to mine, which were bitten to different lengths and shapes.

One day he called and said, "You should probably know that the university's investigating you."

"What? *Why?*"

"You're investigating them, they're investigating you. What, you didn't think this would happen?"

"I guess I thought I was somehow invisible." But of course they'd want to discredit me, along with everyone else who worked this case. I combed my memory for any strange calls. Someone had tried to sell me magazine subscriptions over the phone. There was a wrong number a week ago. "What do they know about me?"

"What is there to know?"

I wasn't sure. I wondered if they'd denounce my investigative work because I wrote fiction, if they'd share my name with the press, if I'd start receiving ominous phone calls in the middle of the night, like Grayson. "Are you still getting death threats?" I asked.

"Don't worry about me," he said. "Just get Riley to talk to me. I can't wait forever." Grayson was raiding his stash of professional favors to get Riley a cream-of-the-bar pro bono lawyer; he was doing the same for Calliope, Daisy, and the trainer who was allegedly attacked at a hotel.

The university leaked Simone's deposition tape to the news, including segments where they made Simone hold a box of condoms from her apartment, and where she cried at the effect of the assaults on her psyche. Grayson scrambled to place the tapes under protective order, but segments had already aired on ESPN and Channel 4.

The magistrate judge subpoenaed Simone's personal diary as evidence and then a rogue reporter with an agenda violated a protective order to leak excerpts of it to the papers, who gleefully printed them. The leaked excerpts said things like "I am happy to know that some of my pain is now being felt by these boys. It gave me so much pleasure to know that those assholes were being arrested and to know that this was going to be something that would follow them forever." Simone's private anger was now everyone's property, for judgment or ridicule. She had to explain to the press, "My journal was a very private place for me where I thought I could release all of my most personal inner feelings."

Simone dropped out of school, one year from graduation.

Three months after Coach Riggs's suspension, the university president felt safe enough to reinstate him, and he was back in his position on the field. The president promised that nobody would lose their jobs over this scandal. According to court documents, a university official lied and told others that Simone had welcomed the football players by standing naked in her doorway the night of her assault. At an athletic department event, a regent asked the football players and their families to stand, assuring them that "no one has suffered more than you."

When Riley met with me again, same time and place, she looked pale in the wan light of early spring. It was dry in the city, but we still had two feet of snow on the ground in the mountains, so I was overdressed for the weather and sweating across from Riley. After we ordered, she rested an elbow on the sticky table and covered her eyes with the back of her wrist. She said, "I'm trying to put this behind me, but it's dragging up a lot for me emotionally and mentally to meet with you. I don't know if I'm ready. I don't want to be selfish."

"You're not being selfish," I said. "No matter what you decide to do."

"I just want to know if getting involved further will be worth the cost to me."

"I get that." Riley was waiting for me to try to convince her to testify, but I wouldn't. Trying to persuade people never worked; it only made them lock down into their most conservative choices. Riley would have to make up her own mind.

Her body was perfectly motionless, so still it seemed like a feat of stillness. She said, "I guess I need to know exactly how disclosed my name will be at each stage in the process until this case is closed, and after that."

This was movement in a positive direction—she had said "will," not "would." I explained that Grayson had a process for keeping names off documents called "filing under seal," and that I didn't understand it, but Grayson could explain it. Riley interrupted, "I think Abner's name should be left out, too. But even then, Coach Riggs will still know. I'm afraid he'll leak my name."

I said, "You're right to feel scared. I don't think Wade Riggs cares about you. I think he cares about himself. Which is why he won't leak your name. That's the exact opposite of what will benefit Riggs, because it shows he knew about your assault, contrary to what he testified under oath. I'd think he'll want to pretend he never talked to you, that you don't exist to him."

"But nobody really knows what will happen with this case," Riley said. "Look at everything that's happened so far. I mean, I used to believe these people were my friends. I thought I could trust them. I thought I could trust Coach Riggs."

There was new despair in her voice. I asked, "Have you seen Riggs since we talked?"

"Last week. I was in the elevator and he got in, just us two."

"That sounds intimidating."

"Tell me about it. Riggs said, 'How is everything, are you doing okay?' I said yes and he got out. And then last Friday, after acting all nice to me in private like that, he turned around and told the football players, 'Some girl is trying to make a million dollars off the university to make her feel better.'" While describing Riggs, Riley had taken on a tinge of the coach's uglier features and his soft Southern accent. I had never seen Riggs anywhere but on TV, never shook the man's hand. But I could say with certainty that I hated him.

Riley asked quietly, "How important is my testimony?"

I didn't want to scare her away. But I didn't want her to compromise her dignity for an imagined career. Riley was twenty-one. I wanted her to choose. I wanted her to stop working with her alleged rapist, and for the people who threatened her future and scared her out of testifying. I wanted her to stop doing what I always did—eat scraps because that's all there is to eat.

Throughout my childhood, I hated sitting across the table from X whenever I had to eat dinner with him. The food felt infected. My mother would begin her guessing game: "Guess who forgot to run the dishwasher last night?" or "Guess who forgot to tell me about the PTA meeting?" I was always Guess Who. X made grimacing faces at the sound of my name, chewed his dinner. My brother and sister tucked their chins and ate quickly; maybe they felt guilty, or lucky. My brother was rarely Guess Who; my sister, never. We all had the unshakable roles my mother had assigned: my sister was Good, I was Evil, and my brother was Invisible. But you can't put food in your mouth and chew it when you have to sit across from your attacker and play Evil Guess Who. Before too long, I'd leave the table without excusing myself and go to my room. Shortly after I left, I'd hear them laughing together, something they never did with me around.

I was so hungry every night this happened, but I always waited until the lights were out at night before I tiptoed to the kitchen and quietly opened the refrigerator, using my fingertips to silently separate the rubber refrigerator seal so it wouldn't make a sucking noise. The fridge breathed cool air on me and illuminated the dark room. I'd find my full plate tightly encased in Saran Wrap and placed on the top right shelf of the refrigerator. That's how I knew how much my mother loved and needed me to be Guess Who, how it relieved something inside her and allowed her to snore more soundly upstairs. I always considered leaving the plate there to shame her, instead foraging in the cabinets where the food I ate might never be traced. But this was her version of love, or perhaps it was as close as she could come to apologizing. Either way, it was all I was going to get from her, so each time I peeled back the plastic and ate. But that kind of love tastes bad, like cold, congealed meat and puckered peas, mashed potatoes flattened by plastic wrap.

It's a lifetime habit, settling for what you can get. I didn't want Riley—so still in contrast to my constant fidgeting—to turn into me.

So I told her, "Your testimony is vital. It could win the whole case. Your rape ties Coach Riggs to the football team's systematic abuse of women. You're the only one. Your testimony could end the problem. It could mean that the next girl doesn't get raped, and the next, and the next."

Riley's dark eyes turned almost black. She hadn't realized her story was so important to anyone but herself. If she had, she might never have met with me in the first place.

I excused myself to go to the bathroom, even though I didn't have to go. I spent as long as I could in there, sitting on the toilet seat with my head in my hands. I needed to give Riley time to think, overthink, rationalize, and become disgusted with herself. I knew if I left her alone, she would berate herself into action more than I ever could.

Sure enough, when I returned, Riley spread her hands flat on the table. They were yellow with cold. She said, "I guess I'll do it. I will. If I can help those other girls."

"Really?"

My surprise seemed to make her second-guess her decision. But Riley wasn't one to give her word and snatch it away. She continued, convincing herself. "Something needs to change. If I can help, I will. But I don't want my privacy violated and my name to go all over the place."

"It won't," I said, hoping it wasn't a lie. "You're doing a good thing." I told Riley that Grayson would be in touch with her and her family, and she gave one brief nod. She said goodbye and left, the weight of her decision trailing heavily behind her like a dragnet. But she didn't know what I knew.

When I was seventeen, X burst into my bedroom yelling about something. He was angry about his wristwatch, I think, which he had found on the floor. He decided I was responsible, although I had been hiding from him in my bedroom, which was part of a converted garage. I yelled back so loudly that my throat seized up and I choked. He pushed me and I spilled backward into my room, backpedaling so

I wouldn't fall. He advanced. As soon as I regained my feet, I grabbed him by both shoulders and shoved him as hard as I could, shouting "No!"

He reeled backward.

I had never struck him before.

I had yelled plenty. Fought with him plenty. Struggled to get away, run out of the house, snuck out, insulted him, avoided him, and committed every antagonistic action I could. But I had never used physical violence.

We stared at each other, both of us shocked at what I had done, what I could do, now that I was bigger. His eyes formed asymmetrical pentagons. I thought, *I just committed suicide.*

But instead, X turned his back on me and left.

I waited for him to come back with a weapon of some kind—a shoe, a belt, a stick, a knife. I tried to remember something useful from my one year of judo. But X didn't return. I waited, barely breathing, until my knees buckled.

Then I closed my door, gently twisting the knob until the latch bolt retracted and silently found its cave. I leaned against the door and crumpled to the floor, crying into the collar of my shirt so nobody would hear me. My life was made of mistakes. If I had just known earlier. That sonofabitch might have left me alone, if I had only pushed back hard enough.

10

Scorch the Earth

I understood why Frank Heidemann, the murderer of the ten-year-old girl, confessed his crime to the roper Carl Neumeister. He didn't want his friend to go away. What's interesting to me is why, once he broke the seal, Heidemann kept confessing and confessing to anyone and everyone, all the way to the electric chair. He was as relentlessly open as he had been secretive. Some of my witnesses often made the same flip, from secretive to confessional (or the reverse), in an instant. It made me wonder if the two behaviors—concealment and confession—are somehow made of the same compulsion.

Some criminals flaunt their crimes, either out of guilt or an underlying conviction that they're invincible. They videotape assaults. A perpetrator in another case once posted on his public Facebook page: "That pussy wants to be fucked until it falls off." And he listed his nickname as "Therapist," an inside joke with his friends—TheRapist.

Sigmund Freud said we're all desperate to be seen for who we are, no matter what we have to hide. He said, "No mortal can keep a secret. If his lips are silent, he chatters with his finger-tips; betrayal oozes out of him at every pore." Our bodies broadcast our deception with gestures and actions, physical "tells" that signal our lies: fearful microexpressions, too much or too little eye contact, tapping feet or bouncing knees. We create barriers via folded arms or crossed legs. We literally become two-faced; the expression on the right side usually deceives and the one on the left side usually tells the truth.

Liars repeatedly touch their faces, groom hair or clothes, lick lips, fidget, twitch, yawn or swallow a lot, clear throats, place their palms facedown on a table or desk. They laugh at something serious, frown at a joke. Many nod while saying no, shake their heads while saying yes. Some self-soothe by rubbing their legs or arms. They shield their mouths, eyes, throats. They have the sticky speech of dry mouths. They can't point with a finger, nor make strong gestures. Some flirt, like Huge did with me, or crack jokes. They glance at exits, and point their toes there. Some create distance by leaning or stepping backward, retracting their heads like turtles, arguing (fight), or making an excuse to ditch the conversation entirely (flight).

These are also signs of fear.

There are verbal "tells," too. Liars stall, answer a question with a question, and divert blame to others. They omit the subjects of sentences, avoid first-person pronouns, use present tense, passive voice, and vague speech. They use oaths of honesty, like "truthfully," "actually," and "to be honest."

Which, *to be honest*, I do all the time, whether I'm lying or telling the truth. That's why it's nearly impossible to tell conclusively if a person is lying. Sometimes a person acts like a liar because she's used to being called a liar. Polygraphs only pick up on inner commotion. Sometimes a person acts honest because he's a sociopath and believes his lies, or his right to tell them. Sometimes we evade our stories because we're afraid of their power.

According to the Association of Certified Fraud Examiners, when someone recounts a true event, it's roughly 20 to 25 percent prologue, 40 to 60 percent "critical event," and 25 to 35 percent aftermath. But when we lie, our stories become unbalanced, perhaps 95 percent prologue and 5 percent event, or 10 percent event and 90 percent aftermath, padded with false or meaningless information. Deceptive sentences are too long or too short—fewer than ten words, more than fifteen. Liars bury the lede under insignificant details, then rush through important events like they're disposing of them. Our need to simultaneously conceal and betray ourselves upsets the balance of our stories. We cannot maintain our own narrative.

Freud said we confess because we project our parents onto the person we confess to. We hope that confessing will provide the parental unconditional love we constantly crave, despite our sins. He said it's also why babies love baths and adults love sex. I'm naked. Love me anyway.

In Flannery O'Connor's short story "A Good Man Is Hard to Find," a serial killer called the Misfit confesses to his victim (before killing her) that in the absence of God's unconditional love, there's "no pleasure but in meanness." Unless we can have faith that we are loved despite our sins, we might as well do whatever we want, and take pleasure in our power over others. We can become our own gods, accountable to nobody.

The football players in our case were treated as gods, "celebrity gods" as Calliope and *Doonesbury* described them. If you're god, who can you look up to? Who can love you unconditionally from above? Even Coach Riggs only cared about the players conditionally—if they scored, if they behaved, if they performed, if they won. This is just my theory. But maybe these players, like the Misfit, confused unconditional power with unconditional love. No pleasure but in meanness. Love me anyway. Or I'll make you.

Sometimes the confession itself is an act of violence.

In my sophomore year I joined a college support group for sexual abuse survivors. There were about ten of us at any given time, sometimes more. We called ourselves "Group," as in, "Are you going to Group tonight?" Group met once a week, and whenever I was sad or scared, I counted down the days and hours until we were together, safety in numbers.

The people in Group were more important to me than almost anyone else in college. I understood them, and I needed to be with people who understood me on that subterranean level, the ones who knew the cost of my pain without my having to tell them. I couldn't tell them. None of us could really talk about what had happened to us. We told our stories only in snippets—brief, vague phrases, always in the mechanical voice we used for anything graphic, anything that might hurt the listener. We had a culture of our own, with a vocabulary of pauses and long gazes. We folded up our pain into origami cranes with coded messages tucked deep inside. We didn't need to explain ourselves, which in itself lightened us, made it possible to breathe the rest of the week. Just showing up to Group was our confession.

But one new member, Morgan, who had been sexually abused by both her parents, couldn't stop telling her story at almost every Group. She described the details over and over: her abusers' naked bodies, the smells, who touched whom where. Far from robotic, Morgan's voice was operatic—slow and low for the grisly parts, then rising high, trembling with charged emotion. She seemed to revel in these recitals, perfecting them with each repetition. At some point my hearing would wither until I only saw Morgan's mouth moving. The other women in Group wrapped their arms tightly around themselves, staring at anomalies in the gray carpet, or at their own shoelaces. Some cried and trembled, but not in sympathy—in rage. We were furious at Morgan for these confessions, for forcing us back to the scene of the crime against her.

People started dropping out of Group and the size halved. As much as I needed it, I started missing meetings, too. I couldn't stand Morgan's weekly dissection of her pain, on top of my own burdens. Regardless, Morgan would track down truant Group members on campus and ask, "Can we talk?" The unspoken Group agreement was that we'd do whatever was necessary—skip a class, show up late to work, postpone studying for an exam—to be there for each other when we really needed each other. But with Morgan, we'd say curtly, "You have ten minutes." Morgan didn't seem to notice, or mind. She'd sequester us in a stairwell and tell her story for the twentieth time to ruin our night.

We had bought the line that telling our story was brave, that we were subverting the paradigm. But some Group members said they had flashbacks and nightmares since Morgan joined. Another member said what many were thinking: "I don't believe her anymore. I think she does this to us because she's trying to get her story straight." I saw her point, but I didn't think Morgan was lying. What would be the point in lying about something that made you a pariah? Instead, I thought the problem was with the story itself. Morgan couldn't fit her story into a world that made sense, so she kept trying and trying. For her to stop, either the story would have to change or the world would. And neither could.

Neuroscientist Daniel Siegel wrote that survivors need a "coherent narrative" to make sense of what happened to them. If not, they keep looping back to their story, trying to craft it into meaning. That's why schizophrenics repeat the same sentence fragments over and over. So if Morgan needed to repeat her story to understand it, I didn't want to silence her. I had grown up silent about my past, unwilling to be a downer around my friends, so they would continue to like me and invite me out of my terrible house. When I tried to talk to my mother, she only interrupted and told me how things had been far worse for her, and then told me a story about eating potatoes raw as a child because gas was too expensive. My brother was four years younger than me, and I hadn't wanted to burden a little kid who still played with LEGOs and watched cartoons.

But my sister was older than me by two years, so sometimes I would chat her up, trying to work the conversation around to my lone- liness, my sadness, and then maybe the deeper, horrible stuff. My sister was poised for what was coming and didn't let me step inside her bed- room, so I stood in the doorway to talk to her. At the first mention of X, she immediately snapped, "Get out of my room and shut the door." I would have to leave midsentence, usually slamming her door and vowing not to try anymore, perhaps lasting a month before buckling to my loneliness again.

I would rather suffer through Morgan's stories than be like my sis- ter. Group held a secret meeting without inviting Morgan. I said inane things about freedom of speech, but the other Group members were long past done. I was relieved to be overruled. We strategized about creating stated rules around our unspoken ones, but didn't settle on any. We felt unsafe, like prey's prey. We didn't know what to do.

In the end, we asked Morgan to please shut the fuck up. She did. She kept showing up to Group, now silent and probably hurt. And after that, none of us told even a fragment of our stories, ever. I felt like we had turned into my own bullying family, enforcing silence for the sake of the herd. Something was ruined for me. I continued going to Group, but less often, until I eventually stopped altogether.

I don't believe in silence, so I've tried countless times to find the right narrative container for my own horror, what X said and did, what went where, how I felt. But no jagged simile, no disjointed paragraph can come close to describing real pain. Pain is its own language. Each description feels false, decorative, like I'm pouring watercolors into the crater of a bomb site (see, I'm failing even now). It was anything but poetry. Anything but that. So I can't describe what it's like to be raped, not because this is as far as I go, but perhaps because this is as far as language goes. Language distorts my memory into something else, its own complete form, separate from the experience. I can't bear it. What X did had no form. It *was*. Sometimes, it *is*.

Did it help Morgan to chronicle her story again and again? I don't think so. It kept her locked in a world of agony, controlled by it, controlling all of us. Each telling only replenished her need and hurt the listener. It hurt me.

But silence hurt me more.

The spring my mother visited me, it was the last year of a multiyear drought that never seemed to end. The state was made to burn, and the fires started early that year. The week of my mother's visit, another nearby college town was burning, not far from the state university that rivaled ours. It was sunset all day long. The overhead sun flattened like an orange yolk. The city tinted to the color of old Rome, and passing faces blurred, as if I were viewing them through a Vaseline-smeared lens. The world was beautiful, but it was hard to breathe.

When I picked up my mother from the airport, she looked older. I hadn't seen her in two years, and she was now in her late sixties. After hello, the first thing she said was, "You can't wear that color." I was wearing a sky-blue halter dress I had found at a thrift store, printed with tiny flowers. I had thought I looked pretty. I pulled on a beige sweater and buttoned it.

My mother talked through the car ride, the hauling of her suitcase up the stairs, the boiling of tea water and delivery of crackers. Books she read, movies she saw, museums she visited. Relatives she disliked. And did I remember her old friend Julia, in England? Julia had a disease that meant she was confined to a wheelchair and couldn't even venture down the street ("Or lane, as they say there"), so my mother visited her a few months ago. She regaled Julia with story after story of her travels: Turkey, the Czech Republic, Hungary, Japan, Nepal, two or three countries a year. She thought it would be nice for Julia to hear about this, as housebound as she was. But Julia was very quiet and couldn't even socialize for more than a few hours each day, so my mother ended up spending much of the week reading in her room, even though she had flown all that way to entertain Julia, who asked to cut the visit short despite the fact that she may die soon and this very well might have been their last chance to see each other.

I remembered this constant chatter from my childhood. My mother had a trick: she'd give every detail and just when the story looked like it might end, she'd release the listener on a cliff-hanger: "That was before she embezzled all that money." And then, of course, I'd ask, "She embezzled money?" and it would start again, another twenty or forty minutes to the next cliff-hanger. I could be anyone at all, any word receptacle, and she would barely notice.

I had gone through a long nervous chatter phase myself, especially during and after college, and sometimes even now. During my worst period, my best friend was the unfortunate main recipient, maybe because she was the only one who would listen. If I didn't tell someone everything, maybe I didn't exist. But even my best friend got tired of it, as anyone would, and frequently cut me off to talk to her boyfriend, who must have felt like an insect plastered against a windshield. It was a relief to stop. I hated the sound of my voice, filling the air with words to shave down the fear of whatever entropy silence held, all the bad things that happened in silence.

This visit was three days of my mother talking, me listening, JD working nonstop into the evening. When JD first met my mother, both were courteous but uncertain, like two leashed dogs approaching each other on the street. They didn't hug or shake hands. JD showed her the same professional interest he reserved for his patients, and she talked in his direction without asking questions, as though he was as disposable as anyone else.

Even though JD was polite and caring and didn't complain when I gave my mother our bed so she'd be more comfortable, I could tell he didn't like her, didn't like what I had told him about her. So I spent the days with my mother alone, taking her places half-shrouded with smoke. I wasn't sure if she noticed anywhere we visited. Like the restaurant with every panel, wall, and ceiling tile intricately painted by master craftsmen over the course of a decade, gifted to the town by its sister city in Tajikistan. Or Rocky Mountain National Park, with fourteeners and elk and eagles and bighorn sheep. Rivers, mountains, parks, food, all went without comment except for an occasional brief "Isn't that something."

She didn't ask me any questions. Instead, she'd talk for an hour or more about her friend Patty's black belt in tae kwon do. Patty's test was very hard, with lots of details that required explanation. When my mother took a sip of water, I volunteered, "I earned my black belt, too," and she said, "That's why I'm telling you about Patty's," and then it was an hour on how much she loved my brother's wife, how he had picked such a great woman, so similar to herself, how my mother gave up her wedding ring and it was now on her daughter-in-law's finger, how angry my sister was about that because she thought that ring would be hers once my mother died. Then an hour about a friend I'd never met who insulted her at a party and said she talked too much ("And she's even a therapist!"), so my mother never spoke to her again, even when the friend got cancer and eventually died, and my mother felt that it was the right decision not to contact her then, even with the cancer. How fat my uncle was and how my mother told my aunt he'd better lose weight or my aunt would end up pushing him around in a wheelchair. A man on the bus she often takes into the city was so obese that he had to occupy two of the seats, but my mother didn't let him get away with that. "He must be four hundred pounds. I always make him move over and I sit next to him, even though it's uncomfortable for me, but he has to learn."

I managed to break through with, "Mom. I'm sure it's painful for him to be overweight. He doesn't need you to show him anything."

She blinked at me. Then she said, "I saw that picture of you in that magazine." I had sold an essay to a fashion magazine, and they had shot a photo of me. "You looked terrible."

I managed to insert, "Um, guess what, Mom? I'm doing private eye work now. I got a job working for a lawyer, investigating cases." My segues with her were always awkward.

"Oh, I read a very good murder mystery last week—"

"I don't do murder. I do rape."

"It's got a hot-pink cover but you shouldn't let that—"

"Mom, it's a rape case. I investigate rape." I just wanted her to hear this one thing. To say *something* about it.

My mother's hazel eyes squinted until they turned brown. Her eyes had always been strange and beautiful—purple at the edges, green and amber near the center. They had lightened with age, as had mine. Someday mine might look like hers.

My mother said, "I'll send you that book. You'll like it." Then, a minute later, "You know, you should really rethink your stance regarding X. Because someday you may need us."

She began talking again and left me no room to remind her of what she used to repeat while I was growing up: "Someday you're going to need me. And I can't wait for that day to happen, because I won't be there for you." Angry at me for something or other, she said it when I was five, then seven, then twelve and sixteen, and then she stopped altogether because we both knew it by heart.

My mother was there for a lot of other people, though. She gave career advice. She gave relationship advice. She told people what to do and they did it, or they should have done it because look at them now. I found myself retreating from her words, even as they multiplied and engulfed me.

I wondered if so much talk was wearing her out, as it was with me. By the last night of the three-day visit, I was brimming with un-spent anxiety, beginning to twitch with it. I was grateful when JD came home and we drove to a fancy Moroccan restaurant, lined with rich wine-red and orange tapestries that smelled faintly of the street's smoke. JD and I had eaten here before on a date, and I wanted to treat my mother to the best dinner I could, to thank her for coming. It was a long meal, five courses: *harira* soup, vinegary eggplant salad, sugar-dusted chicken *b'stilla*, our entrées, fruit, and sweet mint tea. My mother ordered the rabbit, I picked at an artichoke, and JD ate lamb. She talked and we listened. After a while, JD stopped trying to speak at all, chewing metronomically, staring at the families chatting at other tables. When he wordlessly left for the bathroom, my mother said, "He seems disengaged. But stable. Steady." She knew I would hate this, and I did. Then she talked through the rest of the courses about people JD and I had never met.

There was nothing to do but overeat. Then my mother stopped talking. We looked up at the sudden silence, chewing. She indented the tablecloth with her knife, and then drew a prolonged inhale through her nose. "Okay," she said. "So you got me here. Say what you want to say to me."

"What?" I asked.

"You asked me to fly in. I flew in. What do you want?"

What did I want? My tongue dried up.

My mother folded one hand into another and waited, her mouth a straight line that trembled.

In the past, she had disowned me rather than listen to me, or drowned me in nervous talk. But now, here in this restaurant on her last night, she was finally listening, even if she had her about-to-take-a-multivitamin face on. She waited for me to say whatever I needed to say.

And I was completely unprepared.

"I just . . . I wanted to see you," I said, my voice squeaking at the end of the sentence.

She still waited.

I said, "I wanted to see my mother." That was true. I hadn't realized she might have the ability or inclination to see me in return. I had wanted something from her, or for her, but what was it? I blanked. New desires were multiplying inside me, too quickly for me to decipher the words that might connect them. JD looked away, maybe trying to give us some degree of privacy, or maybe he was just miserable.

My mother said, "Oh." Then she quickly stabbed into her smooth, shiny rabbit, relief bubbling into renewed talk. Everything in the room was, in her estimation, wonderful, and look at those tapestries on the wall that reminded her of a trip she took blah blah blah blah blah. She soaked up her sauce with bread. She asked for more sugary mint tea and laughed when the server squirted our faces with rose water after the meal. She complimented the belly dancer's figure and called JD handsome.

I was too stunned to eat or drink anything more. I had asked her to come, and she had flown two thousand miles here. My mother had lied when she said she wouldn't be there for me when I needed her. She was here now. She had offered herself out of—what? Love? Guilt? It didn't matter. It had been brave of her to come.

Rising from my gratitude was the realization that she had just given me a chance, my only chance, to speak to her about my pain. And I had blown it. I hadn't understood what I was supposed to do—tell her what X did again, make her understand what it cost me, present a case, evidence, feelings? Was I supposed to instantly transform into Morgan and start describing horror? Those muscles had atrophied long ago. In splintered pieces over decades, I had already told my mother what had happened. I had confirmed those truths every day I wouldn't speak to X, or look at him, or when I stopped visiting entirely and forever. But there was something else I was supposed to say, right then, and then never again.

My mother was so happy, off the hook she had invented, talking so fast her tea grew cold, and then grasping the goblet and thirstily

drinking the whole thing down. "Altitude," she said. JD poured her
more tea. I almost spilled it when the server slid the pleather check
folder onto the table and my mother and I both grabbed it at the same
time. I pulled hard, but she pulled harder, strengthened by her own
gratitude. JD protested and unsuccessfully tried to pay the server behind her back; he didn't like owing my mother anything. We drove
home. I don't remember what she said in the parking lot, the car, the
living room, before she turned out her light and closed her eyes and
mouth and slept.

"That was a lot. Are you okay?" JD asked me in the dark, after we
turned out the light. I nodded. He listened to my hair swish on the
pillow, kissed me, and went to sleep.

Not having something doesn't mean not wanting it. Hospice nurses
say their patients' last words are "Mama," even when their mothers are
decades gone. Even as my whole body screamed to get away from her,
I still craved my mother. Not *a* mother. Mine.

I once found a copy of a ballpoint picture Genie, the feral child,
had drawn of herself with her mother. Both of them looked like wide-
faced stuffed monkeys, arms splayed for hugs. In repetitive loops, Genie had drawn Mama's hair, eyes, mouth, body, nipples, belly button,
and feet. In one outstretched hand was a smaller version of monkey-
Mama with the same loopy hair, eyes, nose, mouth, nipples, and belly
button, wearing the same checkered pants. Asking the scientists which
letters to use in which order, Genie had painstakingly printed labels:
"Baby Genie" and "Mama Hand." The blind, weak woman who had
abandoned Genie to her father's cruelty, starved and ignored her, and
left her chained to a potty chair all day and night for thirteen years, was
now depicted holding her beloved baby Genie in one hand. Below the
image, Genie had written even more carefully: "I Miss Mama."

I lay awake most of the night, next to JD, and the state continued to
burn around us. But fire is worst when you have a home, or if you're
a bug or tree or rabbit or artichoke. For the greater good of the forest, it's a blessing. Fire cleans the land, converts what's dead or dying
into light and heat. A tree by itself is agitated, no matter how serene
it looks. All those atoms are compressed into a form that it finds

borderline intolerable, so when it combines with flame and oxygen and combusts, I imagine it finds calm. It has purpose, and knows what to do. It destroys itself.

The next day, JD went to work and I rode the bus with my mother to the airport. When we arrived, we were two hours early for her flight. I asked, "Will you visit me again?" and her face twisted, but not in pain. She said, "Maybe. I don't know. I don't need to see you. I want to know you're okay. But I don't need to see you for that."

But her voice was as uncertain as her face, which was tilted away from me as she watched a mother lead a toddler on a halter-leash shaped like a puppy backpack. I wouldn't give up on my mother. I was still the hammer. I had worn down her resistance once, and would do it again until we were part of each other's lives. Even mothers change. Next time she gave me that chance to talk to her, I would be prepared.

Our visit wasn't over yet. Maybe there was still something I was supposed to say, or ask. Her visit had been cake-layered with talk talk talk, but she had told me nothing, and she still knew nothing about me. Before she left, I should ask her something important, something that would make my family make sense.

But my legs wanted to run. My whole body wanted to get away from her, as if she were exhaling ammonia. I wanted cool air, water, rain, a bath. I gave my mother a quick side-hug and left before she could say anything more.

Within steps, I began to run. I ran down the escalator and out of the terminal. Outside, I gulped the smoky air, staring at the pavement.

Then I returned to the terminal through the automatic doors.

In Denver International Airport there is a narrow glassed-in walkway over the escalators to the train that hauls travelers to the gates. You can find that narrow corridor, sit on the floor there, and give a final, surprise wave. It's a locals' secret. JD had discovered it and waved to me when I flew to a wedding we couldn't afford to attend together. I quickly found the windowed spot and sat, waiting for my mother, recovering my breath, nerves vibrating.

I couldn't see her, only other travelers who snuck a quick glance up at me as they rode the escalator down. Men in suits looked homesick and lonely, about to board a metal tube thrusting itself into the sky. My mother didn't appear through the security checkpoint. Had I missed her when I left the airport? Was it possible not to recognize your own mother? I fretted.

And then she appeared. From afar, I recognized her with my body, the way you recognize your reflection. She was small, vulnerable as a worried wren, with her black carry-on bag and salmon-colored short-sleeve shirt and sagging shoulders, her peach-lipsticked lips pressed together in despair. She didn't know I was watching her. She thought I was already on my way home, and she didn't know to glance up. She looked exhausted, perhaps from all the talking, and I wondered if she even liked to talk at all, or if it was what she felt she must do, like visiting the daughter she hadn't seen in years, the daughter she failed.

The escalator carried my mother downward, her ankles pressed together. She stared at her hands, clenching her brown purse. If she didn't look up, she'd never know I was there, that I had come back for her. She would only know I ran away. I hovered above her, waving until my arm hurt.

My mother's gaze finally caught upward. Her face cracked into an openmouthed smile, and she waved back in a flurry, with a little girl's wild delight. "Mommy," I said as her lifted face sank beneath my feet. I kept waving, finally able to love her on the silent side of the safety glass.

11

Grand Jury

After my mother left, I felt renewed vigor for the case, and thrust myself into everything Grayson assigned me. I would carve out my own space in the world and somehow crowd myself into my mother's incessant narrative. If our case was in the news, she would have to think about me, if not talk about me. She had visited me, we hadn't fought about anything, and she had left well fed and happy. I wouldn't lose one centimeter of ground with her and would build on what we now had. I began writing her emails every few weeks, and sometimes called. Things were going well, I thought.

The case had taken a new direction. Daisy's involvement with the recruits spiked local and national news, bruising the reputation of not just the university but also the state government that funded it. The governor ordered a grand jury investigation into the finances of the university's athletic department, to be prosecuted by Colorado Attorney General Ken Salazar. The grand jury would investigate the university's football program recruiting practices, financial transactions, and alleged supply of sex workers to recruits. Daisy was to be their lead witness.

Like anyone who grew up with American TV, I had heard of grand juries, but I didn't really know the difference between that and any other jury except maybe it was bigger? Grander? I did some research. I discovered that a grand jury was completely separate from what we were doing. We were working in the civil branch of the justice system; grand juries are in the criminal branch. I already knew that in our civil suit, the punishment is money, and in a criminal trial, the punishment is jail. But a grand jury is one step before the criminal trial, reserved for special circumstances. In a grand jury, between twelve and twenty-three jurors convene without judges, investigate the situation, and decide if it's likely that a crime took place or not. From there, they vote to either dismiss the case or issue an indictment. The indictment doesn't mean anyone goes to jail yet; it just means that the bad guys are now mandated by law to appear in a criminal trial, with or without the say-so of the DA.

Prosecutors use grand juries for crime systems like drug traffick-ing, auto theft rings, and financial fraud across more than one jurisdic-tion, often when multiple individuals committed the crimes. A grand jury is also closed to the public, so secret that suspects sometimes don't even know they're being investigated until they're indicted. It felt very grassroots to me; the jurors have the power to subpoena witnesses and documents and ask questions themselves. They can also grant immu-nity to help encourage fearful or reluctant witnesses.

To me, criminal law was looking more and more like a poker game: you gather your cards, show them, and three deuces can beat a pair of aces. This was why a DA could pick and choose what she prose-cuted even before all the evidence was in and say that the aces weren't enough, there were too many deuces, and a jury might decide this or that regardless of the evidence. The DA could always say the other side was stronger. If she lacked the courage or the motivation to prosecute, the other side would always look stronger, and that's why the system needed civil cases and lawyers like Grayson.

"Prosecutorial timidity is a huge national problem," Grayson told me. "Check the case closure rates. In the 1960s, it was something like ninety percent. Now it's about sixty percent. That means forty percent of criminals get away with it. Prosecutors don't go to trial because they think, 'Ooh, I might lose.'" Grayson could tolerate a lot of things, but not cowardice.

Long ago, I had complained that none of the bad guys were going to jail, and Grayson had said that our work might lead to a criminal trial. A grand jury had the power to force a DA's hand. If someone was indicted by a grand jury, the DA had no choice—there *had* to be a trial.

Grayson now flew all over the country, taking final depositions from players and recruits at the party, getting ready for our trial. He had particularly hated Fredrick, a player who had been present at both Simone's and Olive's alleged attacks. At lunch, Grayson told me, "Fredrick is a terrible person. At least King and Zachary, they're human beings. They have feelings; they have remorse." Grayson shook his head. "Fredrick is not a human being. He's an evil . . . asshole, really. You know, I asked him what percent of women on campus are groupies who just want to sleep with football players. He said, 'All of them.'"

I was the first to laugh, and Grayson joined in.

"He talked about 'getting sucked' and things like that. Every now and again, he'd smile." Grayson shuddered, a real shudder. "And King didn't admit to assaulting Calliope, but he did say, listen to this— 'Parties and sex, that's what everyone had in mind—that was our hope being a college male, that would be a hope that the recruits meet some girls and you hope that they have some sex.' So when I asked what he had learned that's positive from the experience, he said, 'If a woman gives consent but she is drunk . . . you know, she can say that she was raped. I've learned things such as that.'" Grayson leaned back.

"Can you use that in court?"

Grayson nodded and began to eat. "A few players admitted to sex with Simone but not sexual assault. That's good enough to place them in the bedroom. They don't have to agree that it's sexual assault—we have enough evidence to prove that already, thanks to testimony. And to you," he added. "There's one recruit from the hotel attack I haven't deposed yet who feels terrible about what he did. He found God, I think. I'm grooming him," which was Grayson's shorthand for "hands off."

"But the rest of the recruits were all coached," Grayson said. "In depositions, they took the Fifth on every question. *Every* question. I've never seen that before." He had the quiet incredulity of someone who had the power to expect answers. "I'd ask, 'Did you rape Simone Baker?' They'd say, 'I refuse to answer on the grounds that it may incriminate me.' I put sexual assault in every sentence. 'You knew she wasn't consenting to sex, right?' 'I refuse to answer on the grounds that it may incriminate me.' 'When you had vaginal intercourse against her will and against her consent, etc.?' 'I refuse yada.' I asked about twenty or twenty-five questions just that way, rephrasing it every way I could think of."

"Doesn't the Fifth Amendment imply they're guilty, though?" I remembered this fact from a rerun of 1970s legal dramas: pleading the Fifth meant you were guilty but didn't want to say the words.

Grayson said, "Oh. You don't get it. This is *really* good for us. If a witness takes the Fifth in a deposition for a criminal case, the jury would never know—the witness just won't show up on the stand. But in a deposition for a civil case, especially one that was videotaped like ours, it's our ticket to winning. The jury gets instruction that they're entitled to infer that witnesses are guilty of any crimes they refused to answer about."

"So will the perpetrators go to jail *now*?"

"Only if the DA decides to prosecute."

"I just don't understand how people can hurt women with absolutely no consequences."

Grayson said, "It's a dry-erase world, kid." He forked up a bite of some kind of yellow cream pie that smelled like the refrigerator it had come from.

My head was in my hands. Grayson quietly laid his fork on his plate and leaned over. "Hey, kid," he said. "You know the plan. I'm attacking from the top down. If this grand jury works out, with more evidence out there, the DA might decide to reopen the case against the players and recruits. It's far from over. It's just beginning."

"If everything goes right."

"And it is." He resumed eating. "Especially for you. You're good at this, you know? We should open a firm together. Or you should go to law school. Be a litigator like me."

"Oh, God, no." At his expression, I amended, "I mean, I like what I'm doing now." And I did. I had purpose, not just in the case, but also in what I perceived to be my career. We were winning, winning-ish, in that state of suspended animation before things change for good.

The grand jury took place over three months. It was secret testimony, so we didn't know what they did or said, except that Daisy appeared before them for two hours. But at the end of the investigation, the recruiter Tanner Liddell was the only one they indicted, for allegedly soliciting sex workers and embezzling several hundred dollars of public property by using a university-owned cell phone to make personal calls. Tanner insisted he acted alone, and solicited sex workers only for his personal use. After Riley's experience, I wondered what made Tanner agree to jump under the bus.

"That's it?" I asked Grayson over the phone. "Nothing on Coach Riggs?"

Grayson said, "I understand the university blew off the grand jury subpoenas. They were supposed to provide documentation about their finances, and they just . . . didn't."

"How did they get away with that?"

Grayson told me, "Well, after the investigation, the grand jury filed a report against the university with the trial court. It's supposedly a damning report. Tantamount to an indictment. But not quite an indictment."

"Supposedly?"

"That's the problem. It's sealed. The grand jury isn't supposed to show the record if there's an indictment—Tanner's—and the university president fought to keep it secret."

"So we're not allowed to see that report? Ever?"

"All that evidence, locked up," Grayson said.

What did "sealed" even mean? Someone had to have read it, if only to make sure it wasn't an envelope full of car wash coupons. Grayson said, "If we could get our hands on the report, that would really be something." He paused, almost as if waiting for me to offer to break into the offices of the state court. But he wasn't, of course; he knew better. Still, I felt hobbled by pop culture expectations—I was a PI so that should mean I could do all kinds of illegal shit like pick locks, break and enter, wield a gun, stalk suspects, and slap confessions out of unwilling wrongdoers. But if I broke the law, I'd go to jail just like anyone else. Maybe I could find a temp job at the courthouse, perhaps in the records room with that mousy guy who hated me.

Before I even came up with a strategy, someone leaked the contents of the report and excerpts hit the papers. The grand jury had learned that trainers were regularly sexually abused and harassed in the training room, and that an assistant coach allegedly sexually assaulted two of them—Olive might have been one. One trainer was "coerced to perform sexual favors for players and recruits repeatedly over a two-year period." The report said Tanner had hired between eight and twelve sex workers for recruits, as well as lap dancers three to five times a year as recruiting staples.

The grand jury uncovered a discretionary slush fund Coach Riggs kept in sixteen or seventeen separate cash boxes, each managed by someone different in the football program. The director of football operations said "up to $2,500 could be missing, but not missed" from each cash box. When the press asked Coach Riggs to comment, he said, "There's no slush fund, there's never been a slush fund. All of this is BS." The grand jury report detailed other unexplained transactions uncovered by the state auditor, including $780,000 in deposits to the Wade Riggs Football Technique School, and "large amounts" of undocumented petty cash transactions.

Grayson called me up again. "I wonder what Daisy knows about that money."

"Do you want me to ask her? I thought she's not allowed to talk about the grand jury. She could get in trouble, right?"

"Don't do anything unethical," Grayson said.

"Got it."

That night I scheduled another meeting with Daisy.

"Sorry, I can't say anything," Daisy said at the little café that I now considered to be our place. "I would, but I can't. I'd get in trouble." She

was distracted, slouching in her seat. She had gained some weight. Her perpetual smile was gone, and her skin had lost its color, now looking like lumpy, unrisen dough. "I'm already in enough trouble now."

"New trouble?"

"I'm calling them 'gas station moments,'" Daisy said, one side of her mouth jerking upward. "With all the news and the grand jury, my picture's been in the papers too much. Football fans recognize me when I'm pumping gas. They throw supersize drinks at me with ice in them. Once a middle-aged couple threw boiling hot coffee at my face. And sometimes people spit on me."

I hadn't considered that the lawsuit could endanger her. "Have you called the police?"

"Police? Ha. They're the reason I'm in legal trouble at all," she said.

That, and the fact that she was a madam.

She said, "I could handle it except my kid's getting teased at school. Kids say stuff like 'Your mom's a whore.' My kid's only fourteen. And nobody will hire me for a regular job." Daisy covered her face with her hands, cupping them so she wouldn't ruin her meticulous eye makeup.

When people are ashamed, they cover their faces. The face is where shame lives. My mother once told me an anecdote about a college women's swim team that was showering after practice. While they were bathing, someone broke into the women's dressing room and stole all their clothes and towels. They would have to run across campus to their rooms with nothing but their hands to cover them. Some of them covered their breasts, some covered their vaginas. "But the smartest ones," my mother said, "covered their faces."

Daisy slowly and randomly tore her place mat into a pile of little bits of paper. She rested her head on her hand and blew at the little pile until the pieces scattered. "I need money." Her gaze rose to the level of my chin.

I knew Simone's mother had tried to give Daisy a side of beef, but it wouldn't fit in her freezer. I could have comfortably given her maybe a hundred bucks, but I didn't reach for my wallet. "Have you thought about working an hourly job?" I asked. "Just something until you get on your feet. Like fast food or a big-box store?"

"I worked at a place like that for a week. Then they found out who I was, fired me, and didn't pay me for my time. That's slavery, technically." Daisy brushed her bangs from her eyes. "I get a job, and then they fire me as soon as they find out. With my name, my appearance—I stick out."

"You could cut your hair. Or dye it."

Daisy swung a long lock over her shoulder but said nothing. That's how I knew for certain she hadn't given up sex work. How else would she pay her rent? She needed that shining black hair, and every other asset she had.

"I'm about to be evicted," she said. "A friend found me this condemned place to live out in Coal Creek Canyon, but that's only for a couple of months." Daisy grabbed her hair in her fists and shook it a little. Her nail polish gleamed through the strands of black. "I might move out of state," she said.

It would be better for Daisy and her kid if she moved and started over somewhere else. But we needed Daisy to testify. She was the tawdry face of the lawsuit, a reminder nobody could ignore. If she left the state and disappeared, the case could collapse. Civil cases aren't like criminal ones, Grayson told me often, and it's nearly useless to subpoena a reluctant witness who doesn't want to testify, or who doesn't want to be found.

Of course, Daisy didn't know any of this. "Don't run away," I said. Hurriedly, I named social services: Emergency Family Assistance, Safehouse, Mental Health Center, Family and Children's Services. "Some of them have temporary housing for families."

She told me that with her kid's medical condition, they needed a stable home, not a shelter. "And I have a dog," she said. She stared out the window at the aggressively bright day, and at the women exiting the yoga store buoyed by shopping bags.

Our relationship was shifting and Daisy was speaking to me like a friend. She didn't ask me for money again. Grayson was right—she had attached to me, the way people attach to a scrap of paper with a secret on it, or the losing slot machine that holds all their money and brightly promises a jackpot it will never deliver.

"I really regret coming forward," Daisy said. "I wish I hadn't ever said anything."

I felt sick, but it was my job to lean into her misery, not away. I wanted to, even. Her anguish felt uncut and addictive. I wanted to crawl deep into this woman's strange mind, full of lacerations and broken mirrors. I needed her, and not just for the case. She wasn't allowed to abandon me.

"You can't give up," I said.

Daisy was silent.

And then, hating myself, "We'd just subpoena you anyway."

She flinched.

I was a terrible person. But I didn't unsay the threat, or even soften it. I let it hang there between us.

"What are you going to do, Daisy?" I asked.

Her purple-shaded gaze skittered around the restaurant, away from my treacherous face.

"I want a white picket fence," she whispered. "I just want a normal life."

Daisy had decided to come forward on her own, and the chaos of her life was the kind of thing news spectators loved; it makes them feel safe by comparison. Nothing's more comforting than the sound of rain when you're not in it. But I was no spectator; I got wet. I felt responsible for it all—the costs to Daisy and her kid, the needs of Grayson's case, and the fates of the plaintiffs, two of whom I had never met. I was working for the greater good of survivors, right? That meant I should be working for Daisy as well.

I began job hunting for her, scanning ads and calling department store warehouses. "She could stock inventory in the back," I said. "Nobody would have to see her." I called acquaintances who had small businesses. "Can you use an assistant? A bookkeeper? Someone discreet?" When they asked about her previous experience, I told them, and they politely declined. I called the area's family shelters. "They have a dog. Is that a problem?"

Finally, one of the nonprofit workers said, "Listen. It's real nice that you care. But I've seen this before. You need to let this woman make her own decisions."

"I'm trying to help her."

"Sure. But you're the one who's calling. She's not."

Which only made me more desperate. I imagined Daisy afraid to leave her apartment, crying into a dirty bathrobe, staring into her open refrigerator until it was no longer cold. I imagined her dressing in the dark to meet dangerous men after her kid fell asleep in bed.

But the next time we spoke, Daisy's voice was bright at the other end of the phone line. "I had a great idea. Let's write a book together! All this has got to be worth something. Sex sells, baby! Just tell me who I need to call to get money for this."

I had no doubt Daisy could write. Her similes were better than mine, especially when she described penises. But Daisy needed folding money and didn't have the years and years it takes to write a proposal and approach agents and then go through the blistering process of submitting, waiting, getting rejected, waiting, drinking, waiting, pharmaceuticals. I explained how the publishing industry worked until we were both sad. "But maybe I could pitch an article on you," I said. "I have some magazine contacts, editors I've worked with before." The animation returned to Daisy's voice after I told her we'd split the money down the middle.

I pitched a Daisy story to a magazine editor I was working with at the time. "But can you make it empowering?" the editor asked.

"I—well, it's not an empowering story, exactly. I mean, she's destitute." I told the editor I was going to pay half the money to Daisy.

She used the slow, halting talk that sane people use with the mentally ill. "We don't pay our subjects. That's not really ethical." Then she placed me on hold until I eventually hung up, and she didn't take my calls again.

Calliope wasn't better off. She had stopped returning Grayson's phone calls, so he had asked me to check in. When I called, Calliope said in a frantic voice, "I'm thinking of quitting the case."

"What? Why?" I asked.

"The university lawyers are asking mean questions. I don't want to talk about what happened to me. I don't want to see Zachary. He's a gross guy. He's always pushing and blunt and wrong. King had been a friend, but when I learned he planned all this with Zachary, I realized he was my enemy. He's not a guy you want to be your enemy. Bad things happen to his enemies."

"Bad things?"

"People go above and beyond to get revenge for him. Coaches. Friends." Even though Calliope was two thousand miles away in Pennsylvania, terror sharpened the pitch of her voice to a fine edge. "I'm afraid to go outside. I don't want to testify. I don't want to be called into court. I'm afraid they'll call me a slut. I'm afraid I'll be seen as betraying my race."

She was in an impossible position. All I knew was that silence meant trading short-term relief for long-term pain. I said, "Those men hurt you. You have a right to tell the truth."

"But will I be looked at as an innocent party or a guilty party?"

"Innocent," I said firmly, but I didn't know. I had never even seen a real trial. "It's been decades since wearing a short skirt was used as justification for sexual assault."

"Yeah, you don't need that. All you need is a pair of breasts." I heard the rueful smile in her voice morph into a frown, flattening her voice. "The people I thought I knew, I didn't know at all. I thought they considered me a friend, not just some piece of ass. I don't understand how they could do this, or how they could think that they can treat people like that."

"They can't. That's why you're suing them," I said.

"I'm just one person," she said.

A week later, Calliope quit the case. I found out through the news. Calliope told reporters that the university "condoned a litigation strategy of abusive attacks by [their] lawyers on my character and credibility and private life. These have already begun and threaten to get much worse. It wasn't worth the mental and emotional cost to continue." She compared the experience to guerrilla warfare and she stressed, "I want to make it very clear that my decision to terminate this litigation should not be interpreted as a retraction of what I have identified as having happened to me and others while a student-athlete at the university." She agreed to serve as a witness, so Grayson was relieved, but grim. "I wanted to get her some money," he said.

I of course respected Calliope's decision, but it hit me hard. Was I hurting these women by bringing them forward? Grayson had deposed Leah, the "friend" who brought the football players to Simone's apartment. He said she seemed to be a different person for every question, like she was figuring out what he wanted to hear and then fashioning her personality around it. I had an uneasy feeling that I was a version of Leah, only more skilled at it than she was. Leah was recovering from her own alleged attack, and then invited the players and recruits to the party where Simone was assaulted. Maybe I, too, was splashing around in other people's pain just to avoid drowning in my own. Maybe I was only trying to help them because nobody helped me.

I had damaged Calliope's and Daisy's lives by persuading them to come forward, and I threatened Daisy when she tried to escape the case for her own good. I had become part of the lawyers-guns-and-money machine. I was a good guy turned bad, pretending to be on the right side. Maybe I was only on my own side.

The first private investigator in U.S. history was named Allan Pinkerton. Pinkerton had grown up in a neighborhood of Glasgow, Scotland, called "the Gorbals," the worst slum in Europe. He had to leave school at age ten to work as a cooper. As a young man, he thwarted a Scottish counterfeiting ring and started getting talent-scouted by law enforcement for stings. He then joined the Chartists, social reformers seeking voting rights for non-landowners. They wanted secret ballots, the right to join Parliament, and annual elections. The police began arresting the Chartists for terrorism, and Pinkerton fled to America.

Pinkerton eventually set up a detective agency in Chicago, drawing on his natural ability for crime detection, which he had discovered and honed in Scotland. Pinkerton, with help from his operative Kate Warne, discovered and thwarted the first assassination attempt on Abraham Lincoln. He was the first American PI to hire women. He worked with abolitionist John Brown to transport enslaved people to Canada and used his own home as a stop on the Underground Railroad. His cases became more and more high profile, with new offices opening across the country.

In the early 1890s, Pinkerton's agency grew to two thousand active operatives and thirty thousand reserve officers—larger than the U.S. Army's active military force. The government feared his workforce would become an outright militia, and passed the Anti-Pinkerton Act—still in effect today—to prohibit them from working for the government.

Pinkerton's initial values, the ones that had led him to the spy trade in the first place, completely reversed with his new successes and power. The sought-after Pinkerton now accepted big corporate anti-labor cases. His dogs of war infiltrated, subdued, and decimated the Molly Maguires protesting the slavery conditions in the coal mines of Appalachia, where the miners were paid in scrip that could only be used at the overinflated, extortionist company store. Pinkerton thugs terrorized the miners and lied on the stand to convict and hang nineteen Mollies—ten of them on what they called the "day of rope." Pinkerton had become anti-labor, pro-corporate, anti-underdog. He had started out with good intentions. But he had turned into Them.

12

Turtles All the Way Down

One night, JD stopped me in the middle of a sage field in Estes Park. He held both my hands in his and said a bunch of obscure things about how much I meant to him. I said thank you. He said, "Well?"

"Well what?"

"Are you going to marry me?"

"Wait. You're proposing?" There was no ring, no knee. I shouldn't have been surprised; it was outside JD's character to kneel to anyone. I was vastly unprepared, wearing a jacket I hadn't washed in a year and a thrift store ski hat with the logo of a vibrator company on it.

I said yes. Of course I said yes—I loved him. But I pitied him, even as I kissed him and told him how happy I was. What business did I have marrying anyone?

One day after Brazilian jiu-jitsu training, I invited one of the coaches to our wedding. He stared at the wedding invitation, visibly shocked. "You and JD?" he asked. "*You're* together? Getting married?"

"We live together," I said. "I brought him into this school."

"I didn't know." The school was big and busy, so that wasn't surprising. Then he said, "I knew he lived with someone. But I never in a million years imagined that it was you."

I felt my smile start to harden at the edges.

He blushed. "I mean, once I saw you touch his chest in, like, a romantic kind of way. I thought you were trying to get him to like you. Or maybe . . ."

He paused for so long that I had to say it myself. "You thought we were having an affair?"

"Yeah." He laughed. I laughed, too, worried. Even this guy thought I was an improbable choice for JD to take seriously, to marry.

We decided to elope rather than spend money we didn't have on a traditional wedding, which to me always looked like the same movie with the same costumes and different actors. Besides, who would walk me down the aisle? I needed somewhere aisle-less. We compromised: we'd elope to southern Thailand and have our honeymoon in Japan, where I had lived for four years as a teenager but hadn't been back since. I initially balked at Thailand because when my family had lived in Tokyo, we had repeatedly taken trips to Bangkok. I remembered seeing very little girls stationed on stools outside massage parlors, wearing tube tops and red lipstick, waiting for sex tourists to give their handler some baht and lead them away to a room.

But that shit happened in America, too. A Thai friend told me, "Darling, Bangkok is not Thailand." JD and I agreed on an island five hundred miles south of Bangkok. JD also wanted to celebrate with family and friends, so we planned a pre-elopement barbecue, and decided to invite as many people as would fit in our scrubby, sage-choked yard full of cheatgrass and fireweed.

My mother and I were still speaking regularly when I called and told her we were getting married. She sounded grim and didn't offer congratulations. She didn't ask to speak to JD. I was proving her wrong; she had been so sure when I was young that nobody would ever marry me. Maybe I was encroaching on her married-person turf, or maybe she feared I would need her less, love her less. I invited her to the party, which was turning into a bigger deal than we had anticipated, with JD's family coming and friends planning to fly in. I asked my mother, "Will you come?"

"I will bring X," she said.

For a second, I panicked. After everything, was she really planning to bring him? If so, I'd rather not have the party at all. I said rapidly, "No, he's not welcome. He's not invited. But you are."

She said, as if she had already practiced for it, "I wouldn't have a good time if he wasn't invited. So don't invite me."

"You are invited. He's not. You can RSVP for one. I want you there."

She said, "At some point you're going to have to, you know. Forgive him."

I couldn't resist. "Forgive him for what, Mom? What should I forgive him for?"

She hung up.

I wrote her a pleading letter asking her to come. I knew I was risking something when I wrote, *My wedding isn't about X, or about you. It's about JD and me.* But everything was about her.

We had been getting along, I had thought. I just needed her to support me now, one time in my life. If she wasn't there for me at my wedding, would there ever be any hope for us? I sent off the letter before I had time to change my mind, enclosing the invitation. I'd made them by hand, using the laser printer and paper cutters at a temp job, striped vellum on textured green paper, punctured with a heart-shaped hole puncher and held together with red satin ribbons. I waited for a reply. It didn't come.

Forgiveness, she had said. The same mandate was preached in every self-help book, including the biggest one of all, the Bible. Forgive your enemies their trespasses. I didn't grow up Christian, and the idea of mandatory forgiveness felt foolish, masochistic, dangerous. I've never heard anyone logically explain the Sermon on the Mount. Turn the other cheek because . . . it shows you believe God will protect you, despite all evidence to the contrary? Aristotle said, "Bad men are full of repentance," but I've never seen it. How do you forgive someone who's never asked for forgiveness?

For my mother's sake, I tried to imagine forgiving X, forgiving the person who would hit me and then make me apologize for it, the person I had imagined as thunder, nightmares. Saying "I forgive you" to that smug Dorian Gray face, scarred by self-knowledge. Giving him

my forgiveness unasked, like handing a murderer your soft, pink infant
and hoping he doesn't do what he always does.

I once dated a photographer who said, "If a picture doesn't work,
get closer." I didn't want to look more closely at him, but I would,
if it meant escaping him permanently. He was just a person, with a
heart, brain, blood. Muscle, fat, bone, teeth, brain, nerves, connective
tissue, lymph, urine, gas, shit, skin. Get closer. Water, protein, lipids,
carbohydrates, and DNA. Bacteria. Oxygen, carbon, hydrogen, nitro-
gen, calcium, phosphorus. Closer, smaller. Atoms. Protons and elec-
trons in their automatic dance. No, no dancing with him. Smaller,
smaller. Quarks.

That was a comfort, a quark. Nobody knows what a quark is, really.
Nobody's ever seen one. They're just rumors without form, without
identity, invisible and ubiquitous. They have no personalities, no pasts
or futures. Quarks are tiny, concentrated energies everywhere, in our
hot hearts, and in the hot hearts of stars. *X* was made of this minuscule
stuff, as was everything else in the universe. This idea seemed to ho-
mogenize even him. At *X*'s smallest, most uncomplicated increment,
he was nearly, *nearly* nothing. Just like me.

But I still didn't forgive him.

The entire year of my engagement to JD, from spring 2004 to spring
2005, I couldn't tell if we were winning or losing the case. Or both?
Each season brought what Dorothy Parker would have called "fresh
hell." We collected witnesses to validate what we already knew, and
public opinion of the case zigzagged between extremes.

Despite the highly visible scandal, the Associated Press voted head
coach Wade Riggs "Big 12 Coach of the Year." After all, his team had
a Big 12 North Championship and an 8–5 record. Maybe it was backlash, or maybe they were simply stating their priorities. With a smirk
that didn't reach his eyes, Riggs said, "I hope that by me receiving this
award that everybody gets a healthy dose of satisfaction out of it and
feels as though this is an award to them as much as it is to me." At a Big
12 media session, he said, "I've spent over three hundred hours with

the recruiting party issue myself, so it's very time-consuming. But it's all sorting itself out. It's really brought our team close together, when it could have gone the other way. It's given them a cause."

An auditor uncovered a hidden world of athletic money. A football booster club called the Dear Old [University] Fund had given the football team unauthorized equipment and quiet payoffs of hundreds of thousands of dollars in "incentives" to the previous coach and staff, potentially violating NCAA rules. The auditor also discovered that when Nike abruptly dropped Coach Riggs's contract without saying why, the university secretly moved an extra $60,000 from their auxiliary funds into his salary to cover the shortfall. ESPN estimated Riggs's salary package was worth $1.6 million per year, including $200,000 for football camp and a $2-million payout if he stayed for five years.

Students and faculty protested on campus against the football team, and the local chapter of the National Organization for Women also spoke out. To handle the university's image on the football scandal alone, the regents hired a PR consultant at $350 an hour. The university announced a 19 percent drop in out-of-state enrollment, resulting in a loss of $15 million. Parents didn't want to send their children, female or male, to a rapey school.

The strategy of sex and alcohol recruiting had backfired, and Coach Riggs now had trouble enlisting good incoming players. The team started to lose more games, and ticket sales were down by over fifteen thousand. Riggs had forgotten something basic. All recruits are children, sixteen and seventeen, with parents who didn't want them to hurt girls. The mother of one recruit from the party had told me, "No, no. They wanted my son bad, but he didn't like the atmosphere over there by you, and I didn't want him to go there. I saw about that party on *20/20*. They've got to stop doing that. You know that's bad, when it's on *20/20*. Wade Riggs came to my house after that poor girl was raped and said that my son was a nice boy, a smart boy, they liked him. But I said, what's this about a party? My boy wasn't supposed to go to no party. He's supposed to be looking at the school and what they offer. Nobody told me they were taking him to a party like that. I mean, they're taking my baby there and somebody got raped, I don't like that. No, no, no. That's *not* okay." I kept her on the phone until she almost begged me to hang up so she could go fix dinner. I wanted to talk to her for the rest of my life.

Six lawmakers and the cochair of the university's own Independent Investigative Commission demanded that Coach Riggs be fired. A representative from the U.S. House Judiciary Committee scolded the university president, saying, "Wade Riggs should be gone. Gone, gone, gone. The fact that he isn't is a very loud message." The Office of Civil Rights asked to be forwarded all briefs in the case. When he was questioned why no football player had ever been disciplined or even investigated for sexual assault, the university's director of judicial affairs broke into embarrassed tears.

The university's existence itself could now be at risk. Among all public universities, this one was the fifth-largest recipient in the country of those treasured federal research dollars; state funds covered only 8 percent of their budget. With such severe Title IX violations, the university could lose all federal funding—hundreds of millions of dollars—and go under.

The athletic director resigned under fire. He said his resignation "should not in any way be construed as an admission to having engaged in any activity of wrongdoing. When completely investigated, I feel the record will show that I performed my duties responsibly and in the best interests of the Department of Athletics and the university."

Around this time period and over the next couple of years, top administrative staff left their positions at the university. The CFO/ treasurer resigned, the chancellor resigned, and the foundation CEO resigned. So did half of their vice presidents, among others.

Finally, the university president resigned after receiving criticism for two scandals: failing to fire Coach Riggs, and also failing to fire a professor, allegedly white but posing as a Native American, who called 9/11 victims "little Eichmanns." The president said, "It was becoming increasingly difficult to be strong on the issues that were important in the long run because it kept coming back to questions about me, so I decided I had to take my future, my job, off the table." She left for a different academic position out in the Midwest.

Coach Riggs kept his job.

"Why the hell is he still working?" I asked Grayson at lunch.

"Because he's winning. But so are we." Grayson grinned. "The university's going to settle."

I rolled my eyes. He had been saying this from the beginning of the case, for two years now. "You always say that."

"But this time I mean it," he said, half rising from his chair in emphasis. "They're blowing off their depositions. They didn't even depose half of the victims. They blew off all their motions for trial evidence, and we've served a dozen. We've served forty trial subpoenas, and they've only served one. They're done." I knew settling was the aim—a trial was too risky for all parties. But I had been looking forward to the drama.

My butcher paper was now spangled with stars, circles, and cross-outs in Sharpie, looking more like a finished result, the names there feeling like they belonged to old, neglected friends. We had all the proof we were going to get. With Daisy, Riley, Calliope, Olive, and the other witnesses for Simone and Ivy's case, our investigation was a success.

Other people's investigations, not so much. Unexpectedly and all at once, the regents, state attorney general, and police department all bailed on their respective inquiries into the university and the football players. Grayson and I and his legal team were all alone again, just like when we started.

But that was okay. Grayson and I relaxed, laughing at lunch. The university lost motion after motion before the magistrate judge, and the trial was set to span five weeks beginning at the end of May. It had been a long two years, and we were ready for a change. We needed an outcome, to see these people held accountable. Seven women had committed to taking the stand in court to tell their stories, to their own peril. All the bad guys were subpoenaed. Court TV and ESPN had already booked hotels across from the federal courthouse and were negotiating for parking for their sound trucks. Grayson had the upright shoulders and lightness of someone who was just waiting to win.

And then, eight weeks before the trial, a federal judge threw out the case.

13

Failure Is an Orphan

I don't understand," I said for the third time. "The case is over? Just over?"

For my meeting with Grayson, we leaned against a planter outside the law firm building because it felt better than being in the office. "They knew," Grayson said, his voice cracking with incredulity, his words flanked by traffic noise. "Those . . . the university knew the case would be dropped. They knew before I knew. Someone from the court leaked it to them. That's why they sat on the case and didn't do anything. They've known for weeks. I only found out when the newspapers called me for comment."

"All the women," I said. "All that work."

"The university was ready for it. They had their statements prepared for the press."

"I thought the judge liked us."

"It was a different judge. Until now, the magistrate judge was overseeing the case. He was totally on our side, furious at the university, but magistrate judges don't usually conduct trials. We drew this Article III judge for the trial, a Bush appointee. He had nothing to do with the case. He's nothing but a tourist. That summary judgment request has been sitting on his desk for nine months. Everyone forgot about it. *I* forgot about it."

"How can he throw out a case eight weeks before trial?"

"A federal judge can do what he wants. He never even scheduled a hearing. He just popped up and threw it out." Grayson looked down at the pavement and, unexpectedly, spat.

"I still don't understand what happened."

Grayson said, "The case is based on there being a clear and present risk to students under Title IX. The judge gets to apply the standard to show that risk. And this judge set an impossible standard. He said we'd have to prove that *every* football player on the team presented a risk of sexually assaulting women. 'All or most,' he said."

"But people aren't the same," I said. "That's impossible to prove. And it would never be true." For every King and Zachary there was a Huge and a Gabriel. The majority of the players I talked to seemed like nice people who just wanted to play football and get their degrees. And whether it was one or half or all of the players, women were still getting hurt. Why was it always about the perpetrators' rights, not the victims'?

"Oh, it didn't end there. He said six conditions had to be present to show risk," Grayson said, ticking them off his fingers. "The university had to have knowledge about sexual assaults—'just' harassment didn't count—the victims had to be female university students, the perpetrators had to be part of the recruiting program, the perpetrators had to be drunk, it had to take place on campus, and we had to prove that all or most players *and* all or most recruits present a similar risk.

"Really, he just didn't like Title IX being used this way. He thought it should be limited to stuff like jerseys and buildings. He admitted that 'some of the harassment, abuse, and assaults were shameful at best, and criminal at worst.' And then he threw the case out." Grayson laughed bitterly at the gray sky. "This is some kind of boon from above for the university. They must have sacrificed a goat or some such shit to pull a federal judge who graduated from their own law school."

I said, "Wait. He's an alum? Isn't that a conflict of interest?"

"They do what they want."

Grayson glanced at my face, and his own became fatherly, brisk. "Don't worry, kid. Act like it never happened. We'll win the appeal. We're also going to sue for the documents they withheld, like the reports from the Office of Sexual Harassment. We'll get 'em, and we'll be ready by the appeal." His eyes didn't match his mouth.

I said, "You don't believe what you're saying."

"Don't pull that stuff with me, Erika. Not now." He stared at a tulip.

I tucked my chin. If fury were a chemical element, it would be an unstable one, transforming instantly into despair. "It's just not fair," I said.

"It's the game." A crow cawed on a telephone pole; Grayson looked up at the sound. "And you might as well know. That judge ordered Simone to pay the university's legal fees."

I had no idea what my face was doing.

"It won't come to that," Grayson said. "But, of course, Simone's freaking out."

I tried to keep my voice modulated low. "How much money is that?"

"It won't come to that," Grayson repeated, and paused. "Above three million dollars."

It's possible to get gang-raped by your university's football team and then owe the school all the money you'll ever make for the rest of your life.

The previous week, I had cut through a park playground, one with wood chips scattered on the ground for the falls and accidents that would inevitably happen. Two six-year-olds were arguing by the swing set. One sat on his rubberized swing, kicking violently with each word so he jerked in all directions, his face darkening with subcutaneous blood, the lining of his vocal cords tearing with the acid of his fury as he shouted, "It's just . . . not . . . FAIR!" The other six-year-old walked away, saying wearily, "That's how it goes in the wood chip world, Hamish."

I had always thought I was too cynical to be an idealist. I thought I looked at the world with open eyes, while Grayson made lemonade out of nothing. But talking to Grayson now, I realized which one of us was truly the realist, and which one of us was Hamish.

Grayson patted my shoulder. "Keep working. We're not done." He slumped back to his office doors in his suit, now wrinkled. He would be all right, doing what he could for a case that was already lost. But I wasn't cut out for the wood chip world.

I spent what little fight I had left hating that judge. I researched him online: Juris Doctor degree from the university's law school, and a picture. He had white skin with a cyclist's tan, a lipless smile bracketed by folded facial lines, eyebrows too lazy to fully cover his pale eyes. Spongy hair, and the luxury of an unbroken nose. He looked like he belonged in boat shoes and a fisherman's sweater on a midpriced yacht.

I was a university alum, too. They called me all the time asking for money I didn't have. I had worked that job, asking alums for money. This guy had money. If he was an alum, he might be a donor. And if he was a donor, he'd definitely have to recuse himself, right?

But donation records were usually private. When I worked at the University Foundation there were different levels of clearance, and the woman who dealt with the heavy-money people had her own office with a door that locked from the inside and the outside.

So I called the University Foundation and asked, "Who do I talk to about giving away an entire estate worth millions and millions?"

The receptionist's voice brightened to hot white. "Oh, wonderful! Let me transfer you! Please stay on the line! Stay on the line, okay?"

While I waited, I scratched at a drip of paint on my wood-veneer table from when JD and I had painted the wall Cameo White. It was a color we chose at the paint store because another customer had returned it, it was 50 percent off, and we only hated it a little when the sun set and it turned almost orange.

This isn't illegal, I thought. It wasn't illegal to lie. It was called "pre-texting." PIs did it all the time, misrepresented themselves to connect with someone. "We both went to the same high school." "I want to buy a car." "I need to give away an enormous estate, to you, you, only you." And besides, fuck them anyway.

I was on hold long enough that I could tell another call was being shuffled off for mine. The receptionist's voice was replaced by one I recognized: Barbara, the middle-aged blonde I had temped under a few years ago. She had always worn cheap 1980s-blue suits with white shirts, and she used to swivel back and forth compulsively in her chair while I talked to her. Her muddy voice always sounded like she was in the middle of eating a peanut butter sandwich, like it did now. "To whom am I speaking?"

"My name is Sue," I said. Sue was the fake name I used in bars because, for some reason, I answered to it. "Um, my grandfather just died and my grandmother wants to give away his estate. His entire estate. To the university, she thinks." My mind was moving fast, trying to gather the strings of my lie together and braid them into something appealing.

Peanut Butter Barbara's voice sparked. "I'm so sorry for your loss!"

"The thing is," I said, "my grandmother's in kind of a state right now and doesn't know where their records are, where my grandfather gave to charity in the past. My grandfather was an alumnus, and she thought you were high on his charitable giving list. But she wants to be sure before giving away *all* that money."

"Let me check to see his giving history," Barbara said. "Sue, what's your full name?"

This was too easy. I started to get nervous. I rubbed my finger over the mouthpiece and said into the air, "I'm sorry, Nana. Yeah, I'm finding out now." I uncovered the phone. "Sorry. She's not well since . . . since it happened. I have only a few minutes. Grandpa's name is . . ." and I gave the judge's name. "We just need to know how much he donated to the university last year or this one. She wants to give the estate to the one charity he cared about most and get rid of it all. It's such a lot of money, more than she can handle. A ton of it." I clunked around an empty glass on the coffee table. "Sorry. It's helter-skelter here." I covered the phone again, whispered nonsense into the air.

"Certainly. I understand. I'm checking right now." A short pause and some clicking.

Once I realized that Barbara was going to give me actual private information, I got scared. I knew this woman. She locked her door even when she went to the bathroom, so nobody would have access to these very records she was about to divulge to me over the phone out of greed. Was I breaking the law right now? Was that why I felt so good, for the first time in days? It wasn't against the law to lie except under oath, or to a federal agent. Or if I was trying to defraud someone out of money. Or slander someone. Or if I profited from it. I wondered if five minutes' worth of my hourly salary would be enough to determine "profit." He was a federal judge. Grayson had said, "They do what they want."

Maybe asking wasn't illegal; maybe I only risked trouble if I actually learned something. I needed to hang up the phone right then, before I found out anything concrete. Barbara clicked back on and chirped through the mouthpiece, her voice smiling, "Found him! He's been very—" and I hung up.

I called Grayson. "He's a donor. I think."

"How do you know?"

"I . . . found out. All you have to do is subpoena the University Foundation for his donation records."

"No way I'm doing that." Grayson's voice was iron.

"What?" Grayson usually enjoyed wielding his lawyerly power. "Why not?"

"Because I don't want to get disbarred, that's why!" His voice vibrated the phone, almost angry. "That's career suicide. You never go after a federal judge. Never, if you want a legal career. Even if you don't want a legal career. You just can't. And he might have made the same decision regardless of his affiliation."

"But the donation records are in there. You said it. 'Sunlight is the best disinfectant.'"

"You don't get it," Grayson said. "A federal judge is untouchable." A quick breath. "But good job finding that information out."

"Yeah, well. I might have broken some rules to do it."

"I didn't ask you to do that," Grayson said. "That was your decision." He excused himself and hung up.

Oh, Hamish.

When I told JD about impersonating the judge's granddaughter, he winced like he was in physical pain. He said, "Please, please don't ever do that again."

"There's no point," I said. "We lost, and Grayson won't pursue it."

"There are other reasons not to do what you're doing," he muttered. I could tell he was relieved the case was over, and I resented him for that.

When we moved, I had transferred my butcher paper to our house in the mountains and carefully taped it up in my office. Now, I tore it down. What more was there to prove? We had proven it all and it didn't matter. I crumpled it up, but that didn't make me feel better, so I ripped it into tiny pieces over the trash can, dumped leftovers on it, went outside, and threw the bag into the garbage can without bothering to tie the drawstring. Every time I looked at my bare wall, I did a double-take and remembered all over again that we lost.

Grayson gave me other cases—often Title IX but sometimes medical malpractice, personal injury. Sometimes he just wanted me to find someone's locations or assets, or convince someone to call and trust him. I did the work, but poorly and late. I had trouble remembering why I should care. The university case's former trial date came and passed, just like any other day.

Justice wasn't blind—it was random. I felt sickened by the lost case, like I had the flu. The mountains sank into a deep fog and the mist wafted down the dirt roads in sheets. Fog in the mountains isn't weather; it's a stratus cloud. Vapor condensed on my face, hands, clothes. My feet were cold, my lungs were cold, and the weepy damp crawled down my shirt and up the legs of my pants. I was in the mountains but I couldn't see mountains, only the silhouettes of trees. I smelled sugar water seeping through the cracks of damp bark, phloem feeding the pine beetle larva nestled in their wooden galleries. The tree's food gave the beetles the strength to grow beneath the bark and destroy their host, like tiny Shivas. The dirt on my windows dampened into mud that collected in the corners. Everything melted. Sodden roof shingles hung by one nail. The town-village felt sorry for itself, its cheap wood curling, the grocery store full of unsold vegetables rotting in the middle.

And the Chinooks weren't done with us yet. That spring in the mountains, the winds became a whole other animal: full-bodied, oceanic, tidal, plummeting from the Continental Divide, which dominated my western view. The trees whipped in circles, shaken like babies. The wind didn't howl; it *was* a howl, and I was one, too. I was caught in it, could suffocate in it. Our house swayed and the windows shuddered. The floor thrummed under my feet. I wanted to back away from the wind but there was nowhere to go—we were surrounded at all sides. The wind clobbered us from the west, then curled around the house and shoved it again from the east, like it was saying, "How do you like me now?" Whole moons were choked out by the clouds of dirt hanging in the sky.

Wind tore down our west-facing fence, and JD spent all spring repairing it again and again. The wind pulled weatherstripping from our doors, sucked oxygen from the rooms, pushed smoke back down the chimney and into the house. It threw dirt and rocks at our windows, no matter how high. The gas grill rolled from one side of the deck to another like it was pacing. All our wind chimes and bird feeders fell to the ground, and JD picked them up and hung them again and again. That's what he did—fix things, fix people, and make sure everything held together. I loved him so much for that, and felt that I would never be able to repay him for the thousands of simple things he did for me.

Wind's purpose in life is to remove. Yes, it scatters seeds and assures the diversity of plant species, but I didn't fucking care. It also knocked over school buses and blew birds off course and limited the movement of every species on the planet. Everyone wants a cave when the wind blows, and caves suck, ask Plato. Wind scrapes through your brain and yanks loose all kinds of connections you had previously battened down. My thoughts snarled until it felt like all I could do was cut the threads at their roots and start again.

Before moving here, I should have listened to the trees, gnarled and harried and too tall, their branches combed leeward. The trunks stuck into the air like middle fingers. Two of our lodgepole pines cracked and fell over. I bent over and examined their hearts; they were healthy, light brown without a tinge of rot or pine beetle. They just weren't strong enough. I wondered how long it would be before I myself

cracked and fell. I wondered if JD, who missed nothing, was just waiting out the season until it was safe to leave.

The days finally slid into summer, and with them, perspective. It's
hard to feel crummy in a beautiful place.

One day I was walking on our land, orange-tagging the trees that
appeared to be dead or dying from pine beetle. We would chainsaw
those down later, split the logs, and add them to our woodpile. On our
dense three-quarters of an acre, we had to cut twenty to thirty dead
or dying trees a year, and it was easy to see the wide swath the beetles
traversed through our forest. It was sad but not unpleasant work to
look for sap blisters, smell the pitch, spot the reddening needles. While
I tagged trees, I also went after the invasive vines and shoots, knocking
mistletoe out of trees and pulling up the bindweed that went after my
aspen saplings and tried to drag them to the rotting ground.

The sound of paws on dry leaves. I turned to see a fox trotting
about eight feet from me. Far to my left, a dog streaked toward us from
deeper in the forest. The fox stopped in front of me, one foot raised.
It patiently waited for the dog to galumph up the hill, the promise
of blood in its nose. Once the dog drew near, I could swear the fox
grinned at me, then turned and streaked into the trees to resume the
game, the chase.

That's how this case felt to me. The dog would never catch the fox
because it was the fox's turf, and they both knew it. All the dog could
do was keep the fox on the run.

But I was leaving the case for a while, for Thailand and marriage.
Despite my rotten-mood spring, JD had stuck around. We planned our
front-yard send-off party, and then two weeks later we would board
a plane for our wedding on the other side of the world. We worried
there would be a power outage—frequent in the mountains—during
the party. We also worried about pollen storms, large green tsunami-
like clouds that sped down the west slope of the Continental Divide,
growing larger until they blew through the town-village, drenching
hair, sinuses, cars, trees, and roads in neon-green pollen. But the land-

scape, our frenemy, nevertheless soothed us with the brightening lichen on the tree stumps, the lodgepoles turning light green at their tips, everything always pushing toward life as life pushed back.

People move to the mountains for the summers, when the towns sound like wind chimes and smell like sap. Woodpeckers, chipmunks, foxes, columbine, sage. Aspens shimmer a golden green. It's never hot. The clouds are low and white. When rain comes, it's only for a few minutes to wash the dust away. The smells of life rise from the ground—wild strawberries, rain-rinsed trees, aging wood. Nobody owns a lawn, and weeds are left to do what they do best. Chain saws drone through the days, but nothing interrupts the night. Stars scatter like blown white pepper along the Milky Way. Cars bend along blind curves. The day's heat drains from the sandy soil, and the moonlight and starlight turn the ground into something burnished, to tread carefully. The land is covered in snow so much of the year, battered by wind, it has developed a shell of sandy clay, scrubbed clean. It has been sheltered in abuse, recoiling inside itself. It has withstood and can withstand anything. It needs nobody for its tending, and tends nobody.

I invited every friend and every relative to our front-yard wedding celebration. I wasn't close to my relatives, but now that I wasn't going back home anymore, when else would I have the chance to see those people? JD had a pretty big, informal family, and I wanted at least someone from my family to come up and support me. I wrote "No gifts, please" on the invitation, to lessen the financial burden and make it more likely they would come.

Friends responded immediately, excited. But I was surprised at some of the responses from my relatives. A scrawled "We can't come" or "We regret we are unable to attend," followed by a cold, stingy signature in pencil. No personal note, no congratulations. I wondered if I had done something wrong, misspelled a name or forgotten someone important.

My sister declined the invitation, saying she'd be in Stockholm to begin her MBA program there. She hadn't had a serious boyfriend in a long time, and her relationships had never progressed to the point of proposals or even cohabitation. I didn't think she would want her little sister getting married before she did, and she didn't seem to like me anyway. She might feel that she wasn't allowed to like me; after all, she was Good and I was Evil. Growing up, I only remember her getting spanked once, whereas I was always getting hit or grounded or yelled at. She had kept up the good girl role even as an adult. She never swore or broke traffic rules. Even the one time I managed to drag her to a bar, she ordered a glass of milk and corrected the bartender's grammar. My sister had never gone out of her way for me, or sent me gifts that weren't obvious regifts, or even called on Christmas and my birthday.

But it hurt when my younger brother said, "We're not going to make it, either. It's too hard and expensive. And we have the baby."

Not too long ago, I had told my brother what X did and he immediately said, "I believe you. But I can't remember anything from childhood." This was true. I had often mentioned events I remembered from our shared past—bad things like when X accused my brother of stealing and almost broke his arm in a rage, or good things like private jokes the two of us had. My brother remembered none of it. Since he had grown up, he had told me several times that he didn't care about me or anyone in the family. We weren't close, but I did love him. He was my little brother, and I wanted him to come to my wedding celebration.

"Please come," I said. "Mom's not coming. It'll just be our friends and JD's family. I won't have anyone from my side of the family here." It was the only time I had ever asked him for anything. My brother immediately agreed to come and bring his family. To cut costs, I said they could stay with us.

The party itself was a blur of barbecue smoke, half-burned chicken, burgers, friends, cheap wine, friend-made muddy microbrews, and a neon-pink sunset rimmed in gray. Grayson was there solo, in jeans and his ever-present button-down shirt (it would be fifteen years before I saw him in anything as casual as a T-shirt), enjoying the mountain air and other guests. JD's ninety-eight-year-old grandmother came, and we photographed her like paparazzi. Nobody wanted to go inside.

Drunk neighbors I had never met stumbled over. I wore a short red dress, and JD wore shorts and a red-and-white guayabera. We held hands a lot. He looked happy through his shyness, surrounded by family and our friends and their kids, dogs. I knew he needed a job to do or he'd feel uncomfortable, so I put him in charge of the barbecue, charring chicken and burgers for all. I talked with everyone and forgot to eat.

Some guests stuck around for an extra day, including my brother and his family. They had a late flight, so while JD was at work, we sat around the house talking and admiring the baby as the stay-over guests left one by one. And then a half hour before they had to leave for the airport, my brother said, "There's something I've been meaning to tell you."

He shifted on his cushion and glanced at his wife, who glanced at me. He had rehearsed something, and his wife had coached him. He said, "The thing is . . . Mom just disowned you."

It was like that moment where you're chopping something and the knife slices through your finger. There's blood and adrenaline, but not pain, not yet.

"It was because of your wedding invitations," he said.

I couldn't think. Was it the paper? It was green. Who doesn't like green paper?

My brother kept talking into the empty space. "When the relatives got your invitations, they called Mom and asked her where she was staying. She had to tell them that she wasn't going to go. She said it was humiliating and embarrassing for her to have to explain herself. She said she shouldn't have to explain it."

I didn't understand. "So . . . I wasn't supposed to invite relatives to my wedding celebration?"

"I guess . . . not after she said she wasn't coming. She said you made her look bad. So she told everyone that you only invited them to embarrass her and draw attention to yourself."

This explained some of the cold responses I had gotten. But were all my relatives stupid enough—afraid enough—to actually believe something like that? My mother often exacted wrath on anyone who crossed her in action or thought, via campaigns where she called their mutual friends to flay open the offender's every slight. It was always safer to agree with her, or pretend to. Even my brother's voice implied that this was something he half believed about me, too, that I would get married to a man forever and ever to spite my mother.

I said slowly, "I don't understand. Did Mom expect me to cancel my wedding because she had decided not to come?"

"Listen," he said, "I don't know what you were supposed to do. I'm not even supposed to be here." He kept talking, as if the words were a poison he could shed only if he poured it into my ears. "I just know that you weren't supposed to embarrass her. She told me not to tell you that she disowned you. She wanted you to keep trying to contact her, so she could blow you off. She said, 'Let her wonder.' But I couldn't do that."

"What does that mean, 'disowned'?" This wasn't medieval China. I had no ready-made context for excommunication. "So she doesn't want any contact with me at all?"

"You're out of the family. We're not supposed to talk to you ever again, or about you. We're not supposed to give you any information about any of us." He cleared his throat, clearly uncomfortable. "Mom said, 'Tell her when I die.'"

I could almost hear her voice in his, that clipped French Canadian accent she borrowed from her own mother when she was done with something or someone. I stilled. My mother had quasi-disowned me before, but this time it was different, I could tell. These words were her version of a vow, like the one I had made on that airplane long ago, to never again be in the same room as X.

My hands gripped each other, almost in prayer. "So it's over, then."

"That's why I came," he said. "I thought I should tell you in person."

My brother said he was sorry, looking away. My sister-in-law said she was sorry, and congratulations. They hugged me, loaded their baby into their car seat, asked me to fetch some paper towels for a spill, and then drove away in their rental car down the dirt road.

The stiff face I had been wearing broke into pieces. I curled up, fists to my eyes, kneeling with my head to the floor in a kind of bow. I cried in that position for what must have been an hour, my dog occasionally sniffing my ears, until JD came home. He asked, "What's wrong?" and wrapped himself around me on the floor, as if he could shield me. But there was nothing to protect me from. It had already happened long ago and had finally caught up to me now.

For the next seventy-two hours, my body turned itself inside out. JD stood outside the bathroom door as I vomited over and over. "Are you okay?" I was not okay. He gave me herbs and I threw those up, too. Food ripped through me in a hot, liquid gush. My skin erupted in hives and teenage-grade acne, and sloughed off my arms in strange sunburn-like scales and translucent strips. Sores sprang from my lips and clustered inside my mouth. I had no fever but I sweated through my clothes, foul-smelling, and I kept having to shower. My ears leaked wax and my nose ran. I cried until the capillaries burst under my eyes, covering my skin in black-red pinpricks. I got my period two weeks early, with great, shuddering cramps and clots. I coughed until I peed myself. I cried so much I dehydrated, and my face chapped and peeled. JD tried to heal me, but there was nothing to diagnose. It was as if my body was trying to purge itself of itself.

In my sick, streaming state, I decided to call my sister. My sister was devoted to my mother and to X, even though I couldn't recall X treating her with anything other than eye-rolling disgust.

I had read that after a few generations of ranching, you don't need to install cattle guards; you can just paint the lines on a road and the cows won't stray. My sister never married, never had children. If she took a gig far away from home, she always orbited back. It's a mistake to live that way. You can't get your life back from the people who took it from you. They will starve you to death by meting out one grain of love at a time.

The central theory of Stockholm Syndrome is that the impulse to hate is weaker than the impulse to survive. My sister had plans to pursue her MBA in, of all places, Stockholm, where she had said she would be at the time of my wedding celebration, and therefore would be unable to attend. But my brother had said she was still living back East. She wasn't leaving the country for two more weeks.

Might as well finish that off, too, I thought.

My sister cheerily answered her landline on the second ring. She didn't ask about my wedding celebration, but instead told me about her home repairs. Grout, lots of grout, tiles, mold remediation. Like my mother, like me, when she felt guilty, she talked too much.

When she finally stopped, I said, "So you're not in Stockholm right now."

"No."

"You said you couldn't come to my wedding because you'd be in Stockholm."

"I had a lot of stuff to do here before I leave for—"

"You're not leaving for two weeks," I interrupted.

My sister's voice deflated. "You don't understand the position you're putting me in."

I said, "I'm disappointed you chose not to come."

"Okay." The word sounded crestfallen. She hung up. My brother later reported that she immediately called my mother to say that I had screamed at her, demanding to know why she had ruined my wedding celebration by not being there.

"I didn't scream at her," I told my brother. "Nothing was ruined."

He said, "Well, she doesn't want to talk to you again, either. She's on Mom's side. Nobody's supposed to talk to you. Mom said if I did, she'd take it as an act against her."

I thanked him for taking the risk and hung up.

The hardest part was trying to hide all this from JD. We were eloping in two weeks. I wasn't going to let my mother ruin everything. It was his wedding, too. We were supposed to be happy, but instead he skirted me, watching my face for any changes, trying not to comment inappropriately, or too much, or too little. "I'm totally fine," I said every time he asked. I wondered if, when it came time to actually get married, he would come to his senses and ditch me in Thailand.

In the two weeks between our celebration party and trip to Thailand, space and time folded. I was so disoriented I couldn't drive well, and kept running over curbs, nearly hitting canyon walls, other cars, once braking to a mother's scream after her child ran into the street in front of me just as I was turning left. That near miss made me afraid of my car. Late one night north of town, I braked at a stop sign, distracted by dead leaves scuttling across the street, pushed by the wind, like they were people crossing in front of me. I don't know how long I idled there before a car finally drove up behind me and honked, headlights flashing. I tried to pull over but stalled out. I had sat at the stop sign for so long that my tank was on empty.

"You can't be disowned, because nobody owns you," JD said. But I bore my family's last name. People "have" kids or spouses, or don't have them. My martial arts teachers would say that each punch or grab was a gift. "You gave me this arm," they'd say. "I'm not giving it back. It's mine now," to break or use for leverage. "You totally owned that guy," training partners said if I did well.

BE MINE on the candy heart JD had given me on Valentine's Day.

JD said, "Why is disillusionment a bad thing? You should want to lose your illusions. Then you see reality."

But reality sucked. I had hoped that in our time together, somewhere amid the hundreds of stale peanut butter and jelly sandwiches, my mother had found a way to love me. Instead, I was ghosted two weeks before my wedding by the woman who had taught me how to eat.

Exile was meant for bad guys in a good world, or for good guys in a bad world. Napoleon Bonaparte killed 3.4 million strangers and died of arsenic poisoning while exiled to St. Helena. Dante wrote *The Divine Comedy* in exile. Which ring of hell was exile? None. Exile is exiled even from hell.

But I was only exiled from my old family. I was still held responsible for my new one.

JD and I went to look at wedding rings at a generic jewelry store, the nuptial equivalent of Costco. He picked out a band in white gold, thick, with the edges curving inward. I said, "I'll just have what he's having." They resized the men's ring to fit my finger. It slid up and down from crease to knuckle, very heavy. It never fit right and made my finger sweat.

Then we had to pack for an international trip, take a plane, and somehow get married nine thousand miles away. I was glad for the promise of jet lag, glad for any excuse for my disjointed behavior.

When we landed in southern Thailand at three in the morning, the small airport was dark and empty. Nobody was working at any of the information booths. When we finally found a worker who spoke English, he told us, half in pantomime, that a plane flying to the is- land from Bangkok had crashed on the runway just hours earlier. "Too much rain," he said, and mimed the plane breaking in two with a hard Kkkk sound. "Everyone die."

We had almost booked that flight, connecting in Bangkok. At the last minute, we instead booked a flight two hundred dollars cheaper that added an extra leg and arrived via Seoul. On the Bangkok flight, the one we almost took, only twelve passengers made it out safely; eighty-nine died and twenty-nine were injured. The corpses were burned alive, charred beyond all possibility of identification. *That could have been us*, I thought. *We could have died on the way to our wedding if we hadn't been so cheap and broke.* I knew I should feel scared, not numb like I did.

JD was nearly frantic. "I have to tell my family we're okay," he kept saying. His mother in particular was a worrier and news junkie by na- ture, and would be able to think of nothing else until she heard from him. We had traveled without laptops, and it was a time before afford- able international cell service. All we had were dollars. We roamed the half-darkened airport, looking for a place to buy baht, but everyone was gone, perhaps at the crash site or sleeping at home.

We eventually found a sleepy tuk-tuk driver who would accept dollars and we rode to our small hotel, which wasn't open yet either. We sat on the curb with our suitcases outside the money exchange kiosk, waiting two hours for it to open. Once we had baht in hand, we blearily located an internet café and signed in, trying to navigate keyboards that kept switching between Thai and English alphabets whenever we pressed some unknown mystery key. JD emailed his family that he was safe, that we weren't on that plane. When he finished, I began to do the same. I emailed all the friends I could remember from my wedding celebration, screwing up on half the addresses, I learned later. And then I started another email for my family. I had told them the destination and date of my flight to this small island, and my mother, at least, would have remembered. I typed in my brother's name, my mother's, and my sister's. I wrote that I knew they weren't speaking to me, but they should know that I was safe. My mouse hovered over the Send button.

Then I deleted the email.

I had to know. If they thought I was dead, would they ask about me? I returned to the internet café later that day to check my email, then the next day, then the next. They didn't write to check on me. Not even my brother did.

Maybe they called, I thought. I bought a 500-baht calling card to check my voicemail back home. The infrastructure still hadn't recovered from the 2004 tsunami, and we couldn't find a working pay phone in our town near the beach. Our cheap hotel had no phone in the room. We traveled to other towns in search of pay phones and finally found one a few towns inland. Friends had called, but not my mother, nor my sister, nor my brother.

My brother and sister might not have heard about the crash, but my mother faithfully read the *New York Times* every morning. I could picture her sitting at the table in her salmon-pink waffle-patterned bathrobe, so old that a white fuzz covered the outside. In my mind, she bit into her single slice of wheat toast with nonfat yogurt scraped over its surface. She sipped from a cup of tea that tasted like the filter bag it came in, string curling into the saucer. She flipped the paper over and read the headline AT LEAST 88 KILLED

AS PLANE CRASHES IN THAILAND, just past the fold. And decided not to call, because—

From there, the images faded into whiteout snow.

If a tree almost dies in a forest and nobody cares, did it ever exist to begin with?

I was faking fun the best I could, for JD. I didn't want to ruin his wedding. Maybe I did have fun, I don't know. I was barely there, although there were pictures of us together before our camera broke. We saw elephants grazing by the side of the road, poked with a stick by their handler. We ate noodles in cliffside hut restaurants and threw pork rib bones to stray three-legged dogs who caught them lying down. We bargained over purple and red silk scarves, hot in the sun. We rode a tuk-tuk to a local muay thai tournament in the rain, walked along the windy beach with the red flag waving. We fought viciously over nothing during a monsoon. It all felt like it happened through a layer of damp fabric, the gauzy colors staining life garish: the dragon-fruit pinker and the coconuts greener and the temples redder, whiter, more gold than actual gold could be. Everything was so loud, so close. I couldn't take it in. I was alive, I knew I was, but my family didn't even care. Sometimes I poked my face with a finger to see if I was still there. I blinked through the days, missing nothing, feeling less than nothing, smiling whenever JD looked my way. He was no fool, but he didn't push me. Maybe he hoped that if we had enough fun, he could undo all the damage himself.

The day before we got married in a language we didn't understand, JD rented us a scooter for seven dollars a day. We rode the scooter on roads that cut through jungles, up soft, sloping mountains. We stopped to buy gasoline packaged in soda bottles and eat orange-stained street chicken, soggy with rainwater. The rain was a mist that turned hard and soft and soaked our hair and skin until we were one with it, slicing through it on our scooter, hopelessly drenched in warm water. We rode up a steep hill on the wrong-feeling left side of the road, hugging a steep cliff. The sea swarmed far below us. JD sat in front of me, and I held on to him. He was still there, still loved me, despite everything. We were alive, in Thailand, and we were going to get married tomorrow.

JD pulled over and stopped the scooter. He turned around to stare at me. "There," he said.

"What?" I asked.

"You're laughing," he said.

14

At the Bottom of the Barrel,
Everyone Floats

When I returned from our honeymoon, Grayson was livid. "I read about the crash in the paper! I thought you were dead! You didn't email me to tell me you were okay!"

But I wasn't okay.

It turns out, marriage didn't cure me. When people asked, "How's married life?" I said, "I don't like it," just to shut them up. I didn't think JD liked it, either. Our time together was spiked with awkward silences and bickering over stupid things like the thermostat and how to properly do the dishes. Neither of us knew what to do, how to use the words "wife" or "husband." "You're my wife now," JD said, like he was trying to fit me into a new costume but the zipper kept getting stuck. We had just done something, but what, besides getting me disowned? Our ceremony had been in Thai, and we had signed our marriage license against the dashboard of a rental car. Other than that, I wasn't sure what had changed between us besides the fact that it was finally clear that nobody else in the world but him loved me now.

The case was dead, and I had nothing to spend my despair on. My rage rat spun on her wheel all day and night, running from nothing. I began to twitch uncontrollably—shoulders, neck, left eyelid. My face retracted into weird grimacing tics. I couldn't stop holding my breath, even in my sleep, and I would wake up gasping. I timed my panic attacks on a stopwatch: they recurred every eleven seconds, day and night. It felt like a wind rising and then receding, stirring up old dirt and then regrouping to do the same again a few seconds later. I couldn't sleep, sometimes for multiple days. Sleep loss made me feel so violent that sometimes my vision blurred. When I showed up to karate or jiu-jitsu, I tried to hurt people. Sometimes I hurt people.

That summer, my karate teacher asked me to design a women's self-defense class, so I enrolled in one to see what they were like. Within five minutes, I knew I was never going to teach women what these men were preaching: that if a woman learned a few awkward, unpracticed moves, she would be safe. Nobody was safe. The instructors donned motorcycle helmets and thick RedMan instructor suits that made them look like fat Power Rangers. They weren't safe either, and I would show them.

They lined us up; we were supposed to beat on one of them and then the other. They said, "Punch me as hard as you can," smug in their gear. "As hard as I can?" I asked. "As hard as you can!" they said. Then I broke the first guy's nose through the visor of his motorcycle helmet and sent the second one to the floor; he excused himself and went home immediately afterward.

I should have cared about that.

I steeped in a depression-colored cynicism that made me afraid to go outside, like Calliope, like Daisy. I was a dirty old sponge, and I would soak up whatever disgusting thing I bumped up against. The sunny weather only felt ironic. I didn't go outside except to work at some temp job at an office, and then I rushed home and went to bed, or sat alone in a room rereading *Middlemarch,* or *The Brothers Karamazov,* or *Anna Karenina,* or *Don Quixote,* or *Moby-Dick,* or any very long book where I knew the ending, the problems were at least a hundred years old, and all the characters would have been dead by now anyway.

I avoided JD, turning on the TV when he came home. He watched me, and then he watched the TV, sitting next to me. "Are you okay?" he asked. "I'm okay," I said. Then, an hour later, "Are you okay?" "I'm okay." "Are you okay?" "I'm okay." "Are you okay?" "I'm okay." It felt like he wanted me to apologize for whatever I was doing—or, more likely, not doing. Maybe he wanted me to apologize for being sad when we were supposed to be happy.

But I wasn't sad. I was furious with myself. I had been such a hypocrite all along. With the case, with my life, I had tried so hard to catch everyone else at their deceptions while completely ignoring my own.

I hadn't been trying to prove a rape case to a bunch of white men in black robes who didn't matter to me. I had been trying to prove it to my mother. If we could win, if some judge would smash a gavel and say "This happened and it was wrong," then my mother would have to admit the same thing. It was the law. And then, only then, maybe she would say those words to me. *This happened. And it was wrong.*

That smiley face garbage can where I hid my bloody underwear when I was four? I hadn't thought it through. My mother emptied the garbage cans in the house. When she got to my room, she probably dumped the trash can upside-down into a trash bag. It would be easy to see the spilled contents, blood on her four-year-old daughter's underwear. She might have deliberated. Made calculations. Then she tied up the black plastic bag, threw it into the metal can next to the garage, and dragged the can to the curb.

She might have known from the start, even before I told her, I thought. *She just didn't care, or care enough.*

"Why do you even want that person in your life?" JD asked. He looked hurt, unable to fill the gap of my mother's absence. But my mother herself hadn't even been able to do that.

JD said, "I think it's a good thing she disowned you. Because you wouldn't have let her go otherwise."

But he didn't get it. Good, bad, or ugly, you only get one mother. She was my only parent. I wasn't even sure if I missed her, or just missed her lost ideal. The Mother Form. And I didn't know how to believe in her and myself at the same time.

"There was a solution," I said. "I just couldn't figure out what it was."

"You spent your whole life looking for a solution. Maybe this is the only solution there is. There's nothing you could have done with that person." JD couldn't even call her a mother. "She wasn't going to give you what you wanted."

"What was that?"

JD said, "An apology? You deserved one. But if you keep holding out for any satisfaction from *her*, there will never be an end."

I don't know the last time I was abused because it felt like there would always be a next time. Meanwhile, I held on and braced myself, even into adulthood, even throughout the case and into my marriage. All my life, flashbacks in my days and dreams had readied me by saying, *Don't let your guard down or* this *may happen again*. Without a defined end, the experience became eternal.

I knew an American woman who traveled to Tibet to protest Chinese colonization. The Chinese government imprisoned her. They didn't let her sleep for three days, dousing her with water at random, freezing her in the cell, starving her, pulling her out for hours of questioning. They said, "We told your family you are dead." They said nobody was looking for her, or knew where she was. It was three days before they finally released her.

You might think, *Three days! It's horrible. But I could survive torture for three days.*

However, inside those three days, you don't know it's only three days. It changes you, forever. This is your life now—imprisonment on the opposite side of the world from everything you love. Everyone who cares about you is already mourning you. You have disappeared, but you're still there, and it will never end.

Everyone in Colorado knows Blucifer, the thirty-two-foot-tall cast-fiberglass sculpture of a bright blue horse with black veins and glowing red eyes, anatomically correct, rearing up on his hind legs. Blucifer weighs nine thousand pounds and lives outside the entrance to the Denver International Airport, greeting everyone coming and going. The statue's official name is *Blue Mustang* but everyone calls it Blucifer, both because of its red eyes and its history of murder.

The figure was inspired by the legend of a mythical blue-coated, red-eyed flying mustang of the San Luis Valley of southern Colorado. The mustang was a brilliant leader, always able to find water and grass for the herd. But everyone thinks the horse represents the state's NFL team, the Denver Broncos. The team colors are orange and blue, so sometimes people illegally spray-paint Blucifer's hooves orange before a big football game.

Blucifer killed its creator, artist Luis Jiménez. He had just finished painting Blucifer's head when it fell and severed his femoral artery. Jiménez bled out and died alone in his studio. His family, staff, and two race-car painters eventually completed the statue, and the airport installed it on the median of Peña Boulevard, facing west. Day and night, Blucifer's red eyes glow like neon warnings. Many hate the cursed, ugly horse, but nobody wants it gone, either. We want the reminder that our dreams never die, even if they slice us to death.

That summer, I was a broken mess. But when you're poor, you can't afford a nervous breakdown. You still have to wake early, show up to work, and make money as you fall apart, or else your one problem will multiply into many. I was still working for Grayson on a case-by-case basis, but it was hourly and not enough to live on. In the quest for health insurance that paid for a psychiatrist, I took a boring municipal job answering phones, filing pieces of paper, paying checks, and updating spreadsheets. I wasn't good for much more than that. My new boss was extraordinarily kind and it was a relief to do something easy. Sometimes I opened an empty document and wiggled my fingers in a typing motion while staring into space. Sometimes I worked on Grayson's new cases while pretending to do my other job. It felt like bravado or folly to work on any cases at all while the failed university case still pulsed like a canker in my mind. But at that point, I didn't know what else to do but work.

I tried talk therapy, behavioral cognitive therapy, craniosacral therapy, EMDR, and a kind of therapy where you "grow up" again by traversing Erikson's eight stages of psychosocial development. I hired outrageously expensive psychics promised to be the "real deal." I stared at different shades of blue—blueberry, denim, cornflower—to stimulate alpha brain waves. I said prayers to God that began with "I know I don't believe in you but . . ." I read artificially calm-toned books on PTSD, anxiety, sexual abuse, and personality disorders, dog-eared by previous library patrons and smeared with orange food. I studied psychology articles categorizing four hundred coping mechanisms, hoping one would work for me. I was beginning to understand why so many mentally ill people became therapists; they didn't want to waste all that exhaustive research on just themselves.

Each time a therapy didn't work, I became unreasonable, weeping over the lost ninety-five dollars paid to someone with a nose ring and dreadlocks promising deliverance. This must have been why I had avoided caring for myself all those years; I was exhausting. This was why people committed suicide. They were sick to death of themselves.

I considered suicide.

I considered heroin.

I couldn't talk about what I was going through with JD, even though he knew about X, and maybe he could have helped. But I knew that my pain had become personal to him. He just didn't want me to have it. So I pretended I didn't, and he pretended he believed me, and we both tried to survive the first summer of our marriage.

Nights, I lay awake next to JD, listening to moths tap against the windows. When I slept, I dreamed of battlefields of dead and bloody infants, or enormous plastic bags of frozen baby horse tongues in the supermarket. I had a recurring nightmare that I had misplaced a baby days ago, forgotten or neglected it. It was surely dead by now, starved or dehydrated, but maybe there was some life left. I searched by highways, under semi trucks, in garbage cans under bloody tissues and rags and candy wrappers, but I never found it.

I researched anxiety and eventually designed a checklist of things to do to get me through the day without collapsing in anxious seizures. I ate handfuls of supplements: fish oil, vitamin B complex, GABA, holy basil, SAM-e, 5-HTP, L-lysine, L-theanine, choline, vitamin C, valerian, and kava. I quit dairy and sugar. I dutifully tried whatever scattershot medications some overpriced psychiatrist had prescribed that week: Paxil, Celexa, Lexapro, Zoloft, Prozac, Remeron, Topamax, Valium,

Xanax, Klonopin. The drugs made me stupid and nauseous, and I tried not to vomit them and the supplements up along with my morning eggs (omega oils, protein, more choline).

One therapy showed promise, with a gifted cognitive behavioral therapist I probably owe my life to. She did what I did as a PI—heard not just the words but also the unspoken meanings behind them. She prescribed bilateral stimulation to increase the communication across the corpus callosum between both hemispheres of my brain, so sometimes I typed (slowly) with my hands crossed, and I worked my job wearing headphones that played drippy bilateral music that swept from one ear to the other. The sounds snagged on parts of my brain, wide puddles or rapids they had to jump over. Lunch was turkey for tryptophan, spinach for magnesium and folate, blueberries for antioxidants, chamomile tea all damn day at work and beyond. I felt guilty that I could now afford blueberries and turkey when so many people ate rotting produce out of trash cans. I snuck out of work weekly for cognitive behavioral therapy to talk with the excellent therapist about the blueberries and the trash cans.

Breathing exercises, 4–7–8 breathing, three-part breathing, diaphragm breathing, *ujjayi* breathing, lion's breath. Fucking yoga. More corpus callosum exercises, martial arts moves that crossed the center line of my body. I listened to meditation tapes and the third movement of Prokofiev's piano sonata no. 7, which seemed to gather broken bits of my mind and shelve them where they belonged for a few minutes. To build left-brain muscle, the excellent therapist also prescribed geometry and algebra. My house smelled like "relaxing" lavender aromatherapy spray, and I stuffed lavender sachets into my pillowcase. I hated lavender, that astringent smell paired with the most wishy-washy color ever. I scattered lavender seeds in our yard before the rains. I took lavender epsom salt baths and stank all night of lavender.

When I slept, it was only by first imagining myself sitting straitjacketed in a white padded room. I now dreamed lavender-colored dreams where I couldn't find anything I needed in the grocery store, and woke up exhausted but smiling hard, because I was trying and failing to hide every bit of this madness from the ever-prescient JD, terrified that he was already suffering from buyer's remorse, trapped in the wind tunnel of my life.

Late one night, I asked him, "Why do you love me?"

We were sitting next to each other on the sofa, listening to the mountain wind. JD's rib cage slid against my side in a silent sigh, and then he said, "I can't answer that question."

"I need you to answer the question." I stared straight ahead, afraid to look at his face, scared he might say "I don't love you. This was all a mistake."

But instead, he stood up and turned to face me, hovering so there was nowhere to look but at him.

JD said, "Listen, it's . . . it's not like I like the color red and you're red. It's more like trying to tell someone who's never had a strawberry what a strawberry is like. It's sweet. And a little sour. And it has these seeds that get in your teeth, and it's a little gritty. It's got leaves and it's less sweet the farther up you go. It tastes refreshing, and it's cold even when it's outside in the sun. But I can't describe it because it's a strawberry."

He seemed done, and I didn't even know if he liked strawberries. "Is it . . . good?"

JD half smiled. "Yeah, it's good. And sometimes it isn't. It's like being high—it doesn't always feel good. Erika, I could say things like you're beautiful. You're smart. You're funny. You're interesting. You get me enough, and even when you don't, it's okay because you try. And we connect, and sometimes we don't. You're like me, but different from me, too. And I could say all those things but it won't describe this feeling in me, because I can't describe something so visceral. I can't. It's not enough. Which is why I hate this question." And then he kissed me good night and went to bed, while I stayed up for hours, thinking about what he had said and how he said it, replaying it in my mind until it was permanent.

One day I left my office job and ran and ran and ran west as far as I could. I hated running, but I couldn't stop until I reached the knife-bladed

Flatirons that edge the city. I ran up the valley foothills until I was out of breath, until I was in the mountains' shadow and could turn around to see the fields of nodding switchgrass and big bluestem, the small city far below, the coral-colored roofs of the university marking their domain. The land stretched out below me, like an offering of everything I could and could never have.

Americans hate to admit we can never have something. To say so feels like a failure of imagination, or a disappointment of our ideals. In Japan, the phrase *shō ga nai*—"It can't be helped"—salts daily conversation. If you can't change something, you must accept it. But if you admit so in America, you're often force-fed an inspiring speech about trying hard and never giving up on your dreams no matter the obstacles.

But JD was right—freedom comes from losing our illusions. It's not giving up to see clearly ahead of you. Some things we can't have, even if we try our whole lives. We cannot bring our dead to life. We cannot reverse time. We cannot force another to love us, or parent us, or stay. I can never find a justice today that will erase the lacerations of my past. And I can never have a mother.

That wasn't the whole story, though. I had JD, a home, and maybe even a future. Giving up on my mother might be the only way to claim a little bit of hope for myself. Maybe I could learn to count on a new kind of family if I could finally let go of my old one.

The state was on fire again, the air so full of pollution that I coughed as I panted. When I wiped my nose on my shirt, it smelled like smoke. There was sadness in the hazy orange sun, but only for me, not for the sun. The sun feels only itself and doesn't know what it means to the life that feeds on it. The sun makes the mountain the mountain, the grass the grass, me me. You you. The sun loves only itself, but I love it because I need it, like I loved my mother because I needed her, and needed her. I don't need her anymore.

And still there is motion, and light to see it by. The mountain is still the mountain, the grass the grass, me me. And you you. My mother, you will die, and I will not come. I will survive the crash, and you won't know. Even as I leave you, I still want to pledge undying love to you, knowing it's a lie. My love is dying right now, so I can live.

The whole time I was falling apart, Grayson was working. He won the order for the university to hand over records from the Office of Sexual Harassment, and got ready to argue at the Tenth Circuit Court of Appeals. A three-judge panel would hear the arguments from both sides and make a final decision.

Even though the case was over, people still brought him leads. Through the rumor mill I had inwardly dubbed "the rapevine," we heard about another trainer who was allegedly assaulted, and Grayson found her name in another police report. He emailed, *She was only there for a year. She got reprimanded for dressing like jailbait. She would have been considered easy pickings by players.* Her first name was Waverly, with an extremely common surname. Her age put her in that sweet spot before she owned anything that would place her on people finder lists. After striking out on her full name, I started calling everyone in the country with her last name, hoping to find a relative.

My short list for Waverly's relatives had ninety-eight numbers on it, all in-state or promising numbers from out of state. At around call number seventy, an elderly man claimed to have a granddaughter with the name of Waverly. Or maybe he was just lonely. He said, "Well, let's see, her mother is doing her second tour, stationed overseas. Her dad is somewheres in Louisiana, dunno where." Turns out, that was his son. "Hell. I don't know where any of them are."

I tried all the people in Louisiana with her last name, but none of them had heard of her, or maybe they were just afraid I was a creditor. Certain places—the poor South, fundamentalist Utah, and rich neighborhoods—nobody trusts you over the phone. People with everything to lose, or nothing to lose.

By midsummer, the only items on my short list I hadn't tried were four different addresses with no phone numbers attached, so I typed up a brief letter referencing the case. I said "someone" had mentioned Waverly's name, I was a private investigator, I was interested in her story, and she would be treated with respect. I sent each letter via FedEx, with signature required to heighten drama. This was a technique I had invented, with a pretty high rate of return. People take you seriously when you spend that much money to mail them a single piece of paper.

Sure enough, Waverly called on the day of delivery. It turned out she lived a few hours south from me, within driving distance. "I want to talk to you, too," she said, her mouth close to the speaker so it came out loud, wet, and breathy. "I have a lot to say." She gave me her address and asked me to meet at her apartment that Saturday, at five in the evening.

I felt some of the old excitement come back, tamped down with a kind of cynicism I hadn't felt before. Other interviews used to give me a kind of lottery high right beforehand, like when you've bought your ticket but they hadn't called the numbers yet. But after we lost, I wasn't sure what the payoff could even be.

Waverly lived in Pueblo, Colorado, in a neighborhood that appeared to be a one-stop shop for crack, hookers, and guns. At least four pawnshops within my sight said they WANT TO BUY YOUR GOLD. A Laundromat offered payday loans while clothes dried. I remembered that Pueblo was ranked the most dangerous city in Colorado. It reminded me of a neighborhood where I had lived in Omaha one summer, having to sneak along a back route to my waitressing job early every morning so the sex worker on my corner wouldn't mistake me for competition and chase me down the block. I realized how far I had come, that an unsafe place like this would actually make me feel unsafe.

The entire American West was battling a heat wave, the temperatures slogging upward to 108. Trees sagged under their concrete blankets. Signs blurred. There was no freon in my car's air-conditioning, so I had to lower the windows no matter how shitty the neighborhood or I would pass out. I drove as slowly as I dared, looking for Waverly's address. My car had been in a crunching accident, and instead of fixing it I had just cashed the insurance check to pay for groceries and my new, endless medications and supplements, but I still worried someone would steal it here. I parked in the lot of a tire shop and walked down the street until I reached Waverly's walk-up.

She answered the door with her phone pressed to her ear. "I am *not!*" she said, waving me in with one swipe. The apartment was gray but it was supposed to be white—carpet, kitchen linoleum, blank walls with decades-old paint. Waverly's washed-out features matched her apartment, and both were dim despite the season of light. No air-conditioning here, either, and Waverly's white skin glimmered with sweat. She was the only young woman I had talked to thus far who didn't look perfect. She wore no makeup and her nose was crooked. With my own broken nose, I had developed an eye for them, the odd bumps and curves, the smoothness of the skin as it tried to compensate for old damage.

Waverly said to the caller, "*He's* a she. It's that university lady I told you about." She held the phone to my mouth and said to me, "Tell my boyfriend you're a woman. He thinks I'm cheating on him." I said into the phone, "Um, hello. I'm a woman." But I must not have sounded female enough because she fought with him a little while longer and then clicked off without saying goodbye. She turned to me and rolled her eyes and we smiled at each other.

"I just want you to know up front, I'm not a 'university lady,'" I said. "I work for the survivors. I don't work for the university."

Waverly said, "Good, because I hate that place. Let's go eat."

I followed Waverly downstairs and into the scorching street. Waverly pointed out the shelter where she worked. "It's a high-risk job and doesn't pay much," she said. "I want a different job, or maybe business school." I tried to imagine Waverly in a suit instead of what she was wearing now, a too-big pink tank top with an orange juice stain on the front.

We went to a restaurant I had passed earlier in my car, one that looked clean. I was wrong about that, but the salsa was good. The entire place was turquoise and yellow, a color that tinted Waverly's skin green, and likely mine as well. We ordered and then Waverly asked, "Where did you hear about me?"

"We found your name in a police report."

"Which one?"

"You've been in more than one police report?"

"Several. I had a domestic violence dispute with my ex-boyfriend." I wanted to ask if that was how her nose got broken. Waverly wiggled her flip phone. "This guy's new."

"So you hate the university? You said, 'I hate that place,'" I asked. It was my simplest PI technique. Most people talk in loops, diving deep with one phrase and then diverting with another. All I had to do was remember the dropped thread and repeat it verbatim a few minutes later and people would open up in gratitude. It's rare for anyone to remember what you say.

Waverly said, "Yes. I do hate them. They treated me badly. It was a big waste of time. I think they should pay my student loans. I was a trainer for the football team for a year and it was constant harassment."

"Sexual?"

"Yeah, definitely sexual, and also misogynistic. One player wiped the inside of his helmet with a towel, spat on it, threw it on the ground, and told me, 'Pick it up, bitch.' There are other guys I'd put in that category—" and she named all our suspects for Simone's assault, and other players as well. "Most of the worst guys were defensive backs."

"Their position coach didn't try to fix the environment?"

"Jaden Usher?" she scoffed. "He and the other coaches *created* that environment. He went after Olive and wouldn't stop harassing her for sexual favors. The coaches told players, 'You run like a girl,' or 'You run like a bitch,' even though there were women present. And how do they know the men there don't find it offensive, too? I'm sure some of them didn't want us feeling bad. Probably only a third of the players were truly scandalous." Our food arrived so quickly it was as if the cooks had it all ready in advance.

My head hurt and the restaurant was too hot. "Did you know Olive through the training program?"

"Olive and I became better friends when she started crying and told me about what happened at the hotel. The players started the rumor that she was a slut, so people were saying, 'Did you hear about Olive, she's sleeping with everybody.' She was harassed all the time. All the time. She used to get calls from Coach Usher and players, it was ridiculous. You could check her phone records.

"You know," Waverly said suddenly, "I would love it if something came from all this. I really want something to happen." Over our conversation, she repeated this wish six or seven times, so much that I saw how little she believed anything would happen at all. "Erika, do you think something will happen?"

I pushed away my dinner, a chili-drowned burrito topped with over-refrigerated tomatoes that had turned mealy. "Fuck if I know," I said.

Waverly looked surprised at my swearing, and I guess I was surprised, too. By this point in the case, I had lost all my nuance. If I did a bad job, what was the worst thing that could happen? We could lose? Oh, right, we already lost. I liked Waverly, her mixture of realism and feminist idealism, her self-confidence born of hard work and self-reliance, her vulnerability born of the same. I didn't want to "work" this woman, or use my "We're just talking, here" line. So I just asked, directly, "So, Waverly. What did they do to you?" If she wanted to talk, she'd talk, and if not, I'd leave and try to make it home before the food poisoning hit.

Waverly wanted to talk. She leaned forward, the table pressing against her rib cage. "OK, so it was my ex-roommate's birthday party. All those guys were there, and a player named Umar was really drunk and about to leave." I wrote "Umar" in my steno pad, and Waverly spelled his last name for me in a clear voice. "I said I'd drive him home because he was drunk and I don't think anyone should drive intoxicated. I knew him pretty well. It's not like he was a stranger or anything.

"Umar told me to pull around the back to drop him off, so I did. Then he forcibly pulled me into the back of the car by the wrist." Waverly grabbed my wrist and pulled so hard my skin burned. "Like that, but harder. I told him I didn't want to do that, it was inappropriate, and besides I didn't want to anyway. He pressured me, saying, 'Come on, come on,' and kept holding on to me without letting go. I said, 'I'm not going to have sex with you,' and he said, 'I wouldn't have sex anyway because I don't have a condom,' but he kept me trapped in the back of the car until I finally gave him a hand job."

As soon as we started talking about sexual assault, some guy revved up a keyboard and a band began playing some kind of Latin carnival music that got louder and louder until we were yelling. "I'm so sorry that happened to you," I shouted.

She leaned forward to shout, "I didn't want to do it, but . . . well. That is one big man. I've seen what those guys can do. I tried to get out of the car twice or three times, but he kept pulling me back in. Later, I found out he did that to lots of women, including Olive. He and I never spoke about it. I reported it to the police."

"Did they charge him?"

"A detective looked for physical evidence in the back seat of the car, but he didn't find any. They told me to try to get a confession, so I wrote some emails. Umar wrote back saying that he was sorry if something happened but he didn't remember. I'll send you the emails. I was looking at them just the other day."

"Did you tell anyone? Your boss?"

"Oh, no. No." There was a break in the music, and her "No" ricocheted loudly around the restaurant. Waverly lowered her voice but soon had to shout again once the band began playing a new song. "It wasn't okay for trainers to have sexual relations with players. They never got punished for anything. I'd be blamed.

"Besides, my boss was all about the players. He would tell them one week ahead of time when they were going to get drug tests. There was a rumor that the players used to force someone else's urine into their bladders to pass the tests. I don't know how they'd do that. But they did a lot of drugs, a ton, and I never heard of a player failing a drug test. There was no way that would happen if it was random like they said it was."

"After the police, what happened?"

"I talked to the Office of Sexual Harassment. They got really mad on my behalf when I told them everything. But nobody ever contacted me afterward. Nothing ever happened. Not with them or the police."

This was something else we could use, if we ever got our voice back. Waverly traced her face to clear errant hairs and said, "You know, that player was someone I knew. He was in a position of trust. And then I told those university people, and I trusted them to look after me. At first I was just excited that someone wanted to listen. But now I want something to happen."

I admired this girl, her hope and determination. She was so different from the well-cared-for students I had spoken to. Waverly had a soldier mother overseas somewhere, scattered family, nobody paying her rent or guarding her interests. She was on her own, but she didn't have the hard edge I'd expect. "So what do you think?" Waverly asked. "Is something going to finally happen?"

I wasn't going to lie to this woman. "I don't know. I mean, the courts threw out the case. Nobody cares."

"I care," she said.

"You're not the problem."

"Am I part of the solution?"

"Maybe. We have to prove something called 'deliberate indifference' to a bunch of people who are deliberately indifferent."

"Deliberate indifference," Waverly said. "I like that. The university is deliberately indifferent."

"But so are the courts. They deliberately do not care about these women." I wanted to lay my head on the table rather than look into Waverly's washed-clean eyes. I said, "The university, coaches, perpetrators, players, DA, lawyers, everyone with any power. They don't care about truth. Only money. Sometimes I wonder why we're even trying."

"You have to try," Waverly said firmly.

"Why?"

"Because *you* care, right?" Waverly asked. "Don't you care about me?"

15

Victory Has a Thousand Fathers

Some people become private investigators to cope with their own pain. John Walsh is one. His six-year-old son was abducted from a Sears across from a police station. Police eventually found the child's severed head in a drainage canal, sixteen unimaginable days later.

The Walsh family advocated for legislation to protect children and later launched the TV show *America's Most Wanted*, to help catch criminal suspects. Over twenty-five seasons, tips from the show led to 1,154 arrests, including the capture of seventeen of the FBI's most wanted fugitives. Over 550 FBI cases were solved. Bad things can turn into good things. Not for John Walsh, who would never get his son back, nor bring the killer to justice. But I think perhaps he found hope by looking directly at what he'd lost and trying to make the world safer. Maybe that was a good enough reason to live when you don't want to anymore.

I was still wobbly but functional, and I stopped entertaining thoughts of ending the life my mother had given me. You can't give back a gift. I felt strangely better, lighter. I stopped the anxiety medications, which didn't work anyway, and the spinning in my chest slowed a bit as the chemicals left my body. I still followed my grid with the stu-

pid blueberries and supplements and weird exercises, but sometimes I
forgot. I slept much more often than I didn't.

I continued to work my cases for Grayson. We were now investigating another university two states away for a similar alleged football
rape, but everything was different. Witnesses came forward openly—
women and men. Players talked to me and said what happened was
wrong. The opposing counsel's disclosures were accurate and complete. Nobody seemed to blame the victim, and everyone I spoke to
held the university responsible for their football culture. It was almost
as if we had earned this ease with the hardships of the first case, which
was still a cataract on my conscience, blurring my perspective. "Don't
worry, kid," Grayson said. "We still have the appeal." But he was paid
to feel that way, or would be if he hadn't been working the case for
free.

Football head coach Wade Riggs, the last administrator standing,
was finally fired in the winter of 2005, four years and one day after
Simone's attack. The news was embittered by the fact that the university awarded him a three-million-dollar buyout. Riggs said, "In the
last twenty-four hours, [the athletic director] has made a decision to
change the football coach at the university. I respect that decision, I
didn't like that decision . . . I didn't resign my position . . . He felt like
he had to make this decision." Riggs said he had been looking forward
to his contract being extended, but then, "It's pretty simple. We lost.
We ran out of juice. The well went dry." And then he moved west to
play a lot of golf. The news of his firing dominated the news, over-
shadowing the two Nobel Prizes awarded to the university's physics
faculty that month.

"They didn't fire Wade Riggs over the case," Grayson said. "They
fired him because he lost three games in a row. One score was seventy
to three."

Unexpectedly, football safety Zachary Mooney—who had allegedly
videotaped Olive, attacked Calliope in tandem with King, and was in the
bedroom with Simone—walked into 9News one day and gave a two-
hour confessional. He corroborated Calliope's claims, after previously

denying all sexual contact with her. He also said Wade Riggs had lied
on TV when he said he didn't know about any sexual assault claims,
because Zachary had a previous record from high school. Coach Riggs
had assured Zachary that they'd take care of legal concerns and asked
defensive backs coach Jaden Usher to find Zachary a lawyer. And then
Coach Riggs gave an alleged rapist a football scholarship and brought
him to campus.

Zachary's criminal record began twenty miles away from the university, the weekend he graduated from high school. A high school
student named Hannah had woken up in the woods in pain, wearing
strange clothes, covered in mud. She got a rape kit, which was positive;
semen DNA evidence linked her to Zachary and another man. Hannah
didn't press charges at first because her father was dying of cancer, but
when she discovered that Zachary was implicated at the university, she
asked for her case to be reopened. The DA ignored Hannah's request
for years. They had everything they needed to convict; DNA plus a
positive rape kit equals the gold standard in physical evidence. But the
district attorney eventually declined to prosecute because "we don't
want to look like we're jumping on the [university] bandwagon."

After Zachary confessed, I found Hannah's whereabouts for
Grayson, and he started working with her. I did work on other cases
for Grayson during the fall of 2005 and into the next two years. The
university case was still on appeal, and every now and then Grayson
asked me to find someone or document something. But it always felt
like I was performing CPR on a dead body.

And then, in autumn 2007, Grayson called.

He said, "The Tenth Circuit reinstated the case. They reversed the
lower court's decision. The trial's back on."

"So Simone doesn't have to pay the university?"

"No." From the pause before he spoke, I guessed that he had forgotten that part. "Do you know how big this is? It's a landmark decision.
It legally expands Title IX law in protections for women in schools
everywhere. High schools, even." His professorial tone disintegrated
as a nose-laugh shot through the wire. "Erika, I wish you were there.
The judges were so pissed off."

Grayson had spent two months preparing for a fifteen-minute argument to take place in a baroque appellate courtroom in downtown Denver. He ran three different "moot courts," mock situations where law professors question you rapid-fire to prepare you for the big show. This kind of appeal was what they call a "hot court," with the three-judge panel assailing each side with questions. Grayson would have little time to do anything but react, and then they would cut him off at the fifteen-minute point. The judges come prepared, having already read the briefs and attachments, which leaves them the intellectual room to interrogate and harass.

The university case was the last to be argued that day. "I was getting really nervous," Grayson said. "Two of the three panelists on the Tenth Circuit were George W. Bush appointees and Federalist Society members. I anticipated hostility, and I had only fifteen minutes to turn this case around. The courtroom was packed with three hundred people. Those long bench seats were filled with top judges and litigators who had come to watch. The press was there, the *New York Times*, the *Washington Post*.

"So it's my turn. I start arguing, waiting for them to interrupt me. You usually get ten to twenty seconds, then they interrupt, and it goes like that until your fifteen minutes are up. And the entire future of your case rests on it.

"But this time, there were no questions. I'm talking, and five minutes goes by. They're just listening. That never happens. I'm thinking something's really wrong. Was this case going to amount to anything? Was it all for nothing?

"Then one of the judges asks a question in a kind voice. 'Mr. Grayson, say I agreed with you'—*long* pause—'and we reversed the district court's decision, do we even need to address your appeal for sanctions regarding the university withholding evidence?' At that point, I knew we'd won. They had already made up their minds! They'd already decided for us.

"They encouraged me to continue with smiles and nods, very few interruptions. I kept talking until I saw the yellow warning light blinking—only a minute left—and I said I was done. Astonishingly, one judge told me to keep going, and said, 'We're going to thoroughly vet this.' That's just unheard of at the Tenth Circuit, to go over your time. So I was up there for a half hour, talking. In twenty-five years of trial practice, I've never even heard of such a thing. It turned into an intellectual give-and-take. 'This is an interesting issue, have you considered this,' etc. I was actually enjoying myself.

"Then it was time for the university lawyer's argument. Thirty seconds into it, they attacked him. Those guys were pissed off. They were fathers. They weren't having any of the bullshit that the university lawyer was putting out there. Riley in particular was the one who got to them. There was blood on the floor."

I later had the chance to listen to an audio recording of the hearing. In an echoing courtroom, Grayson's voice was thin and scratchy at first, fear constricting his vocal cords. He accidentally used the word "detest" instead of "arrest," correcting himself with an embarrassed half laugh. The judges spoke to him in soft tones, the ends of their sentences drawled to encourage Grayson's reply. When Grayson apologized for a possible oversight in his argument, one judge rushed in with, "No, no, no, you're being very helpful! Please!" They liked him. I couldn't understand any of Grayson's technical-sounding argument, nor any of the amiable legal banter among them. After Grayson paused on a question, I remembered his hearing disability from the war. How scary that must have been for him, hoping he had caught every word from three judges inside an echo chamber while trying to save the multiyear case on which he had risked his career.

They let him talk as long as he needed to, and Grayson concluded his argument on the emotional note: "That's the consequence of rape in this environment. Nothing. *There are no consequences.*" He was so quietly convincing that when the university attorney took the stand, the judges continued arguing Grayson's point for him.

They said, "There's a culture in the football program that women are available for their sexual desires and [the players are] going to be protected by the coach; they're not subject to the usual rules. Would that *not* be enough to require the university to take steps to change that culture?" The university lawyer tried to argue that there was no evidence for a rape culture, that all the attacks on women were unrelated, and they were the responsibility of the individual players—Defense Dog 1: "That's not my dog." A judge retorted, "You cannot discriminate. *You* cannot discriminate. You start piling things and it gets hard to say, 'This is one thing in discrete isolation.'"

The judges kept asking, "What would have been enough?" If one attack wasn't enough, if three or five or seven weren't, the judges wanted to know what would finally spur a need for change. "So this series of events isn't enough for them to do something other than sweep it under the rug?" Then, "No, no, no, put all the series of events that we have together, if that's not enough, what is? This plus what?"

The judges openly mocked the attorney's answer, calling it "thin soup." They asked, "Does this problem persist with the Frisbee team or the fencing squad?" They pitched Grayson's facts and asked the university lawyer, "How do you deal with that?" or "That's evidence, right?" One judge countered the university attorney's arguments with a rude "So?" Another quoted the lawyer's words back to him using a dopey-sounding voice.

The questions got even more emotional when they talked about Riley. One judge raised his voice to demand, "You're not actually defending—saying that the head coach's response was appropriate, here. Are you?" The university lawyer had to admit, "I am not."

By now, the university attorney seemed angry, too, slowing his speech and speaking metronomically, as if the three judges were thick-headed children. He overenunciated words, loudly stressing "to," or pronouncing "a" with the hard vowel: "*A* incident by *a* player." He tried Defense Dog 2, "My dog didn't bite you," calling the attacks "foolish decisions made by players and college students where they drink too much and make sexual decisions they regret." He said they were "not necessarily nonconsensual," or "a sexual experience," or "sexual relationships which [the woman] may not have wished to be involved with."

His euphemisms made the judges drop theirs, directly asking, "How many sexual assaults were there before the plaintiffs were assaulted? Why don't you go through them and explain why they're not enough?" Through each excruciating account, the judges argued that each assault mattered, before, after, and including Simone's, that each attack was enough on its own to justify change. Every time they said "enough," it felt like a missing piece of me locked into place where it belonged.

The judicial panel barbecued the university lawyer for thirty-seven minutes. The most fervent judge eventually concluded, "That can't be the law, that we have to have the whole football team engaging in sexual assault and the head coach knowing about it before there's liability." He said, "The risk doesn't have to be that great when the damage is that great." And then, as if realizing the resonance of his own words, he repeated them.

Only recently, I learned the impassioned judge had been Neil Gorsuch, who later became one of Donald Trump's appointees to today's Supreme Court. As our country became polarized into two opposite ends of the political spectrum, I realized what had happened back then with our case: a conservative judge sided with women's rights. This time, he dropped his political stance, thought of his two daughters, and made an instinctive, human choice to care.

After we won the appeal, the university fought it again, requesting a rehearing in front of the entire appellate court. They were denied. Then they were rejected by the U.S. Supreme Court. They had no legal options left. We were going to trial and the court date was set.

By now, I was doing more boutiquey work. I had discovered that Amazon Wish Lists defaulted to the "public" setting at that time. If you know what someone wants, you know who they are. I shared that information with Grayson and pulled up wish lists of everyone we wanted to discredit, looking for weird books, fetish porn, anything. "Even if it's not damning," Grayson said. "Even if it's a book about home repairs, or a cello CD. Then I can unsettle them on the stand, saying, 'So when you're lying in bed, listening to Yo-Yo Ma, thinking about the deck you're going to remodel, etc.' They'll think I'm already inside their heads."

Grayson was about to fly to Bangkok to take on a new lawsuit with a client he had never met. I worked his cases, did my clerical job, and escaped to my mountain home whenever I could. The foothills were in an inversion, gray and overcast below in town and blue skies above in the mountains, once I drove through the clouds that lined the canyon. JD was still around. And we would have our five weeks in court. I wasn't happy, but I was finally pointed in that direction.

When victory came, it was as silent as an email:

Hey kid. It's 2:20 a.m. in Bangkok and I can't sleep. Been here since Saturday midnight. My depositions blew up over the seamiest of revelations. Sort of a *Death in Venice* scenario, though "One Night in Bangkok" says it all. Too much so for even your tender ears. [*He had no idea.*] A lesson in this is I should have hired you to investigate my own client. The other side sure did. Maybe there's a story in this, too. Sure as hell ain't no lawsuit.

I realized some hours ago that now I know what it feels like to be a lawyer for the university, which brings up what we have to celebrate: Just before leaving I settled the case!

I'll save the war stories for the celebration, and I hope you're around next week for one. The final deal, which will NOT be confidential, is total shock-and-awe victory: $2.5 million to Simone, $350K for Ivy, and they agree to appoint a full-time Title IX Coordinator and fund two more positions. The university will be supervised for five years by an outside consultant of *our* choosing, and they have to implement all their recommendations. Plus they agree to substantially increase the budget of its Victims Assistance Office on an ongoing basis. Plus they will issue a press statement with astoundingly great and historic language praising Simone for advancing women's safety on campus and at universities around the country, and other good stuff. Will likely be made public end of this week or next.

Hope to see ya soon.
Grayson

I felt ebullient, and just a little cheated. I had been looking forward
to the moment where Grayson threw all the evidence in the faces of
those responsible, in front of an appalled jury. But you take justice any
way it comes. Six years almost to the day of Simone's attack, the university signed the settlement. As Grayson said, they paid Simone $2.5
million plus $350,000 to Ivy, the other plaintiff. Calliope had left the
lawsuit as a plaintiff, so she got nothing—the same was true for Riley,
Waverly, Daisy, and all the other witnesses.

The university settled under duress. If we had gone to court as
ordered by the Tenth Circuit, under Title IX rules, they risked losing
many more millions. Shortly after the settlement, the second university president in three years gave his resignation notice. Besides the
new mandated positions for hire, the university also implemented
seventeen major changes to their athletic program, and ten new recruiting rules. The NCAA rewrote its rules for recruiting visits and
the university made policy changes that led them to become an undis-
puted leader in campus student safety. But to my eyes, the university
still did not seem to acknowledge responsibility, only that "Ms. Baker
underwent a very traumatic experience while a member of our university community."

Regardless, it was over. I mostly felt relief, compounded by a nee-
dling sense that I had left something undone. When Daisy called, I
realized she was a source of that feeling. "I'm so glad you guys won the
case," Daisy said and waited for me to ask how she was. She answered,
"I'm broke."

Gently, subtly, she asked if I got a payout from the win. I explained
that no, I was just an hourly worker. "Oh," she said. She didn't say that
she had made all this money for everyone but herself. She didn't have
to say it.

"I'll see what I can do," I said.

I respected all the women, but I respected Daisy most. Despite our clear differences, I identified with her and wished I was brave like her. So when Grayson returned from Thailand, I called to congratulate him, and then asked if he would help Daisy.

"How?" he asked. I could hear him thinking, *And why?*

"I don't know. Everyone's profiting from her testimony. But her life has completely fallen apart. She still can't get a job."

Grayson said, "She did come forward on her own. She didn't ask for anonymity when she dealt with the press. She made every one of those choices herself, Erika."

He was right. These were what appropriate boundaries looked like. I just didn't care.

In *The Journalist and the Murderer*, Janet Malcolm describes the rapacity of the writer-subject relationship, in both directions. Despite the journalist's transparent greed and deceit, Malcolm insists, "No subject is naive . . . [he] knows on some level what is in store for him, and remains in the relationship anyway, impelled by something stronger than his reason." I agreed with Malcolm about the illogic of the confessional relationship, but I thought we were responsible for the consequences nevertheless. As Riley pointed out long ago, none of us could have predicted the events of this case.

"I feel bad about Daisy, too," Grayson said, but that was it. After all, he had gotten her a pro bono lawyer for her prostitution charge, and she didn't have to do time. He was too kind to tell me I was being inappropriate. Instead, he invited me to the celebration party.

The party was at the large lobby of the firm, which had been remodeled in natural wood and brushed metal, with gorgeous paintings Grayson had curated as head of the in-house art committee. The space implied success and elegance. The party was crowded and all but a few of the lawyers were strangers to me. I recognized some reporters, and some players even arrived with their parents because they believed in the case. One ex-player who'd supported the women had been a Pro-Bowl running back in the NFL, and his jersey hung in the university's Athletic Hall of Fame.

I'm socially awkward in large groups, preferring one-on-one conversations. I mostly walked laps between the drink table and the food table, loading my plate with spring rolls and satay prepared by the chef of a three-night Thai cooking class Grayson had taken once. I listened to the soundtrack Grayson had asked me to prepare for the party, Regina Spektor crooning her promise that it was going to get better. JD was my date. He was never comfortable in groups either unless he had something to do, someone to teach or heal. He never saw the point of standing around with a small cup in his large hand. He suffered next to me in his nice clothes that looked itchy on him. "How long do you want to stay?" he asked me three times within the first half hour.

Grayson chatted amiably with JD, whom he had met at our wedding celebration, and introduced me to Simone for the first time. She looked like Jackie Kennedy Onassis. She also reminded me of someone else, and it took me a few minutes to realize that her face resembled a picture I had seen of Coach Riggs's wife when she was young.

Simone had an earthy air, like someone who had earned her confidence by enduring the reverse. The cautious warmth with which she shook my hand showed me that she had no idea who I was. "Erika's the private eye who worked on the case!" Grayson said, and from the flex of Simone's eyebrows, I could tell she was thinking, *I had a private eye?* She was gracious and didn't ask questions. She didn't want to make me feel bad that she had no idea what I had done for her.

This party was our moment. But I felt a strange dissociation from the scene, which was so public when my feelings were so private. This case was personal, and full of my own ideals, and not mine to claim, and too long, and over before I was quite finished with it. But like my mother, would I have ever let this case go if it hadn't let go of me? I felt a little bit like crying and instead ate more cheese.

Daisy had arrived at the party, thinner now, in a snug royal-blue dress. She sidled up to JD and me. I liked her so much, but we weren't friends, exactly—what were we? Our relationship had no label. My party-discomfort coping mechanism was to crack inappropriate jokes and eat everything. Daisy's was to hint at a possible three-way with JD and me.

I admired her skill, her up-and-down looks at JD that somehow included me and complimented me on my taste. Sex was layered beneath every comment. Her gaze deftly lingered on our lips and fingers, so each of us would feel like we were the one she wanted. I had never seen her like this. In her blue dress, Daisy had transformed into her working self, an all-inclusive sexual force with its own gravitational field. There were no clear lines to her. She was as permeable as air.

Daisy was talking about nothing—parties, tricks, sex so casual that it was "like shaking hands" (she said this while shaking JD's hand, and JD dropped hers). But beneath her words and her blue dress, I heard, *Take me home with you. There are no rules here. Nothing is normal. Show me your darkest secrets; I'll keep them. Pay this small fee; I'll be your container.*

I do what she does, I suddenly realized. I just keep my clothes on while I do it. She solicited money for secrets; I solicited secrets for money.

"How long do you want to stay?" JD asked for the tenth time, and I said, "Let's go." We excused ourselves and left.

For days afterward I felt ashamed, or maybe angry. Daisy had treated me like one of her tricks, her Adult Babies, her Shower Curtain Guys. Was that what she thought of me? She had never tried to play me like that before. But maybe that was because I had been the one playing her. Maybe she was the one who was angry.

Living in the mountains, I usually got two sunsets. The first one was down in the foothills, in the city where I worked, with the mountains hovering over me. The sun would stay down until I drove up the creek-side road, rising 2,900 feet in elevation, into the sunlight again. Then I saw my second sunset at the top, as the sun bent downward over the Continental Divide, the larger vista.

Not this day. No sunsets at all as autumn became winter. To save gas money, I had parked my car at the Park-n-Ride station near home and rode the bus down to work in the city, and now I was taking the bus back up to the mountains and my waiting car. As we rose in eleva-tion, gray skies in the city transformed into a whipping, whirling snow, hard crystals in the air and slush in the tires. The bus pushed its worn body up the hill, wipers straining. The driver sweated and cursed. She couldn't stop to knock that oily, slippery snow off the chains on her tires or her wheel rims. "It's lard," she said over her shoulder. "Pure lard." I had driven in that kind of snow plenty; if you stop on a hill, you're there until the thaw, and so is every car behind you. The whole drive is a steep uphill climb for fifteen miles on a two-lane road with blind curves until you hit the reservoir.

In the half dark, we finally swung around the last curve, into a whirl of white powder. The wind blew too hard for the snow to land anywhere, and I could barely make out the tracings of the familiar reservoir, the dam, the frosted evergreens on the mountains. The surface of the water was beginning to freeze and crack into giant polygons that turned blue in the dusk light. Up the mountain, the frozen dead man lay alone in his Tuff Shed. That wasn't me. I was alive, and I had done something with my life. The case was over, and we had won. JD was tucked in our house just out of view, cooking something warm, waiting for me.

I'm home, I thought. *This is my home.*

I felt strange. The outside was the same mess of snow and wind. But inside that dirty bus, my hand slowly found my chest, which felt different from the way it had just a second before, or ever.

The spinning in my chest had stopped. It was gone.

It had been faltering ever since we won the case. Sometimes it had paused for a second before resuming again, uneven, weak. But this hushed, still feeling was new. Nothing whirred inside me. I was quiet inside, for the first time in my living memory.

I have never been a forgiving person. But then again, no one ever asked me for forgiveness. Was this what forgiveness was like? A rat that ran and ran until it dropped dead? It didn't matter. It was a lot easier to breathe without the running.

I didn't forgive X, not necessarily. It was more like everything over the past five years—the case, my life—had added up to an equation that no longer included him. Or maybe my DNA had changed. He no longer owned any part of me. *You can't be disowned, because nobody owns you*, JD had said. Maybe I forgave myself.

It's possible to forgive without condoning, without connection, nor the desire for it. Perhaps it's a form of exile, shoving your enemies out the door of your mind and into the snow—not with malice or denial, but simply because they don't belong on your bus.

This bus, the real bus that I was on, slid into the Park-n-Ride lot and the brakes finally caught. It was time for us all to leave, climb into our cars, and drive the short distances home. The doors shucked open, shocking us with cold. Behind commuters with hats and tucked chins, I stepped into the swirl of snow that scoured my teeth and lined my ears with ice particles. Fine-grit sandpaper snow. Everyone hurried to their cars and trucks, but I stood, cold, watching the bus rumble away from me, leaving behind nothing but exhaust.

I was fine until I made it safely inside my car, lit only by the single streetlight and the taillights of vehicles as they drove away from the parking lot. And then I wasn't fine at all. I couldn't grip the frozen steering wheel. My hands shook too much to hold the key and stick it in the ignition. I knew JD would be worrying about me at home, checking his watch against the bus schedule, unable to call because there was no cell phone reception in the mountains. But time was stuck.

My feet and hands went numb as snow covered my car and wind blew it off, over and again. I cried as if the tears were ripped from me, in raw, private noises that bounced against the frigid glass windows, already frosting inside from my breath. Impossible that these terrible sounds came from me. They sounded like flesh tearing from an animal, like a motor breaking, like violence. It wasn't catharsis. It was new grief. Why? I still don't know for sure. But I think I was crying for that rat.

I've found my way here by following the trail of heat to its source, the beginning of my story, which was not the violence, but what happened after. This is one of my first memories:

I was four or five years old. The abuse had been going on for a long time, and I was beginning to settle into a new kind of feeling— bitterness, which I was too young for and didn't understand. It settled in my chest and stomach. It felt like abandon, like there was nothing left to lose. I had already lost it. I didn't know what "it" was.

After one time, I sat on the edge of a bed. I had been toweled off, washed out from shower water, and numb. X was in the room, drying himself off. So I wouldn't have to look at him, I stared instead at a Modigliani print that hung on the wall. I've since learned that it's called *The Woman of Algiers,* or sometimes, *The Algerian Almaisa.* The woman in the picture had smooth, black hair parted on the side, properly tucked back into a bun, a pristine white collar lining her neck. She faced slightly right, but her gaze was on me. She was my only witness. Her mouth turned slightly upward but her eyes were sad at what I was transforming into in front of her.

X dressed himself, picking up his collapsed clothes from the chair in the corner—button-down shirt, khaki pants over his boxers. The bathroom was behind him, a beige shower with frosted glass you can't see out of, where nobody outside can see what's happening inside. I remember he was pleased, mildly embarrassed at his pleasure. I couldn't feel my body's contact with the bed. Something stirred within my stomach, and then my chest, and then the question was out of my mouth before I knew I was going to ask it, or speak at all: "Do you love me?"

Whatever he expected me to say, it wasn't that. I was surprised, too. This was the only time I ever asked about his feelings. He never asked about mine. I was afraid of his answer, but also curious and so, so numb now, as numb as a seashell. He stilled, perhaps seeing me for the first time, or his version of me. His pause was only a couple of seconds, but I thought my veins might crack at the silence. I thought I might die.

"Yes," he finally said, curt, and resumed buckling his belt.

I stared at the Algerian Almaisa. We had both heard it. Not the answer. The pause before the answer.

It's taken me decades to unpack what I learned in those two seconds. With my question, I had just given him the power to hurt me again, if I had cared about how he felt. I didn't care anymore how he felt. I also didn't care anymore how I felt.

But I cared what he said.

If he said "Yes, I love you so much," gave me a look of pain and devotion, apologized, or did anything that made me believe he loved me, then I would die. Because it would mean love was such a ruinous thing. I would never escape because there was nothing better to escape to. Inside this house, outside this house, love was so greedy and opaque that you use up a child and then discard whatever remains. With love, you hear her beg "no," and you don't care. You take pleasure in her pain. Love was a perfect masterpiece of a person's private horror, witnessed only by a dead painting and an empty-shelled girl.

Or he could have said, "No, I don't love you." Then I was unloved by someone who at least had the integrity to tell me the truth.

But X didn't choose either of those two things.

Instead, *he lied*.

That pause. Two long seconds while he formulated his answer. His shoulders retreating away from me, his feet still planted, as if afraid he might move and give himself away. The twist of his suddenly uneven face, a yellow cast misting the surface. His truncated, tinny voice, blood and oxygen abandoning his vocal cords and shrinking them, the sound squeezed through a constricted windpipe. His eyes ticking to the side—not to the left, where you remember a feeling, but to the right, where you invent one. His lips pressed together right after he spoke his "yes," swallowing the "no" he concealed inside himself.

This was how I learned what a lie looks like. It looks like X.

On this terrible day, it was a double gift. He *didn't* love me, and he was a liar. He was full of shit, and that house was full of shit. I was disillusioned, released from the burden of false faith. I didn't have to believe him, or in him, ever again.

X wouldn't stop abusing me for years, until I aged out of it at six or seven. Maybe he imagined I wouldn't remember if he stopped then. I don't know if he was drawn to younger prey elsewhere. He sometimes indulged in the more mundane abuses—hitting and shoving and yelling and insults—when he found the opportunity and spare rage. They hurt, too.

But his lie had given me hope, my concealed weapon. If the lie of love was there, the truth of love had to be somewhere else. It just wasn't in that house. And rather than kill myself, or kill him, I just had to survive until I was old enough to leave. I could have a life. It saved me, and saves me still: the sudden gift of sight, where I can spot a lie and know what it means.

My first time. My first case.

Epilogue: The Job

The first-ever female private eyes and spies were probably sex workers. A shell-shocked soldier would need someone to talk to, someone in the dark, and the information within those confessions would have cash value. Daisy had often said, "My clients tell me everything. Sometimes all they want to do is talk." Talking to a sex worker might feel as safe as confessing into the abandoned well where you threw your trash.

The first documented female private eye in America was not a sex worker, however. Kate Warne got her job as an operative at the Pinkerton National Detective Agency in Chicago by posing as a widow, although she was more likely just a single woman in need of a job. At age twenty-three, she showed up at the agency to answer an advertisement for a secretarial position, and when Pinkerton told her the job was filled, she insisted that he hire her as an operative. She argued that a woman could discover things a male operative couldn't, by gossiping with wives and listening to men show off.

It would be sixty-four years until women had the right to vote, and thirty-five years until women were allowed to join the police force. Pinkerton had never heard of a female detective. But he hired her because of her face, which, he said, "would cause one in distress instinctively to select her as a confidante."

Kate Warne helped uncover and foil the first assassination attempt on president-elect Abraham Lincoln on the journey to his inauguration. Under food-themed aliases—Mrs. Cherry, Mrs. Barley—she flirted with secessionists and gossiped with their wives until she discovered the details of the assassination plan. Fifteen thousand insurrectionists would protest at Lincoln's stop in Baltimore, and while he changed trains, several different assassins would try to kill him.

Warne armed herself, wrapped Lincoln in an old overcoat and shawl, and replaced his trademark stovepipe with a floppy hat. Now he just looked like someone tall. Joined by Allan Pinkerton, Warne nursed Lincoln as her invalid brother for the entire trip, cooing over his poor health. She helped coordinate decoy transportation and designed an alternative three-leg detour, arranging for horses to quietly drag the train car through Baltimore at 3:00 A.M. The newspapers later called her "the lady unknown."

Because Warne refused to close her eyes while safeguarding the president-elect, she inspired the Pinkerton logo, "We Never Sleep." Some speculate the pen-and-ink androgynous eye in their logo was hers, inspiring the job title, *my* job title, "private eye."

Pinkerton appointed Warne as superintendent of the Lady Pinkertons, a new workforce of female operatives that included the agency's first mixed-race operative, Hattie Lewis. Warne's "Lady Pinks" built identities, established pretexts for contact, hand-coded messages, and sewed documents into dresses. Pinkerton wrote in his memoirs, "I must [use women] or sacrifice my theory, practice and truth."

Warne worked as a Pinkerton operative for twelve years, living under a dozen aliases, changing accents, and establishing identities that ranged from wealthy secessionist sympathizer to fortune-teller, and perhaps even posing as a man. She solved murders and bank heists. She was one of Pinkerton's top five operatives in a workforce of thirty-two thousand. Warne conducted entire operations with no oversight while Allan Pinkerton served in the army. In 1861, Pinkerton placed Warne in charge of the Union Intelligence Service, a precursor to the U.S. Secret Service, to spy on the Confederacy. Many of the nation's first Secret Service agents were women.

Historians have tried to write about Kate Warne's identity, but there's little to say. She was a shape-shifter, a conglomeration of identities. All records of her cases burned in the Great Chicago Fire of 1871, and no confirmed photographs remain of her. We do know she died in Chicago at about age thirty-four of a lung infection, possibly pneumonia. Allan Pinkerton held vigil by her deathbed while she died. In an 1868 obituary ironically mistitled "General Intellicenge," the *Democratic Enquirer* reported, "She was undoubtably the best female detective in America, if not the world . . . Her first impulses were almost always right. In her career while she lived she developed that her sex could do much more than had ever before been ascribed to their sphere."

Pinkerton buried Kate Warne in the Pinkerton family plot at the Graceland Cemetery in Chicago. On her gravestone, he misspelled her last name: Warn.

All my years of physical fighting paid off in early cataracts: one big cataract in my right eye, a wisp of one in my left. It turns out that getting punched and elbowed in the face isn't good for your vision, and I now had the eyes of a middle-aged boxer. Every light source turned into a cloud, and the letters of street signs, books, and name tags blurred into something unreadable. There was a strange relaxation that came with not being able to see, as if my blindness meant I were invisible myself. My flaws smoothed over in the mirror. The world became abstract and pastel, which was pleasant, although I kept almost getting into car accidents. Even then, I was too squeamish to allow myself to go unconscious while a stranger stabbed my eyes with a laser. I could no longer read faces, and I broke my toe because I couldn't see the floor. I waited until I was unable to read at all, even with glasses, and then JD all but forced me onto the operating table.

After the surgeries I could see again, which was worth anything. But what I initially felt was loss. It was as if my body knew what had been done to me. The clouds had been vacuumed from my eyes and along with them, my lenses—the actual lenses through which I had seen the world for the first half of my life. My new eyes see at a fixed focal length, and I have to use different glasses to see far away or close up. I must constantly decide where I want to look, what I want to see, and to what degree of clarity. I am no longer porous, taking in everything whether I want to or not. Every observation is also a decision—to know, or not to know.

I continued working for Grayson, mostly on Title IX sexual assault cases. Each new case seemed shockingly easy. Witnesses were generous and open, the backlash was minimal, and I didn't feel afraid. Our success rate together was 100 percent. Every civil case I helped Grayson with settled in favor of the plaintiffs. Nothing went to court. And because the district attorneys never pursued the perpetrators in criminal court, none of them ever went to prison for sexual assault, or were even charged for their alleged crimes. So each win only felt partial, compromised by the knowledge that the perpetrators were still out there and might hurt someone else. I wondered how I could ever fully heal from my own abuse if I was thinking about sexual violence all the time.

Working on a later case that closely resembled Simone Baker's, I met with a potential witness who looked like me—that is, she looked like nobody in particular. "I could swear I know you from somewhere," I said.

"That happens to me a lot," she said. She had brown hair, light olive skin, brown eyes, and her build was slight. When we ordered, the waitress asked if we were sisters. We smiled no, and the waitress asked, "Cousins?"

"So you're a private investigator," the potential witness said, cheeks firming into a genuine smile. "What's that like?"

I told her about the job, my first big case, the confusion, Grayson. I had never gotten this personal with a witness before. She asked more questions, and I mentioned my rough childhood, getting disowned, my grief over my mother. She listened. I did everything wrong: got personal, talked too much, showed personality, had opinions, expressed feelings. I felt the same dissociation as I had that first time I met with Calliope, as if I were floating above myself, except this time I wasn't watching the creation of a PI—I was watching a person completely fall apart. But it didn't feel like I was falling apart. Instead, it felt like I was falling together, joining all these strange fragments of myself in the telling of my story.

I thought, *This is what it feels like to talk to me.*

It was better than talking with JD, better than any therapy I'd ever had. Because this pink-cheeked attentive woman was a stranger. She would go away, taking my troubles with her. They were hers now. She was as disposable as a razor blade, shaving off my sins; my new skin surfaced smooth under the edge of her gaze. It was such a delicious relief, I couldn't stop. I didn't stop. I was like Heidemann, the child-murderer in 1910, confessing all the way to my own electric chair. Because when you keep secrets for a living, all you want to do is tell the truth.

By the end of the meal I bought us, the interview was completely blown. I had asked her maybe ten questions total. She was still interested in the case, and maybe we were friends-of-the-moment, but she wasn't going to tell me anything important. How could she? I had taken up all the space.

"I'm sorry for talking so much," I said as I paid the bill. "I didn't mean to dump on you like that. I don't know what happened. I never do that."

"That's okay, it happens a lot," she said. She was three beers in, so she blurted, "You're not very good at this job, are you?"

I was. I just didn't want to be anymore.

Despite all his misgivings about my line of work, JD and I survived my PI career intact. Sometimes we celebrate Ringworm Day by printing out disgusting pictures of coral-red ringworm scars on our printers and folding them into homemade cards to mark the day we met. Perhaps he's fascinated by the same part of me he wants to heal. Or maybe we both like the reminder of the ugly places we've been, and how far we've come together.

For years, Grayson kept an eight-foot bookcase stuffed with over a thousand news articles about our first big case together. The docket contains well over a thousand legal documents. Grayson and his co-workers logged more than ten thousand billable hours over five and a half years of overtime uncompensated pay for three attorneys, many paralegals and admins, my time and expenses, plus vast clerical resources, travel, deposition costs, and court fees. Grayson alone put in 3,500 hours on the case. Even after he finally got paid, it was a fraction of his usual fee.

The case dominated over five years of our lives and six of Simone's, from her attack on December 7, 2001, until the settlement on December 5, 2007. According to Grayson's estimate, the lawsuit cost the university eight figures, maybe even nine. Costs included insurance premiums that quadrupled from three to twelve million dollars a year, legal costs of over three million spread out over ten white shoe law firms, PR fees of at least that much, Coach Riggs's buyout at three million, Simone and Ivy's settlement of $2.85 million, and the costs of the two new hires. As only 8 percent of the university's budget was supported by the state, out-of-state tuition is the university's lifeblood, and Grayson estimated those losses at fifty million. Over five years, they lost most of their top administrators, including two presidents, the chancellor, CFO, foundation CEO, athletic director, football head coach, and others. Grayson told me they paid one of their outside PR firms one million dollars to crisis-manage this scandal alone.

Their insurance company only covered $4.85 million of the loss. Between the filing of the lawsuit and their budget after settling, the university had increased out-of-state tuition by 40 percent and in-state tuition by 85 percent in six years, once hiking it by 28 percent in a single year, to the rage of students and the governor. So the students ended up paying for the university's mistakes.

"We would have settled for as little as three or four hundred thousand," Grayson said. "They could have made this case go away for one percent of what it ended up costing them." But apparently the sentence "We were wrong and we're sorry" is priceless. Growing up, I would have dumped out my piggy bank to hear X say it to me just one time, but thanks to this case, I no longer needed that now. What had healed me most wasn't time; it was action.

Our case was regularly reported on TV by ESPN, network and cable news, CBS, *Nightline*, *Today Show*, and *Larry King Live*. *Good Morning America* flew Simone to New York for a live interview, and Calliope was on *20/20*. Besides local press, the story was heavily covered in the *Washington Post*, *New York Times*, *Los Angeles Times*, *Chicago Tribune*, *Sports Illustrated*, *ESPN*, and *USA Today*. Since this case, there have been numerous significant Title IX sexual assault cases, the movie *The Hunting Ground*, and a vicious backlash from Donald Trump's secretary of education, Betsy DeVos, as she bemoaned how accused rapists "had their lives ruined" by potentially losing their scholarships. Last month I mentioned the case and a very progressive university professor said, "I taught Simone. She was my student. And what I just don't understand is why she invited those football players to her apartment. What did she think was going to happen?"

I said, "She didn't invite them. They crashed her party. She didn't do anything wrong." The professor shrugged, eyebrows leaping in a visual "whatever."

Even if public memory is shortsighted, I have to hope that the case made a difference for the women, the survivors. By the end, eleven women came forward to be counted. There was an equal number we knew about who refused involvement (as was their absolute right). And more that I didn't know about and never will.

The women from the case now lead quiet lives. Hannah (whom Zachary had allegedly attacked the night of her high school graduation) and Calliope bonded over their common horror at the hands of the same man. Nina, the female kicker, outlived death threats and hate mail from university fans, and went on to play in the Continental Indoor Football League as the second female professional football player in history. She devotes her life to nonprofit advocacy and pro bono counseling for sexual assault, domestic violence, and child abuse survivors. A decade after she came forward, she reported to the *Washington Post* that people were still calling her a liar. Her former team has had a losing record every year but one since Wade Riggs was fired, and they call their losing streak the "Curse of Nina."

Other women from the case have gone completely dark. Little or no social media, names changed. Their justice wasn't clean, nor re-demptive, and nobody can even find them to say thank you for making us safer. I wonder who they would have become if they hadn't been attacked—what parts of them are identity, and what parts are survival. I wonder the same thing about myself.

DA Beatrice Hull met her term limit in 2009 and opened a law firm, switching sides to become a defense lawyer. She told the press, "We're not getting guilty people off. It's about having people assume responsibility and turn their lives around, and it's pretty gratifying." Most of the top administrators from the university went on to posi-tions at other schools, sometimes with a title promotion. The football team's intermediary with the police, "Duke" Dumond, was accused of verbally, physically, and sexually abusing a thirteen-year-old in the Ramsey home where he lived. He allegedly did things like punch her in the kidneys and touch her breasts, and she said that about twenty times he held her face in a pillow and told her he wished she was dead. Duke denied the accusations, and the young girl decided not to press charges. Duke was later inducted into the USA Strength and Condi-tioning Coaches Hall of Fame. In his sixties now, Duke is living in a memory care unit in Mississippi, forgetting his life.

To my knowledge, nobody held Coach Riggs accountable for his testimony under oath that he knew nothing about Riley's alleged at-tack. And of his comments about Nina, Riggs only said, "I would have said that differently. We did everything imaginable to make it work for her. Other than that, there isn't one thing I would have changed." The university hired him back as a radio color commentator for his former team. Two years ago, at age seventy-three, Wade Riggs was inducted into the university's Athletic Hall of Fame. Riggs said he for-gave everyone who wronged him while he was a coach there. "You've just got to go on. Life's too short. You've got to go on, and you've got to forgive. That's the way it was with me . . . You're just better off taking the high road and moving on and trying to be the person that you think you are."

I'm still good friends with Grayson, and I sent him the article. He emailed back to ask, *Has Coach forgiven you and me?*

As for the players and recruits, I'd love to say someone went to jail for any of the alleged sexual assaults, but nobody I investigated ever did. Today, all the suspected perpetrators are still enjoying sunshine and fresh air.

After spending years periodically crying and apologizing to his ex-girlfriend over the phone, King found a way to live with himself as he went pro and played for two top NFL teams. Zachary had five children and suffered a debilitating but non-fatal stroke in his midthirties. Umar, Waverly's abuser, went pro and bought businesses. Abner, Riley's alleged rapist, worked for the university for many years in a salaried middle-management administrative position, with his name and picture displayed on their staff website. Jaden Usher—the defensive backs coach who allegedly sexually assaulted Olive—became a head coach in the NFL. Before hiring him, the NFL team claimed they investigated all accusations against him, but decided "it was not something that was going to influence our decision on who Jaden was."

Of the recruits suspected of sexual assault, one was drafted to the NFL but failed the drug test. Another received a scholarship to a Pac-12 university, only to get arrested his sophomore year for felony and misdemeanor weapons charges. Ten months later, he called a nineteen-year-old stranger "Chewbacca," because she wouldn't go out with him and his friend. The interaction then escalated until another football player fatally shot her.

Except for Grayson, I lost contact with everyone from the case. The same is true with my own family, although my brother and I occasionally talk by phone on birthdays. Even with Daisy, almost everything I know about her is from the internet and the newspapers.

Daisy got her white picket fence, but first she had to undergo years of more barbed wire. Daisy set up a workplace in a motel room and saw clients there, using the lobby computer every morning to schedule her Craigslist dates. She hated it. The motel owner finally took pity on her tear-stained face and offered her a job on the night shift so she could quit the life.

They fell in love. He married her. She joined a professional folk dance troupe. She moved to the suburbs and does public speaking against human trafficking and sexual abuse. A Christian nonprofit agency took credit for turning her life around, and a newspaper wrote an article about it. In the photo, Daisy stood smiling in a beige kitchen, glossy hair cropped to her shoulders, using oven mitts to proffer the camera a cherry pie.

With her family's support, Daisy did much safer webcam sex work, and spoke at the Women's March in Denver, advocating for the decriminalization and destigmatization of sex work. Her husband passed away, but she bounced back into a new relationship, ever resilient.

I saw Daisy one more time, at an outdoor festival just a few years ago. Between acts there was an "Open Dance" where festival hippies were invited to climb onstage and dance in front of the crowd. The emcee heckled everyone who walked by: "You, with the walker! Get up here! Mama, push that stroller onstage! Shake what the Lord gave you! I know you can!" The microphone rasped with feedback every time the emcee veered close, as if she were electrified by static. That emcee—herself unmoving as hippies danced around her like they were climbing invisible walls—was Daisy.

Daisy was now skinny. I was at least fifty meters away from her and in a crowd, but at one point she fell silent and cocked her head, staring in my direction. I wanted to approach her, but I felt too shy. What would we say to each other? Still, staring at her unmoving figure on the stage, I thought about how nice it must feel to be one of those lunatics dancing around her. Daisy let people be themselves. That's what a sex worker is, after all: someone who makes the world safe for everyone but herself.

I made mistakes with Daisy, but I'm not certain exactly what they were. I know I was part of an engine in a vast legal machine that hurt her. So was she. We did it for a cause. I worked for five years to help two students win a lawsuit to keep young women safe from sexual exploitation. In doing so, I may have hurt a rape survivor, taking everything I could from her. Or, rather, she offered it all up for free, and I accepted, as I was paid to do. My choices added up to something that helped save thousands of women, but not Daisy. And I'd do the same thing again.

In *Beyond Good and Evil*, Nietzsche wrote, "Whoever fights monsters should see to it that in the process he does not become a monster. And if you gaze long enough into an abyss, the abyss will gaze back into you." What Nietzsche didn't mention is how easy it is for the abyss to disguise itself. It woos us with the greater good. It sounds like a nice person asking for your secrets. It feels like connection, redemption, even comfort. It looks like my face.

You know all my tricks now, but it doesn't matter. Give me twenty minutes alone with you, and you'll still tell me all your secrets.

You won't even notice you're doing it at first. After all, we're just talking, here. It will feel free, like you've taken off your clothes to feel the sun on your skin. Then, a little too late, you'll realize you're naked, and wonder if you're getting burned in your most private places. You can back away from me, the stranger who now owns the partial truth of your story. That will bother you—partial truth. You'll choose to keep going. You'll tell me everything.

Which is why, after fifteen years, I decided to finally quit PI work for good. I can't control my face, but I can control what I do. In this job, I became a manipulator, a liar, an information thief, an agoraphobe, an intruder, a panic-ridden insomniac, a depressive, an exploiter, an avenger, and nearly a suicide. I also became a first-rate private investigator. I found missing people, exposed truths, and contributed to national systemic change to protect women from horrific violence. I've never been able to reconcile the two realities—the good I did versus the person I became to do it.

Shortly after I made the decision to quit, Grayson offered me a career case, a rural cold-case murder of a woman, covered up by local authorities. The details, the vicious cruelty, the narcissism of the suspected perpetrator, the institutional corruption—this was PI candy, and I was perfect for this case. I felt the old high, the itch of the puzzle, and the manic happiness it would give me.

But I told him no. I know myself now, that I'd stop at nothing, not even collateral damage. I was too good at persuading people to tell me everything, no matter their personal cost and mine.

When you're abused, one person disposes of you with deliberate indifference. When nobody helps you, the whole world disposes of you with deliberate indifference. Before this case, I thought nobody cared about people like me, girls and women who had been used to wipe up other people's pain. But this case showed me something new. Grayson, the survivors, witnesses, Daisy, and even the appellate court judges were not indifferent. They cared about us all, even people they hadn't met. They live in this world and transformed it according to their ethics. They showed me that, in tiny but vital increments, the world can change. And if there was hope for the world to change, there had to be hope for me.

Even after quitting the job, habits remain. I still do dossiers on people who intimidate me—aggressive acquaintances, suspicious neighbors. I still ask personal questions of complete strangers based on hunches, like, "Why are you lying?" or "How long have you been sober?" I might be better at investigative work than ever—more perceptive, more accurate, more insightful. But being good at something doesn't mean you should do it.

Instead, I'm trying something new. I'm still using those old skills, but simply to connect with people, not to steal information from them. I try to listen to what they say, and, beneath that, what they're aching to say. Maybe this is the real human magic: listening to a person as she struggles to speak her most painful truth, and sharing my own truths in turn. Because I can only belong to the world if I trust people enough to show them my true face, who I am between the seams of my scars. To tell them everything, too.

Author's Note

Raymond Chandler said, "There are two kinds of truth: the truth that lights the way and the truth that warms the heart. The first of these is science, and the second is art. Neither is independent of the other or more important than the other. Without art, science would be as useless as a pair of high forceps in the hands of a plumber. Without science, art would become a crude mess of folklore and emotional quackery. The truth of art keeps science from becoming inhuman, and the truth of science keeps art from becoming ridiculous."

I reconstructed this story from five years of work materials, court documents, and archived newspaper articles. However, the narrative arcs of life and art rarely align perfectly. In our jobs, "Grayson" and I often followed concurrent leads, and vast expanses of time elapsed between steps while other storylines and cases slipped in. We had to retain multiple facts, stories, timelines, people, and contexts in our consciousnesses at all times and in all situations, as all these elements knotted themselves into a case. This degree of obsession and confusion would be too much to ask of even the most dedicated reader, so I rearranged the timeline to increase clarity and fit into the larger truth of the story. However I rearranged the events, I took no liberties with the veracity of the events themselves.

With respect to my personal history, this is the truth I know. I acknowledge that my former family's memories may be different from mine. I have no intent to cause harm or hurt anyone. I am only telling my story according to my individual and unique understanding, with a wish to help others who have had similar experiences.

To protect the innocent (and to protect myself from the guilty), I disguised and changed the names of most of the characters in this memoir. The biggest irony of this book is that I cannot name my abuser (called "X" here) because he is still alive. Perhaps he doesn't deserve a name.

Given the elements above, I strove to tell this story as faithfully as I could. Every event here—every conversation, every violent and non-violent act, and every kindness—happened in my direct experience, to the best of my ability to remember it. I wrote this book in awe of this fact, and in gratitude for our resiliency as human beings. Thank you for reading it.

Acknowledgments

Buckle up, because this is going to be long.

This book was under attack before it even made it to print. I am so grateful to the following people who fought for this book and helped me during that difficult time. First and foremost are Ken Rossman and Abby Harder, who protected this book pro bono. I don't know what I would have done without your help and expertise, given so freely and generously. Thanks also to those who offered or facilitated more help and support: Veronica Rossman, Jennifer Sullivan, Bill and Kim Hayashi, Regina Drexler, Kim O'Connor, Andrea Dupree, Scott Nelson, Rick Bailey, and several others I can't name here for fear of compromising their jobs. Ellis Levine was meticulous and indefatigable in his legal edits, which made the book much stronger and more accurate. You all gave me courage when I was scared and bullied. There is no way to repay you.

I want to express gratitude for the courageous women I wrote about in this book. Each of them came forward to tell their stories at great physical and emotional risk to themselves and their safety. Their altruism renews my faith in humanity.

Thank you to my genius agent, Mary Evans, who has stuck by me through dramatic career swings since 1999. You are always on my side, you have seen it all, and you have been a champion for this book ever since it was a mere idea. Caroline Bleeke, you are a generous, brilliant, and truly gifted editor. Your instincts are perfect. You made this book infinitely better, and I am so lucky to travel this road with you. Thank you to Sydney Jeon, the star who worked so hard and so often behind the scenes, contributing editorial insight while organizing and managing *everything* perfectly.

I owe a ridiculous debt of gratitude to the many other people who have helped me revise this book in its earlier and uglier stages. Thank you to Baine Kerr, a great friend whose help on this manuscript was immeasurable and necessary. You made the difference. Thank you to the Murphies Group (Jennifer Sullivan again, Rachel Weaver, Jenny Shank, and Paula Younger, who all suffered through early full versions), and the Worriers (Andrea Dupree again, Amanda Rea, Tiffany Quay Tyson, and Jenny Itell and Karen Palmer, who read the entire manuscript). Thank you to all my other friends who supported me in this project, sharing your ideas and experiences.

Thank you to everyone at Lighthouse Writers Workshop (especially Mike Henry and, again, Andrea Dupree—I owe you triple), and all my amazing and inspiring students and clients whom I love so much. Thank you to Steve Almond and Susan Curtiss for your insights about particular elements of this book. For kind and generous writing support, many thanks to Ellen and Jim Anderman; Scott Harrison and Ellen Moore; Caroline and Tony Grant; Sarah Ringler and Steve Kettmann at the Wellstone Center in the Redwoods; and Eve and Mike, who pitched in countless times. You all gave me much-needed peace of mind.

Thank you to the many other people at Flatiron and beyond who contributed their extraordinary talents to this book: Sarah Murphy, who chose this book from the pile and helped me with early visioning; publisher Megan Lynch, who didn't give up on this project when times got hard; Zoe Norvell, for her incredible cover design work, and Keith Hayes for his spot-on art direction; copy editor Shelly Perron for her meticulous work (sorry for the errors!); Donna Noetzel, for the badass interior design; Michael Horner, for the cover photograph; producer Callum Plews, for his audiobook work; as well as senior publicist Claire McLaughlin, marketing manager Erin Kibby, marketing director Nancy Trypuc, production editors Jeremy Pink and Morgan Mitchell, proofreaders Rima Weinberg and Lisa Cowley, production manager Eva Diaz, associate publisher Malati Chavali, and president/publisher Bob Miller. This book is in such capable and creative hands, and I apologize if I'm leaving anyone out. Also thank you to Scott Huff at Playground Entertainment for optioning this book, and David Colden for making it happen. Thank you to Luke Neima at *Granta* for contracting the essay that made me realize this was a story in the first place.

I would not have survived any part of the events in this book without Jackie Szablewski.

Last and most, I want to thank my chosen family. You're everything. I love you.

If you are a survivor of sexual violence,
a list of resources is available at
www.erikakrousewriter.com/resources.

About the Author

Erika Krouse is the author of *Come Up and See Me Sometime*, a *New York Times* Notable Book, and *Contenders*, a finalist for the VCU Cabell First Novelist Award. Erika's fiction has been published in *The New Yorker*, *The Atlantic*, *Ploughshares*, *One Story*, and more. She teaches creative writing at the Lighthouse Writers Workshop and lives in Colorado. *Tell Me Everything* is her debut memoir.